This family story was written for
Rachael Eileen Agha and Richard Jason Agha
and for the many generations to follow.

Photographs: Family of the author
Book design: Gorila Grafica
Typset in Monotype Amasis 10/13pt

Jason Agha

PROLOGUE

MY NAME IS Jason Agha and I feel compelled to write this true account of a small part of my family's history before it is lost in the annals of time. I have come to believe that if a true story is to be told it needs to be written down soon after those actual events have occurred, and by someone who has had first hand knowledge of those events. This is one such story.

Many stories we are told that are true throughout history and have been written long after those events have supposedly happened can easily be distorted.

Take the Bible for instance, the first five books are attributed to Moses and are commonly known as the five scrolls. Moses lived between 1500 and 1300 BC, though he recounts events long before his time, but were they correct?

These events were handed down from generation to generation in songs and narratives which could be, and probably were, very easily distorted over hundreds of years, due to the fact the written word had not been discovered by man as yet. It was for reasons similar to the one above that I have decided to put down on paper this story so that future generations of my family and others, will be able to read a true account of the facts and events that happened in a small section of our family history, events that you will think to yourself — this can't be true? But I can tell you they all are.

I have been told that all good stories usually have a beginning, middle and an end to give it structure and I suppose this story is no different but we must start where I began and that is in the very middle of this true story.

CHAPTER 1

My Birth

IN A SMALL two-bedroom bungalow, on the eleventh of January 1962, in the county of Northamptonshire, I was brought into this world by a man, who over time I would admire and deem in my view to be one of life's unsung heroes.

I can say that literally due to the heavy snow that lay outside in our little cul-de-sac in the middle of England, with my mother Eileen well into the final stages of labour, the midwife who was called over an hour earlier was nowhere to be seen.

The event about to happen in the front bedroom of this bungalow was totally in the hands of a thirty-three year old man, who years earlier had travelled halfway across the world to deliver me safely on this cold and bleak winter's day.

This man firmly instructed my elder brother by five years, to remain in the front room of the house until otherwise told as he helped my mother to deliver me safely.

As the snow continued to fall outside, I was now being held securely but tenderly in the arms of this man and at that precise moment in time that I entered into our world this man became my father; Sardar, Hassan, Agha.

In the warmth and security of my mother, my brother Alexander was allowed to see me and was told, 'this is your baby brother, Jason'.

For several hours we stayed together as a family in the warmth of that front bedroom and maybe this single moment in time was when this family truly felt bonded as one, for as time passed this family would be tragically split apart, but as it did it would reveal how it struggled to reach this single moment in time on a bed in the middle of England in 1962.

A loud knock at the door signalled the eventual arrival of a very cold and bedraggled middle aged lady who announced herself as the midwife explaining how she has been trying to reach our small village from the main road and having had to walk through the snow on the icy roads over the past hour.

After a warm cup of tea, she proceeded to do all the relevant checks on my mother and myself, and then offered my father to cut the umbilical cord which he duly obliged — then praised him on a job well done at delivering me hours earlier.

Life seemed to be very happy and normal for our family living in the 1960s, although I had been born with asthma and struggled a lot of the time, especially when it was damp, but like most families back then there was no central heating in our small bungalow, we had a coal fire in the lounge and a couple of two bar electric fires in the bedrooms, as well as a Flatley clothes dryer.

Our doctor, Dr McFarland said I was more than likely born with asthma due to my mother having eczema as it was believed in the medical world at that time these were somehow related to each other.

Family life in Northampton, visiting Gran's house, 1965

CHAPTER 2

School Days

IF I HAVE ONE good attribute in life it is said that I have a very good memory, but my memories of that time did not really come to light until I first attended primary school at the age of five in 1967, but for whatever reason any lasting memories of the period leading up to my first day at school do not seem to come to light very easily.

It is said that a child's memory does not form until around ages four to six unless an incident is ingrained in their small memory bank, this is since a child's brain cannot process all it's early life's activities.

I remember my mother taking me to school, at the age of five and on my first day in 1967 everything looked big, from the school steps leading to the bottom playground to the old blue school door which my mother, still clutching my hand struggled to pull open. She guided me through the first door on our right which was to be my classroom for the next school year.

There were many children in this room and it just seemed utter chaos; lots of noise, children were shouting and crying. I was led to a desk by my mother and sat down, there was an old chalkboard and chalks on the desk to use, but I didn't think I did, instead I just watched all the commotion around me.

My mother stopped for a little while then said, 'be a good boy', and that she would be back later in the day to collect me. She then rose from my side, my gaze transfixed on her as she made her way out of the building past the classroom windows and out of sight. My brother Alexander had left this school and had gone on to start secondary school that very same day I had started primary school, due to the five years difference in our age.

School life was pretty good considering and I remember every day we used to get a small bottle of milk with a straw, which was equal to one third of a pint.

Throughout the winter months these were extremely cold due to the fact the milkman would leave them outside the school very early in morning. There were around sixteen children in my class, but when one or more children were absent the class took it in turns alphabetically and were given the option to have an extra bottle of milk, which was a real treat. I remember how all the children would look round in the morning to see if everyone had come to school with the hope of getting that extra bottle of milk.

School dinners were provided if required; as the school had its own kitchen and I would attend lunchtime meals as both my parents went to work. These meals were cooked by several middle-aged women from the village and it was all good hearty food, just right for a growing boy.

CHAPTER 3

Memories

MY MEMORIES were of good things during that period, Mum dragging me round Adnitts department store, then the market in Northampton on a Saturday morning, before going into the health clinic to pick up a bottle of Delarosa Syrup, it was supposed to be good for you and give you vitamins, but was guaranteed to rot your teeth because it was so sweet with all the sugar it contained.

I looked forward to our visits to my mother's parents on Sunday mornings after going swimming at the Mounts Baths, which was a full-size swimming pool in the middle of Northampton. The shallow end was not at all shallow for a small boy like me and at the deep end where I did not dare venture for many a year there were three diving boards, one nearly touching the ceiling.

My brother and I only had one set of grandparents, unlike most other children we knew, most had two sets and the reason being our father's parents were now both deceased and had lived on the other side of the world, so we never got the chance to meet them. Our mother's parents were Granny and Grandad Blaney, good old Irish Catholics. At that time Granny Blaney worked in a factory for a company called Mettoy in Northampton producing large quantities of different types of toys. They lived very near to the factory in a little terraced house, Althorpe Road, St James to be exact, (the area was known as Jimmy's end to the locals), A two-up two-down house, the kitchen and bathroom at the back on the lower floor leading to a small back yard.

It was in the late sixties or early seventies that they moved to a small village called Blisworth near Northampton and that house was in a very similar style.

Visits to them, mainly on a Sunday, were always exciting for two young boys. My brother and I would sit quietly whilst my parents would discuss the events of the past week with our grandparents, all in front of an open lit fire.

Then there would be that moment we both had been waiting for since we had arrived, and one that we had got so used to and had expected nearly every visit. Gran would rise from her chair and say we can go into the parlour now.

Alexander and I following eagerly, as she led the way to the front of the house, opening the door to the parlour, A room kept for special occasions and visitors, not family mind you, the insurance man was one such visitor allowed, so I was told?

Then my brother and I would peer round the parlour door as it was gradually opened by Gran, our eyes looking straight across to the other side of the room to see what was on top of the sideboard. We used to be so transfixed that we were totally oblivious to anything else other than this large glass fronted sideboard.

Most weeks there was an array of toy cars carefully lined up in front of their boxes and our eyes scanned them individually one by one, but we were not allowed to touch. Then Gran would ask us which item we would like, as we took it in turns on each visit to go first and choose — but only one mind you.

I remember collecting the whole of the Chipperfield Circus set whilst Alexander collected all the cars from the television programs and films of that period, *Chitty Chitty Bang Bang, James Bond, The Man from Uncle, Thunderbirds* and *the Monkeys,* to name just a few.

We were also the first in our village to get those orange Space Hoppers. Alexander and I were very popular with the

other children; we had footballs, pogo sticks, cricket sets, our pillowcases at Christmas were stacked to the top, we were very lucky boys to say the least.

Sundays just seemed to fly by after a visit to Gran's, home for dinner, then in the afternoon either a trip to Salcey Forest for a walk through the woods or a trip to Abington Park to walk around the lakes and go on the swings and slides. Whichever we did it was to get us some fresh air before going home and having tea while listening to *Sing Something Simple* with Cliff Adams and his Singers followed by *Pick of the Pops* chart show.

After tea we were to have a bath, then get ready for bed as it was school the next day. My brother and I would share the bath water which was not uncommon back then. Luckily enough for me I always went in first, mind you that bathroom was cold in winter as the two bar heater tucked high upon the wall opposite hardly gave out any heat at first, so although my brother got slightly colder and dirtier water he had the warmer room, fair's fair as they say.

Just a normal family day out in the car

We as a family did most things any other family did in the late sixties during a normal year such as go on holiday in our little red Triumph Herald estate to Pontins in Devon for a week in a chalet or to a static caravan on California Sands near Great Yarmouth.

We took family visits to the circus when it arrived in Northampton, they had real live lions, tigers and bears (oh my). In the school holidays Alexander and I played in our cul-de-sac with friends from our street. There was Mark Page from next door who had an older sister and two brothers, the Pragnell boys, Richard Wolf and many more besides. We would play cricket and football every chance we could.

I remember the old couple at number thirty-three, the Beryl's, old Ma Beryl, as we would call her, would be peeping behind the blinds in her front room to see if the ball went in their garden then bang on the window when you tried to retrieve it. I think every street had an old Ma Beryl, but all we did was go to the shed in our garden and get another ball as we had an endless supply courtesy of Grandma and Mettoy in Northampton. I think that's what got to her more than anything — we could play all day, what fun!

On one occasion playing in the street with my brother, one of the children threw a stone catching Alexander full in the face hitting his glasses shattering glass into his left eye. A mad dash to the hospital in Northampton saw us all sitting in a room, Alexander in front of us on a separate chair as the doctor under a bright light began to clean his eye. The creepy thing about this is the doctor then removed the eye, leaving it to hang down on the cheek of my brother while he cleaned the back of it and the socket from whence it came. The doctor then asked my brother if he would like to see behind himself, so not to miss this extraordinary chance and following the old saying 'seeing is believing' the doctor lifted up his eye and as Alexander leaned to his right Dad, Mum and I all saw his eyeball peering around to look at us like something out of the H. G. Wells film *War of the Worlds*. Alexander telling us he could see backwards as well as straight ahead at the same time, as I said, creepy.

The fun fair came every year to our village; it set up on the local recreational ground for a week and proved very popular.

We celebrated bonfire night at Simpson Barracks, an army training camp on the outskirts of our village, a good night out, food, a large fire and plenty of fireworks to stand and look up at in awe. At the end of the year we always had a trip to the pantomime at the Old Rep Theatre in Northampton. (Oh yes, we did!)

CHAPTER 4

London

MY FATHER HAD received a letter in the February of 1969 instructing him to visit London in early March for an all-important meeting.

So it was March 1969 that normal life as I had known it started to change for this run of the mill family from middle England. It was on a bright Tuesday morning after breakfast we set off down the M1 in our little red Triumph Herald towards London.

The bonnet vibrating vigorously due to the speed we were travelling at and the flimsy clips it was being held down by on each side. We were doing between 60 and 70 mph. This was fast for us as the car was normally used just to potter its way around Northampton. Alexander and I were trying to see how many other red cars we could count on the way. Although the motorway was quite empty it still took us around an hour to reach the end of the motorway and the outskirts of London.

Now heading towards central London, my father pointed out to us the landmarks of Swiss Cottage and Lords cricket ground as we passed them by, London being very busy with all the taxis and Routemaster buses going about their daily business. With all the hustle and bustle of what was going on out of my window it didn't seem very long before we reached our destination.

This was a very large red brick building which seemed to stretch halfway down the street and around the corner, it had large flags reaching right out over the pavement in the street from the first floor waving lightly as they did so. As you looked up, the building just seemed to go on for ever and touch the sky — it was that big.

As we pulled up outside the entrance in our little Triumph and stopped we were approached by a man dressed in a long green overcoat with brass buttons and an embroidered top hat. He proceeded to open the car door on my father's side and as he did so uttered the words, 'welcome to Claridge's'.

The night before, Mum had packed two suitcases, just the same as if we were going on our summer holidays, and these were removed from the boot of the car by a younger man and taken immediately inside.

No sooner than my father had announced our arrival at the front desk of this plush hotel he was greeted by two foreign looking men in suits, just like out of a scene from the TV show *The Man from Uncle,* very strange indeed.

This was still all a mystery to my brother and I but all would be explained very soon as we were ushered through the foyer and into a lift by these two men in suits. The door was closed by a rather tall lift operator dressed in a green suit and matching hat, then once we were all inside he proceeded to slam a secondary gate shut making me jump,

I watched him intensely as he pressed a button that made the lift begin its ascent. My father then began talking to one of the men in the lift in a language which I had never heard before, let alone my father speak..

I did not even know he could speak another language, to me he was just plain old Dad. He was speaking fluently in what I later came to know as Pashto, which was what you would call his mother tongue.

I had never considered my father as being from anywhere else, other than in our own little world in a bungalow in Northamptonshire but now all that had changed in my head by one trip to London and the sound of his voice.

I now know that my father was born and brought up in the North West Frontier of India, which going back centuries was part of the Persian Empire, Pashto was the language commonly spoken in those parts and had been passed down the generations, although most of the population in that region now speak Punjabi or Urdu or a mix of them both.

My father arrived in Great Britain in 1947 as a young Muslim boy and had met my mother in the early 1950s, my brother was born in 1957 and myself in 1962.

There was no hint of any kind of religion in our house and the only real religious contact I had encountered was on Friday mornings in primary school. This was when our local rector would read a story from the Bible, which did not really sink into any of us too well in our class, all we could do was giggle and snigger, for on most occasions you could tell the rector had eaten egg for breakfast, due to most of it ending up down the top of his black tunic. Religion on my mother's side of the family was Catholic, my grandparents went every Sunday evening to the cathedral in Northampton but again my brother and I were not ushered by our parents into that world either.

My father had lost both of his parents while he was in Britain but failed to return for any of their funerals, his father's in the 1950s and his mother's in the early 1960s.

The reason which I had later in life found out, why a young man had not returned to his native home for either funerals of

Dad's father, my grandfather and Dad's mother, my grandmother

his parents like most children would in those circumstances, was all to do with religion.

My father's family are Muslims and religion plays a significant role in that part of the world. My father had not only left his immediate family but under Muslim law had chosen to leave an arranged marriage.

Although my father had left for Britain when he was seventeen for education purposes, he was also expected to return and fulfill his family duties as a Muslim boy and marry his cousin. My father had rarely met his proposed bride, probably once or twice when they were both very young and only then at some large family gathering. This breach of Muslim law not accepting his arranged marriage rocked his family to the core which led my father to become known, as what we would say in this country a 'black sheep' of the family.

So, returning was not in reality an option for him although his heart must have been severely hurt knowing he could not pay his last respects to either of his parents. He also must have known that in marrying our mother his life could be in danger, as people have been known to be killed for this or even less in that part of the world.

He was not an only child; he was one of four boys and a girl all older than him and although they kept in touch by letters this thing called religion kept them apart.

So, my father lived his life in Britain with his new family and learnt to enjoy his life in the western world and all it could offer him, while his family lived many thousands of miles away, but he must have always had a special thought for them in the back of his mind.

We continued our upward journey in the lift as I held my mother's hand standing next to my brother. Both of us looking upwards to my father for reassurance, who was still in deep conversation with these two men, the lift operator standing like a statue in front waiting to move when we had reached our destination. A sudden stop triggered the operator to life, sliding the gate back as the door opened, we all then exited into a long brightly lavished corridor that had small but ornate tables and chairs spread out along its length. After a short walk from the lift my mother was asked to wait along with my brother and me and to sit by one of the tables. My father walked down the corridor with the two strange men and disappeared into a room on the right. Then what seemed like ages my father returned and proceeded to lead us down the corridor and into this room.

There was no one in the room other than the men who my father had followed from the lift earlier and who were now standing in front of some large double wooden doors. My father then began to explain in simple terms to my brother and me what this strange and mysterious trip was all about. Our mother already aware of what to expect, as she tried to tidy my hair with her hand and telling my brother to do up his tie. My father told us that there were people in the next room and one was my father's cousin from Pakistan and that we were to be on our best behaviour and speak to him if we are asked to do so, if not we must remain silent and at our mother's side.

At that point the large double doors began to open, and we were beckoned in by another man in a suit standing further back in the room.

As we entered my eyes were drawn to what I would perceive to be a large man sitting on a couch with cigarette in his hand and next to him a lady dressed in a brightly coloured dress which was actually a sari with very lavish gold embroidery on it, Mum had actually tried one of these on back in Springfield much to our amusement, further around the room there was another lady sitting on a single chair and she also was wearing a bright sari, very smart indeed.

My father and mother sat down while my brother and I remained standing directly opposite this man on the couch.

Mum in her sari in 18 Springfield, Wootton

My father said to us, 'this gentleman in front of you is your uncle Agha Muhammad Yahya Khan, but to most people who know of him, he is the current President of Pakistan'.

We were told the lady sitting next to him was his wife, but time has told me that my uncle wasn't married, and this was one of his many lady companions, but we still called her Auntie out of respect. The lady in the single chair was one of his closest cousins and there were also more family members who had travelled, but they were all out shopping in London. I was later told that this close cousin of the president, was also a cousin of my father and she was the woman who he most likely would have married if he had returned home after his education many years ago.

We had afternoon tea with my uncle and a lot of discussions took place which were both in English, Pashto and Punjabi which went right over my head. I just did not understand any of it but that didn't matter as I was more interested in the array of wonderful cakes that were being continually supplied by the hotel staff, the likes of which I had never ever seen before. Then around late afternoon we left my uncle's suite and proceeded back down the corridor and at the far end two rooms had been set aside for us to stay.

These two rooms had connecting doors and the room my brother and I were in had two large single beds which we found most exciting, this was due to the fact it was bunkbeds for us boys back home.

After relaxing a while in the rooms watching some TV, I began to get tired from the long day I had endured, so my parents ordered food for Alexander and myself which was delivered directly to the room.

Hamburger and chips, which in those days was a real treat, unless you were lucky enough to be taken to a Wimpy restaurant on a special occasion. The only problem was I couldn't eat it all, due to the fact I had stuffed myself with cakes all afternoon.

We got a goodnight's sleep, but I do remember my brother and me looking out of the window for what felt like ages at the busy street below, until Mum checked in on us and ordered us back to bed.

The next morning we all went downstairs to the dining room for breakfast, this was a very grand room with waiters to serve you. I remember having fresh orange juice and scrabbled egg on toast. The other family members who we had not met the day before came for breakfast and we were all introduced to them. I did not realise I had so many aunties! We had arranged to go for a stroll in Hyde Park with them that morning to get to know each other a little better as we were just as new to them as they were to us, Dad catching up on all the news from back home as we strolled. We reached a place called Speaker's Corner next to Marble Arch, where anybody could come, stand on a box on a Sunday and rant on about anything they liked. They must have been prepared to get heckled as the crowd can be very unforgiving though, today being Wednesday there wasn't anyone there anyway.

Rather than going back to Claridge's we all crossed Hyde Park to what was called Hyde Park Corner and viewed Wellingtons Arch.

Then we headed through some side streets which had some very affluent houses and entered a large building with the Pakistan flag flying outside just as it had done over Claridge's. This was the Pakistan High Commission in Belgravia where the High Commissioner to London lived and worked.

On entering we were shown into a room which had tables laid out with food and drink and we were then joined by my uncle the President of Pakistan and the High Commissioner to London to have lunch, which again was fantastic, such an array of food all with different smells and tastes and far too much for all of us to eat, even though there were around twelve or so of us. My father had matters to discuss with my uncle and the commissioner, so it was suggested that with our mother we could go out into London for the remainder of that day. My uncle had arranged for us to use the High Commissioner's car, jet black with leather seats and a wooden dashboard, very regal and with it's own driver. The driver wore a cap and opened the door for us to enter to take us anywhere in London we would like to go, but first he had a surprise for us to go and see.

Apparently, the day before we arrived in London the same car we were now in had been used as one of the cars in a film and had gone on location to Wormwood Scrubs and the Royal Lancashire Hotel. The chauffeur now driving us to the Oakhurst film studios, where they needed the car to film the last required scene. Oakhurst film studio must have been located south of the River Thames because we had to cross it by a stunning bridge which now I know to be Hammersmith Bridge.

We arrived at the studio which looked like the Mettoy factory building my Gran worked at in Northampton, holding my mother's hand we were all led inside by a man who introduced himself as Peter. He explained to my Mum what was going to happen. This was one of the last scenes to be shot before the film would eventually be completed and go off to editing and hopefully be released by the end of that year.

This film, by the way, was to be an all-time British classic *The Italian Job* which at the time didn't mean anything to me at all. After going down a corridor with offices each side that had frosted glass windows as walls, we reached a very large open area that had a huge cinema screen on the wall with a picture of a street scene on it. The High Commissioner's car was brought in through a large door to our left and placed in front of this large screen. My mother got quite excited at the appearance of a man to our right and whispered to us that he was a famous actor, his name is Michael Caine.

We watched as he walked towards the car being followed by a woman who was speaking to one of the film crew in a very loud American accent.

For what seemed to me like ages the actors and the crew stood around the car talking, they then called our driver over and after a while the driver went to the car and from inside produced a small flag and a hat which Michael Caine then tried on.

A short while later everybody dispersed, and Michael Caine went round and got in the passenger side while the loud American speaking actress (Margret Bly) got in the driver's side. The man, Peter, we had met earlier talked to the actors in the car through the window, then a large camera with two men operating it on wheels was brought up to the outside of the car window a short distance from the driver's side where the woman was sitting, it looked all too complicated to me I can tell you.

We all watched as Peter shouted 'QUIET' and 'ACTION', and at that moment the screen at the back began to move from left to right, this looked as though the car was moving along a street and with two men at the back of the car slowly rocking the stationary vehicle to simulate the car was in motion.

This went on for over an hour stopping and starting repeated calls for silence, then action with one guy slamming a chalk board every time it happened.

By the time they had finished I was really getting quite bored, as all I could see were two people in a car being rocked repeatedly for no apparent reason.

We didn't meet any of the actors as they left all rather quickly with their individual entourages in tow but we were thanked by Peter who was actually the director of the film and allowed us to get into the car before it drove out of the studio building.

Mother had arranged to meet the president's lady companion and his cousin, the lady my Dad could have married, at Harrods for some shopping after we had finished at the studio about four o'clock.

So, any ideas my brother and I had of lording it around the sites and streets of London, chauffeur driven, and in a limousine went right out of the window.

It was now late afternoon and we were off back across the river to Harrods so Mum could go shopping as arranged earlier.

We arrived outside the store, the concierge opened the door of the car for us to exit, now due to the fact that the pathways were quite busy and the department store was very close to the road I could not really get any sort of perspective of the size of this building, only that each window as far as the eye could see in each direction had a green coloured canopy over them with the name, Harrods, written in gold letters. These canopies darkened the footway but in doing so made the large windows and their content stand out even more with all lights on. We entered through a revolving door, my hand held tightly by my mother.

Harrods was just so big, packed with so many people and counter after counter going on for ages, it was like a town inside a building. What a madhouse I thought as both my brother and I were being dragged up and down each aisle.

Eventually we met our so called auntie and Dad's cousin in the fur coat department. This was temporarily closed off to the general public while we were in this area, I supposed for security reasons, but the relief to eventually have some breathing space was very welcoming. I am sure looking at some of the items here in this department that they were still alive, my brother and I actually laughed at some of the fur hats that really looked like plenty of the cats back home in our village that sat on many a window sill. My auntie could also see the funny side to our jokes but seeing that we were very uninterested in that sort of thing suggested that we go and find the pet department while my mother and our Dad's cousin continued to shop.

Now, you have heard the saying you can buy anything in Harrods, well in the pet kingdom department this was true in the 1960s. Alongside all the normal household pets there were several different types of parrot, and a rather funny looking racoon that you could touch and feed, it was more like a zoo than a shop. Again, they shut the whole department to the general public and my brother and I had the whole area to ourselves. We sat on a large couch and were brought books to look through, these books had photographs in them of lions, cheetahs and other wild cats which you could purchase at a price, they even had a small monkey all kitted out in a bell suit if you so wished, and a baby elephant but where on earth would you keep that in a two bedroom bungalow back in Northampton? I was not sure of the time, but we eventually met up with my mother again and they all agreed that it was time to head back to the hotel.

I know I was very tired and just wasn't in any mood to start walking again, but what I did not realise was the car was waiting for us exactly where it dropped us off, apparently the car could be parked anywhere in London due to the fact it had special *corps diplomatique* licence plates; I was so pleased it was there.

My mother and my two aunties sat in the back of the car and in front of them there was a little pull down seat built into the back of the passenger's side that I sat on, which was funny because I would be going backwards when the car moved forward, never done that before. My brother got to sit in the front by the driver and he then showed my aunties the items they used in the film, the hat and the small flag on a metal rod which fitted on the front of the car, but only when the High Commissioner was on official business in London.

We arrived back at Claridge's where we were met by my father and uncle, and it was arranged for us boys to have food in our room again and watch television, as we were both quite exhausted from todays hectic but enjoyable events.

My mother and father dressed up that evening for dinner in the hotel restaurant with the President and his family while my brother and I were looked after by the hotel babysitter, well I say looked after, you could ring a number if you needed her. In fact I never saw her, I suppose it was for our parents peace of mind if anything.

The next day mother woke us boys and we all went down to breakfast, my father said we were leaving for home today but would visit Woburn Abbey on the way back as an extra treat to see all the animals for real and not in a book. After getting ready to leave and with our bags taken down to the reception area, we went to say our goodbyes to my uncle and his companion and the rest of our extended family.

We entered the suite and were met by the High Commissioner and his wife who said that we could visit them at their London residence any time.

Our uncle came through from the next room and beckoned

my brother and me to him and after giving him a big cuddle and shaking his hand he then gave us a present each in a box which we were asked to open.

These gifts were the flag and the hat from the car that Michael Caine used in the film *The Italian Job* the day before.

My brother was given the flag and I was given the hat, which was called a 'Jinnah Cap', and originated from the tribal areas of the North West Frontier. The Jinnah Cap became part of the national dress and was worn by many Pakistani politicians.

How everyone laughed as I tried the hat on because it was much too big for me, but in 2020 it now fits just right, what a memento to have kept!

We then left Claridge's and London, what an exceptional few days that came out of the blue, how would I tell my friends back home in our little village of Wootton? They would never believe me but it was real, and that's all that matters. I knew it and nobody, but nobody, could take away the memories from the last few days.

Family life got back to normal after our visit to London, my brother and I went back to school and told all our friends our stories. At the end of the summer we all went to the cinema, to watch *The Italian Job*, seeing the exact scene in the film which we were lucky enough but also bored to view in person.

CHAPTER 5

Family Life

DAD BOUGHT a new car in September 1969, that's when the new registration came out. He kept the same make, Triumph, but went for a more sporty model with a more powerful two litre engine, he bought a Triumph Vitesse in dark blue, a very similar shape to our red Herald and it had an eight track cassette put in it as an extra under the dashboard rather than just having a two band radio, (very up market).

He then bought the soundtrack from the musical *Hair*, and played it very loud every time we went out on a family outing in the countryside, I remember all of us singing along to *Let the Sunshine in*.

One of the family outings we would go on quite regularly was to Leicester, over an hour away to visit our Auntie Gladys, she wasn't our real auntie, we just called her that out of respect. We would spend time with her family and have Sunday tea, Mum and Dad seemed to get on well with Auntie Gladys for some unknown reason and had known her way before I was born. The only real auntie we had was Auntie Deirdre, she was our mother's sister but we had to call her Auntie Dee as she didn't like her given name, she was much younger than Mum but looked up to her older sister for a lot of guidance.

There was a large age gap between the two of them since Mum was the first child of four and Dee was the last of the bunch. Mum also had another sister and brother, but Gran lost her second child Moira when she was a baby so that left our uncle Seamus definitely one of life's characters, to say the least.

It was now late January 1970 and I can remember we had

our usual covering of deep snow, so school was cancelled, and all the village children just had fun sledging and snowball fighting before finally going back to school several days later. My brother told my father he could get tickets through friends to see our local team Northampton Town play football against the mighty Manchester United in February that year, in a FA cup match at the local stadium. My father said that he could only go if he took me and fortunately a ticket was available, so along with a few of my brothers' friends we headed off on a cold crisp morning, by bus, to the County Ground in Northampton used both for cricket and football.

The game was being played on Saturday afternoon at three o'clock on February the seventh and I didn't know what I expected to see that day, but what I witnessed on that cold sunny February afternoon on what I can only describe as a muddy field, would shape the way a part of my life would lead in the future.

We all knew and had heard of George Best, I even remembered him from the television the year before advertising eggs for breakfast, and the slogan went; 'E for B, and Georgie Best'. That afternoon he turned out for Manchester United after a four-week suspension for kicking the ball out of a referee's hand, and took all his frustrations out on Northampton Town by scoring six goals in an eight-two victory over them, what a player and what a day for a young boy to remember.

Going to school on Monday all I could do was talk about George Best and what I witnessed two days before, everybody wanted to be that player, kicking the ball around a concrete playground on another cold February lunchtime, everyone became a Manchester United supporter in our area after that astonishing weekend.

Events came quick and fast in 1970. We all watched the Apollo 13 Space mission take off in April for another landing on the moon, but this had to be aborted four days into the journey due to an explosion on board and returned to Earth, a bit of a disappointment for everyone.

Then at the end of May and into June I remember every boy in our village rushing home from school as fast as we could to watch the World cup from Mexico on the TV. England were there as the reigning World Champions; the whole country was excited. I even got Dad to buy his petrol from the Esso garage so I could collect the silver coins they gave you with every gallon of petrol bought. I used to swap them with the other boys at school, but I still never managed to get Jeff Astle.

In July, the last day of the school year, all the children in our

18 Springfield, Wootton, 1970

school would move up one year and for me I was going into year three. All my classmates were allocated a new desk and someone to sit next to by our then new teacher for the following academic year.

I was to sit next to John Metcalf, a boy who lived two streets away from me in our village, he had several brothers and a sister who went to the secondary school with my brother. In early September when we returned to school and the class sat at their new desks, the seat next to mine was vacant and would be for the remainder of that year. Unfortunately, and very tragically for his family, John would not return to school again, due to him drowning that summer in a pond not far from our house in the grounds of Simpson Barracks. This was the Army training camp which was attached to our village. He slipped into the water while trying to catch frogs, it could have happened to any one of us, perish the thought. I could not imagine how a mother could cope losing a child so young or losing someone from your own close family, only seven years old and with his whole life before him. Life went on in our village and a lot of people tended to forget about John but for me the empty chair each school morning would not allow me to become one of those people.

Mum had started a new job in the September of that year, a, shorthand typist for Barclaycard in Northampton. She would drop me off at the school gates then head off into Northampton, finishing at two o'clock so she could be home when my brother and I returned from our schools.

In mid-December just before we broke for the Christmas holidays I got home from school and instead of Mum being there it was Dad, we waited for my brother then Dad told us Mum has had a car accident that very morning, skidding on black ice and rolling down an embankment.

It could have been a lot worse, we could have actually lost her, as the car was a total right off, rolling completely on to its

Dad's pride and joy, a bit worse for wear,
recovered but not salvageable

roof crushing it down.

Fortunately for us she wasn't wearing a seat belt, it was not compulsory to do so back then, and she was able to lay flat across the two front seats and in doing so she saved herself. There's a saying when your numbers up your numbers up, but for Mum it wasn't this time or was it just lady luck. It might have been her Catholic faith and all those trips to church on a Sunday, but what we do know is she ended up with a lot of internal and external bruising, who knows what's round the next corner but one thing's for sure, you only get one go at life.

The insurance paid out but quite a few weeks later in early January, and they could only replace the car with a saffron yellow coloured version, one of the last Triumph Vitesses left as production was coming to an end for that particular model.

The good thing about this model was it now had overdrive, which was better for the engine, and had a built-in radio cassette player very 'posh'!

After another typical English winter which was gauged by

31

how cold the milk was at school in the morning or how many days off you would get either by the bad weather, such as deep snow or indeed electricity outages so the heating didn't work and no school dinners could be provided.

1971 seemed to slip in very quietly how very different the year end would be for our family if only there was such a thing as a crystal ball, and you could change what lay ahead? The only time we thought we could see into the future was on a Saturday evening watching John Pertwee in *Doctor Who* and most of that for a young boy was seen staring from behind a cushion or even the settee. The Americans launched Apollos 14 and 15, in their space race and landed both on the moon, while Russia sends up the space station Salyut then two rockets to dock with it, and a Mars probe, all this was really good stuff for a young boy growing up in that period. The world was changing very fast indeed, and we were all going along for the ride.

During the following months my father would take several trips to London on weekdays to see the High commissioner, and on several occasions the four of us went and visited him and his family on a Sunday playing in their house or garden. Sometimes we would go out and see all the sights that London had to offer, the zoo, Tower Bridge, the Houses of Parliament and even Speakers' Corner, watching one man on a box rant on about the Vietnam War. These visits were very exciting for a small boy but also very tiring and I would usually fall asleep in the back of the car on the way home.

Summer was the usual long holiday for me and my brother playing out all day in the street and the surrounding area with all our friends from the village.

What we either couldn't have foreseen or even tried to predict was how that summer was going to end for the two of us.

School was due to start around the third week of September but about a week before we were due to go back and start another typical school year, the both of us were told by our parents that we would not be attending school until well into the New Year of 1972. This was because my father and mother had decided that we would all be going on a trip to Pakistan, to see where my father was brought up and to meet the rest of his and our extended family. Now, normally even back then this meant getting on a flight in London, then several hours later getting off a plane in another country on the other side of the world. No, not us, whether it was the hippie era of the sixties coming out in Mum and Dad, or they were just that 'go for it' type, in other words totally mad.

Dad's trips to London in the week with the High Commissioner this year and the year before were to secure visas for different countries that we needed to drive through, because they decided for whatever reason we were going to go in our saffron yellow Triumph Vitesse. Perhaps Mum and Dad had been listening to the music of The Beatles and *Sergeant Pepper* too much, tripped out and got confused between a yellow submarine and a yellow Triumph Vitesse. Who knows? – but at that moment, to my brother and I, the American and Russian space trips looked more easier to do, as we were told we would be also leaving the following week, travelling over five thousand miles, across two continents, taking in eight different countries, to reach our destination in our small Triumph? Mum had already told the two schools that we would not be attending until the following spring. They also booked us an appointment with the doctor for vaccinations, keeping this from us so we would not worry about having them.

Dad had been to the doctors early that year and had the injections he required. Now at the doctors my brother had his injections first; they were for yellow fever, followed by malaria, smallpox, hepatitis A and B, tetanus, typhoid, diphtheria and rabies, all very vital for the areas of the world we were heading for. I'm sure there would be fewer injections if you were going to the moon! Mum and I had our vaccinations together, we were told by our doctor that we could not have the smallpox injection due to Mum's eczema and my asthma. How I ribbed my brother that he had to have more injections than Mum and me, because he was more likely to catch all these diseases, it just seemed funny at the time but beware, 'he who laughs first, laughs last', as they say, but one thing we both knew and felt was very numb arms for the next few days and beyond, but we were told it was for our own good. The last week was very busy going round visiting family and friends to say our goodbyes and to explain to them what we were about to do and how, I think they all thought we were barmy.

Mum and I went to the AA shop in Northampton where she had ordered all the latest road maps that were needed and a GB badge for the back of the car. Dad had taken Alexander

The day before we leave, new roof rack on tying ropes at the ready.

to pick up all the important items we needed for this trip including a new roof rack to store our belongings on.

The day before we left we said goodbye to our near neighbours and our friends in the street. Dad had taken most of that day loading up the car, which sat very low to the ground with all the weight and that's before we would get in.

The boot was well crammed with items mainly for the car itself that we might need, this left the roof rack for the cases with our clothes and personal items all covered with a tarpaulin. Doing it this way meant Dad could take everything off the top of the car every night and take it in to where we would be stopping, leaving the car looking as normal as possible, but then having to reload it all again every time before we set off the next day, quite a chore for him quite a chore indeed. That night it was to bed early for my brother and I, not sure if it was excitement or trepidation for what was to come but both of us could not get off to sleep straight away but then eventually the sandman came.

CHAPTER 6

The Journey

Day 1: Leaving England

AT HALF-PAST FOUR in the morning on the fourteenth of September 1971, both my brother and I were woken suddenly in our bunk beds by our Dad, get dressed he said we are due to leave in about half an hour's time, although it felt as though we had just gone to bed.

Our parents had left us sleeping for as long as possible, with our eyes barely open and our clothes for the journey laid at the end of our beds the night before, we tried to spring into action as best we could. Now the only thing I can remember left at the end of my bed that was important, before this day, was my pillowcase full of presents from Father Christmas, but now it was time to grow up and grow up fast.

Teeth cleaned and face washed, clothes on and out the back door leaving that child in me well and truly back in the bedroom. It was pitch black and cold as was the car, due to the fact Dad did not want to start the engine and leave it running in case he woke any of our near neighbours. I climbed into the back seat of our two door car and sat on the driver's side, Mum passing me the pillow off my bed and a blanket, try and go back to sleep she whispered quietly, easier said than done I thought. House all locked, Alexander was in the back behind Mum with his pillow and blanket, we had two large rucksacks between us as a divider stacked full of food to use for the first few days. Dad climbed in and said here we go no turning back now, of which I thought was strange as he did exactly that, proceeding to start the engine and turn back looking over his shoulder to reverse the car up the incline of our drive. As we reached the top and our car tilted backwards to descend onto the road our headlights caught the number and name of our house, (18 Manzil). We all looked and wondered when we would see this iconic sign again?

We then turned and headed down our cul-de-sac known as Springfield, leaving our nearest neighbours the Pages at number 16, the Pragnells and Wolfs at numbers 12 & 10 respectively. Everything was quiet apart from our little car still on choke, and the rough concrete road vibrating beneath us, an orange glow catching my face from the dim light of the lamposts, the ones I had played around innocently many times with those friends. We slipped gently out of the village, not one of the many residents had noticed our departure, life for them would probably go on as normal as they woke from their sleep in an hour or two, just as our epic adventure was beginning.

Onto the M1, a trip done many times but not this early, there was hardly a vehicle on the road, just the odd lorry here and there as we proceeded towards London.

We had started our journey at some ungodly hour so as to miss the traffic build up in London, as we had to cross the whole of the city to catch the four o'clock ferry from Dover, which would then be heading for the port of Ostend in Belgium. We entered the outskirts of London around six in the morning, passing Swiss Cottage, which I had recognised, as we continued deeper into the capital city.

They say some large cities never sleep but what I saw out of my window was quite a sleepy environment, with a few cars and taxis starting their normal morning routines along with the usual milk float and dustbin lorries.

We passed Marble Arch and proceeded along Park Lane, where the large and expensive hotels were just springing into life. We then circumnavigated Wellingtons Arch where my family and I walked with the President's family two years earlier on that most memorable visit. All of a sudden London seemed to rise from its slumber as we approached the Victoria station area this was a real hub for commuters heading into the city by train bus and underground. We were now crossing the river Thames, via Vauxhall Bridge, the river below looked black cold and uninviting as it shimmered from the ever dwindling lights of the city above. The traffic got slightly heavier heading for South East London and the A2, which would eventually guide us to our destination of Dover along with Mum's reliable map reading. The city of London appeared to stretch for an eternity as we continued and getting busier with every passing minute. We had now reached an area called Blackheath. Dad pulled the car over on a small slip road so we could all take a break, but also checking that the car was running fine.

Mum broke out the thermos so we could have a warm drink, as we all leant on the boot of the car whilst looking across London, watching the lights of the city which seemed to go out one by one as the dawn light crept slowly over this capital city.

It was now around eight o'clock, Dad said another hour and we would be clear of London. As we headed down the A2 towards Canterbury Mum got out the egg sandwiches she had made the night before, and after eating them I must have fallen asleep, my head resting on the pillow taken from my bed hours earlier. I awoke to find us parked in a queue of cars, alongside us was a queue of large lorries, most of which were foreign registered, travelling back to their country of origin and back to their home and families. Just the opposite for us, we were leaving the comfort of our home and country and heading into the unknown and whatever that may bring.

All the vehicles were waiting to board the Sealink ferry to take us onward on our individual journeys, loading would begin around half-past two, ready for the four o'clock sailing, to catch the afternoon tide. The ferry looked huge compared to our little Triumph parked below, and now with its front end gapping open like some giant mouth, we proceeded to load and as our car drove up the ramp to enter its large cavity, it was then that I thought back to that famous film *The Italian Job* when Michael Cane was ushering the cars on to the ferry to cross the channel, it just seemed so familiar as we were being directed onto the ferry.

Dad parked the car as instructed on the car deck, there was a separate deck for the Lorries, and then we made our way up the well-worn metal stairs to the rear deck area for passengers which faced out to sea. Then no sooner had we stood against the white rear railings, the engines started churning and the whole ferry began to shudder and lurch backwards before turning in the harbour. As we cleared the harbour entrance and the water below us turned white from the force of the propellers, we all looked back towards Dover, the evening light catching the white cliffs as well as the castle that sat above overlooking the whole scene. Slowly the large cliffs just shrank into the distance and it left us again pondering if and when we would see them again.Then whilst holding my mother's hand we made our way inside to find a place to sit for the three-and-a-half-hour journey across the English Channel to Belgium.

Darkness fell as the lights of the near continent and the port of Ostend drew closer to our ferry and eventually, we docked, after disembarking and going through customs it was past eight o'clock. Dad had booked our first night in a town called Ghent about an hour from the port. We were now driving on the other side of the road which in the back of our car didn't really make much difference but as a driver and in the dark concentration was at the up most importance. As we entered Ghent it started to drizzle making the cobble stoned road glisten while our little car rumbled along under the streetlamps until we finally reached the corner of a tiny square where the hotel was located.

Dad had booked a room in the hotel with one double bed and a single, the bathroom was down at the end of the corridor. The décor in the room was very old and it had like a velvet wallpaper with a red pattern, but it was now quite late and for only one night the room was not too important. Dad brought up the suitcases while, Mum, my brother and I used the bathroom quickly and put on our pyjamas.

Alexander slept in the single bed and I slept between Mum and Dad that night but when I woke in the morning Dad had moved and slept on a funny shaped settee in the room which now I know was called a chaise longue, this was due to the fact the double bed was very small compared to an English double and he couldn't get comfortable with me in the bed as well.

Day 2: Germany and Wurtzburg

It was around eight in the morning when we left the hotel, Dad had loaded the cases on the roof rack and we headed out of Ghent for Brussels, one of the many large cities we would either pass through or skirt round on our journey.

Dad had the cassette player on a lot of the time, and I remembered it was either The Supremes or The Seekers, we would listen to as we trundled across Europe *(rock and rolling out across the bay, all bound for Morningtown)* or in our case the North West Frontier many miles away.

With Brussels behind us, the German border soon approached, and as we passed through customs I heard my mother speak for the first time in German to the control guard, as she passed the passports through the window for him to view. Apparently, Mum had been taught German at the Notre Dame School for Roman Catholic girls in Abington Street Northampton and was quite fluent although up until now she probably didn't have much call to use it. But with the end of the Second World War only twenty-five years earlier, most of Europe, and even Turkey was more likely to have German rather than English as a second language, so this attribute would hopefully come in very handy.

As we entered Germany it was obvious that the roads were much better, going from being small A roads in Belgium to large motorways called *autobahns*, this would also help us to achieve greater distances. Mum decided to drive to give Dad a bit of a breather and to catch up on his sleep, although she still needed him to look at the maps when required. We passed Cologne and we could see the twin towers of its cathedral in the distance as we headed south deeper and deeper into Germany, only stopping for petrol or a comfort break but eating all that the rucksacks could offer us, not really healthy, crisps, biscuits and chocolate, but just what a nine year old loves, so no complaints from me.

It was late afternoon as we skirted round Frankfurt, and as the night would be closing in soon, Dad said at the next major town we would stop and look for accommodation for the night. That stop ended up being the small town of Wurzburg, right beside the Autobahn and dominated by a large Bavarian castle overlooking the town and river. It was here we found a bed and breakfast to stop for the night, and after Mum had spoken to the lady at the door in German, we unloaded the car for the night. My brother and I had two single beds in the same room while Mum and Dad were in the room next to us. The lady had agreed to supply us with a supper which consisted of soup, which had large potatoes in it, along with nice crusty bread. Soon after that we all got ready for bed as we had another long day ahead of us tomorrow. As I climbed into the bed I can remember how heavy the blankets were, so once you were in bed it was hard to move but it kept you very warm, apparently it can get very cold in mid-winter in this part of Germany, much much colder than when the milk freezes outside our school gates back home in Wootton.

Day 3: The Mountains of Austria

Up early for breakfast which was cold meats and bread with a hot drink, load up the car and off we trot back on to the *autobahn* with Mum driving again heading towards Munich. Our Triumph Vitesse MK 2, made in Coventry, with all this weight on board held it's own on these marvellous German roads eating up the tarmac mile after mile with no problem. The two-litre engine in overdrive singing its own merry tune on roads with no speed limits, passing inferior foreign cars as if to say, 'look at me I'm British made and proud of it'. After about two hours we were going round the city of Nuremberg, then it was about another three hours when we stopped for lunch on the outskirts of Munich, very close to the Olympic Stadium. This was then under construction ready for the 1972 summer Olympics, what a sight! I had never seen so many high rise cranes in one place before, there must have been at least ten or twelve of them all going about their business, like robots dancing in the sky.

Dad said all being well by late afternoon we would be crossing the German border into Austria, and so it proved to be, not bad going crossing Germany in around two days in our little Triumph, the magnificent motorways helping enormously. It made you wonder who actually won the war twenty-six years ago? (To drive twelve hours from Northampton to Dover, around 150 miles, or driving the whole of Germany, around 500 miles in fifteen hours).

Austria was a completely different country once we had cleared the area of Salzburg, it turned into small winding roads set between huge snow-capped mountains rolling down to lush green meadows, covered with wooden chalets of all different sizes.It was in one such chalet that we found a bed and breakfast, and again they spoke German and the breakfast they served was very similar apart from the milk,

Dad, Mum and me near the Austrian-German border

which taste like no other milk I had tasted before, apparently although cold in a jug out of the fridge, this was fresh from the cows the night before, never seeing or knowing what a bottle was.

Day 4: Goodbye Austria, Hello Yugoslavia

Again, Dad loaded the roof rack and off we set, winding down the valleys with the sun shining on one side turning waterfalls into glistening rainbows as we passed, and the cold of the shade on the other. We stopped along the way about mid morning, and I remembered whilst out of the car shouting out my name, and hearing my voice returning in ever decreasing volumes as though I was some were up in the mountains; this was most likely the first time I had heard my own echo.

By mid-day Austria was to be no more for us as we began the process of entering the country of Yugoslavia, stuck behind lorry after lorry. We queued for what seemed ages, armed guards watching everybody with intense interest, pulling out of the queue one van with Dutch number plates and taking it into a large shed nearby. After about three hours, with our boot and roof rack completely unpacked checked and repacked, we were again on our way. Dad was hoping to get past Zagreb, but with the delay at the border and the state of the roads, potholes by the dozen, Zagreb became our destination for the night.

Yugoslavia was a communist country and you could tell this even when you are only nine years old, from the brightness and freshness of Austria that we left behind, to the dull and drab colour of Yugoslavia with very few cars on the roads, and those that were, spewing large quantities of smoke from their exhausts. In the city there were trolley buses crammed to the gunnels, full of worn out faces, I am sure in their own way they were just as happy as the rest of Europe but you wouldn't have known it, someone needed to tell their faces that!

The hotel we found to stay at was very drab with furniture older than Grans in her parlour back in Northampton, dark walls and very dull lighting, it was hard to see why you would want to smile and be happy if this is what they went home to every day. It was only for one night for us, simple soup and bread for our evening meal, and fried egg and bread for breakfast after a somewhat decent night's sleep.

Day 5: Zagreb to Belgrade

Car packed early in the morning, we headed out of Zagreb slightly getting lost as the road signs made no sense at all or Mums map reading skills had taken a turn for the worst, on only day five and still in Europe?

Belgrade would be the next destination we were heading for after the extra hour spent touring the streets of Zagreb, my brother saying there's that monument again for the third time, what fun we had laughing until Mum turned round and gave us both a quick slap on our bare legs, (ouch). Again, due to the rather bad condition of the roads and being stuck behind numerous smoke belching lorries, Belgrade eventually came into view, this city was much larger than Zagreb, and was the capital city of Yugoslavia, but again just as drab. This city had a lot more traffic and most alarming, armed soldiers that seemed to appear on every street corner.

Although the city looked dull and grey as I peered from my window you had the feeling everybody was watching us, but then who wouldn't as this saffron yellow car was most likely the brightest car in the city at that time, went slowly down its streets.

This time Dad decided to reach the far side of the capital before finding a small hotel so that leaving the city and heading for the Bulgarian border in the morning would be less of a trauma than today's episode, thus saving our bare legs in the process.

Another dark and uninviting hotel was our shelter for the night, although they gave us nice grilled sausages and tomato's for supper.

We all went to sleep early around eight o'clock it was dark then anyway, and the lighting was poor in our rooms, apparently a good night's sleep was had by all, and much needed.

Day 6: Pushing on through Bulgaria

Breakfast was milk and cold meat, not that appealing, no bread or cereal because of an oil crisis that had hit the country at that time, as everybody was short of just the basic items. Breakfast eaten, the car loaded, and just four hours to the Bulgarian border.

The traffic got lighter and lighter the further away from Belgrade, and very fewer lorries. Dad stopped for petrol but was only allowed half a tank due to the shortages, and if you had half a tank already, you were refused any at all. We reached the border crossing with Bulgaria and there were a lot of armed guards, all the foreign vehicles were queued in one line and were surprisingly processed rather quickly, and allowed through without much delay, but the Yugoslavian vehicles that queued were thoroughly searched.

Bulgaria was another communist country in 1971 but it appeared to be less developed and more relaxed than the more modern state of Yugoslavia.

From the border we reached the outskirts of the capital city Sofia within two hours as the traffic was much lighter than in Yugoslavia. We then pushed on further into the country, eventually stopping in the small town of Kostenets, set at the foot of a very dominant mountain. I can remember very little of the place we stayed in it must have been either very boring, or was it just the routine we were now set in. For a nine year old if nothing exciting happens that day, well it's just another night's sleep in another hotel, after a long day sitting in the back of a small car.

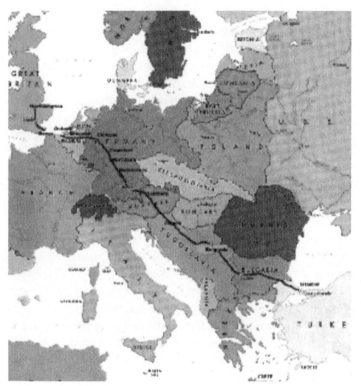

Europe conquered by the Aghas, 1971

Day 7: Istanbul, full of Eastern promise

Dad had the car ready to go when Mum woke me from a deep sleep, she helped me to get dressed and told me we would be entering Turkey sometime today, she explained that Turkey sits on two continents, Europe and Asia, and that we would have to cross a section of water by ferry called the Bosphorus, to reach the continent of Asia. We headed out of the town and into the countryside, it was apparent that the people were quite poor as the majority of the transport we came across was a cart, pulled by a donkey or horse, one even had cows pulling it. Motorised vehicles were military lorries or local buses and there were very few private cars and if you saw one it usually had foreign number plates on it.

After reaching the Turkish border around midday, we eventually crossed over which took us about an hour having to go through customs. We stopped for lunch in a town called Edirne, it is where my brother and I enjoyed our first real lamb kebab and Coke made with fresh pita bread straight out of a hot oven by the side of the road — delicious.

Dad explained to us over lunch that the next part of our journey could become very dangerous indeed once we had crossed into Asia, if we did not stick to a very simple but important rule. This being that we would never drive at night, and if we could not reach the next major town by dusk, we would not move until the next day, this was because the likelihood of tribal bandits preying on night travellers, especially foreign ones. Only in exceptional circumstances and as a last resort, if a hotel could not be found, we would stop in a lorry park with the international lorry drivers, with our car safely parked between them and letting the drivers know we were there.

Dad was also hoping to cross the Bosphorus that day, but he thought that time will beat us due to the expected hustle and bustle of the city of Istanbul, a very strategic and ancient city, formerly known as Constantinople.

Turkey was a complete contrast to Bulgaria and Yugoslavia probably due to it not being a communist country. It was vibrant and loud, with what seemed like everybody who had a horn fixed to their vehicle simultaneously using it, what a noise continuously ringing out as we travelled ever closer to Istanbul.

The sun shone brightly that day and what was noticeable, were the number of minarets that pointed to the sky high above the height of all the other the buildings. This was the first indication that in religious terms, we had started to leave a mainly Christian led world and entering the Muslim world, one my mother was raised in and the other my father, two worlds that rarely meet in marriage, but for my brother and I we were happy they did. It was the middle of the afternoon, ahead of our predicted time that the Bosphorus loomed upon us suddenly from the closeness of Istanbul's narrow streets; a large body of water appeared gleaming bright in the afternoon sunshine of day seven.

We reached one of the many ferry crossings that graced the banks of this distinctive stretch of water, and as we waited for a ferry to take us onward on our journey we stood and gazed across and got our first look at the continent of Asia. Maybe it felt like the right time or now we were at the right age for us to understand what we were about to be told. Our parents began to explain to us both that three hundred years before Jesus Christ was born, a Greek King named Alexander the Great also stood here looking at Asia when he was a young man. He went on to conquer it and the whole of the Persian Empire, all the way to the Indus river in India, the same second part of our journey that we were about to do. My brother, Alexander was then told that he was named after him and they hoped he would go on to do great things in life just as he had done, well time will be the judge of that one, that's for sure!

It was explained to me that I was named Jason after a Greek mythological hero who travelled across the ancient world to retrieve a Golden Fleece, and they hoped that I would also travel the world, well from where I was standing, I was well on my way to doing that and had only been on the planet nine years.

Our parents explained to us that due to them both being brought up in different religious families, it was agreed between them that when they eventually had children, no religion was to be pushed on to us or even a religious name. So, it was easier to name us both after Greek heroes, rather than cause a scene with their two families.

The Bosporus itself was very busy indeed, with all different types and sizes of vessels going back and forth in all directions, how they managed to miss each other only they know, but some sort of manic system seemed to be working out on the water.

We embarked onto one of the many small car ferries touting for our business, and it wasn't long before we headed out into the mayhem to join them. As our little craft edged further from the shoreline the vastness of the city started to reveal itself. Dominating this view was the grandeur of the Blue Mosque, with its six towering minarets like rockets around a space station, Dad saying we would all visit this iconic building on our return journey, when we had more time. As our ferry crept further towards Asia another large mosque gradually seemed to appear from behind the first one, this also dominated the skyline with its four towers and large topped dome. Dad said that this one was called the Hagia Sophia and was originally a Christian church until the middle of the thirteenth century, when it became a mosque after the fall of Constantinople by the Ottoman Empire.

From the middle of the Bosporus you got some sort of perspective of how large this city really was, stretching the whole length of the shoreline both sides, rising up in height from the water's edge as far as your eyes could see and dominated by minarets from the vast numbers of mosques dotted among the colourful rooftops.

The water out in the middle was quite choppy from all the wakes of the various crafts, but it wasn't long before our little ferry slowly bumped into the large continent of Asia and we disembarked. This side of the Bosporus was just as noisy and busy as the European side and I don't think the people of Istanbul thought or worried about if they were in Asia or Europe, as they went about their daily life.

We headed up and out away from the shoreline as dusk

started to close in, so a hotel was the priority for us to find in this area of Istanbul, and it wasn't long before one was found and importantly, where Dad could park the car safely in a gated compound, along with other vehicles belonging to travellers like ourselves.

We had two rooms, with two single beds in each of them and the bathroom was across the hallway, shared with all six rooms on this level. It was agreed that I would sleep in a room with Mum and Alexander would go with Dad to the other room. Mum and Dad were not sure how safe this hotel was due to it having lots of foreign visitors all in the middle of an unknown part of Istanbul. We went down to the small restaurant attached to the hotel and had a meal of lamb, pita bread and salad, it was here that we met some of the people who also were travelling like us.

There were three young Americans, two girls and a man who we got talking to and they told us that after flying into Luxemburg and taking the train to Berlin in Germany they bought a VW camper van and were heading to India and Nepal on what was known as the hippie trail, apparently all different nationalities have been doing this for many years, and we were more than likely to meet many others doing the same thing, as our journey would mirror many of the places the trail passed through.

Not long after our meal we all headed for a good night's sleep if it was possible, because it seemed that everyone in a car on the streets, were still pressing their horns. With the windows shut and thinking about the huge exciting day I had just experienced, and the fan on the ceiling above me producing a constant humming, it wasn't long before I drifted away into a deep sleep. That was until I was awoken sharply at around five by the call of the local mosque, right at the back of our hotel. Then like echoes, the wailing across the city as every mosque was calling it's followers to prayer, but at least with this noise, those horns of the cars had been silenced, as I slipped back to sleep once more.

Day 8: Ankara, Capital City of Turkey

Two hours later we all were heading down for breakfast, consisting of fruit juice scrambled eggs and large flat bread. Dad had the car packed and ready, and as soon as we could we started out on our Asian journey.

After clearing the suburbs of Istanbul we headed for the capital Ankara, but less than an hour into our journey we suddenly got a shock, as the wonderful tarmac roads our little Triumph had driven on since day one, had ceased to exist. In front of us lay just a dirt road reasonably flat but still just dirt, and with the heat of the day starting to emerge this dirt became a dust trail, especially if you happened to be stuck behind any sort of motorised vehicle. When we were on the tarmac roads in the heat, you could at least roll down the front windows to give some relief, as our Triumph Vitesse had only two that opened, but on such dusty roads keeping the windows closed was a must. With the car having no air conditioning, and the cool blower from the front dashboard practically doing nothing for those in the back but moving the existing air around the car, we all started to feel very uncomfortable.

We kept urging Dad to overtake the vehicle in front as soon as it was safe to do so, allowing the windows to be wound down once more for some relief, before we started to catch the next vehicle up. The dust created another problem for us, coating the windscreen with a layer of grime and the only way to see through the glass after a time, was for Dad to wash it, with the windscreen wipers and water jets.

After about two hours driving the water bottle ran dry, so the need to fill this became rather vital, Dad deciding to stop at the side of the road next to a smallholding to ask for some water. Carrying our thermos flask to hold the water in, Dad started to proceed through a small gate towards the property closing it behind him.

The property consisted of a medium size dwelling with windows, and a couple of small outhouses to its left-hand side. At first all we could hear was the bleating of a few goats that were in front of this dwelling, but then all of a sudden there was such a commotion, all we saw at first was Dad running as fast as he could, for behind him and from out of one of these small outhouses appeared a very large dog, and he was definitely not going to take any prisoners, that`s for sure.

Mum shouted, 'run, Hassan run!', and Dad, although the better side of thirty-five, managed to reach the gate just in time, not bothering to open it, he just leapt into the air as though his life depended on it, dropping the flask as he sailed over the top of the gate like Dick Fosbury, in the '68 Olympic games, landing in a dusty pile on the hard ground and not some soft mattress, as we all saw on TV. As I stared through the window on my side of the car, the dog was at the gate barking very furiously, but what I had never seen before on any dog, was the white foam continually spouting from its mouth.

Dad quickly picked himself up as well as the flask and jumped in the car, taking off without any hesitation. Dad then explained that a dog, as mad and angry as that one and foaming from the mouth was more likely to have had rabies, especially in this part of the world. Not long after that episode, we arrived at a small garage so we could fill up the car with water, Dad also went to fill the flask up in case we ran out again, but found out it was broken inside from when it was dropped, so luckily, only a broken flask, it could have been a lot worse or even fatal for Dad if the dog had bitten him.

With the dirt road slowing our progress down we would

now have to stop in Ankara, Dad was hoping to clear the capital and stop further on. About thirty miles from Ankara the road suddenly changed back to tarmac and we could speed up our progress, thus allowing tonight's stop to at least be on the far side of this capital city.

Ankara appeared less hectic than Istanbul but just as noisy. This city is set among small hills filled by rooftop, after rooftop, and dominated by a large temple-like building. Dad explained to us that this was a mausoleum dedicated to Ataturk, he was first president of the republic of Turkey in 1923 and was built to honour him.

We trundled around Ankara, Mum looking at her maps to find the route we would be taking out of the city the next day.

Dad had decided to follow the trucking route used by the TIR international lorries across the middle of Turkey heading for Iran, on the basis that the roads were likely to be in a better condition than other routes going on today's experience. Once this was established, we looked for a hotel and eventually found another travellers hotel with availability. This was advertised as a motel, the first one we had stopped at, where you could park your car right outside your room for the night. Mum speaking in German to the man on the desk, arranged two rooms next to each other for that night, with both having a small bathroom attached which was really nice for a change.

Dad unpacked the roof rack again, which must now seem like a real burden, carrying the cases to the rooms night after night. It was dark now as we strolled out into the street to look for some food, and in the distance we could see Ataturk's Mausoleum lit up brightly against the night sky, as though it was announcing itself to the Turkish people.

We decided to have what is known around the world as street food, little portable kitchens selling all different types of cuisine on the side of the road.

I remember the smells of the spices got your taste buds

dancing and made you even hungrier. Mum and Dad like their spices, with Alexander and I, having to become more accustomed to them especially on a trip like this. After a good bowl of lamb with rice washed down with a bottle of orange Fanta, it was back to the motel for a good night's sleep. The two rooms were okay but nothing special, and we decided to keep the same sleeping arrangements as the night before, the room though was extremely hot, just like the whole day had been. Our rooms just had small portable fans, which we had to pay extra for at the front desk to give some relief throughout the night. Well you couldn't blame the hotel, a nice little extra earner, in a difficult world.

Day 9: The road to Sivas

Awoken by the call of prayer again at around five in the morning echoing loudly amongst the vast number of buildings in this city, we decided to make an earlier start of around five thirty on the road to try and cover as many miles as possible before the real heat of the day set upon us. Our target of the day on Mum's map was to reach Sivas, a small city in central Turkey, set on the Red River.

After leaving the motel and buying some fruit from a local stall holder, to have as our breakfast whilst travelling, we left Ankara before it had properly awoken.

The roads were of tarmac construction up until the town of Kirikkale around half an hours' drive from the motel, after that we were back on to the sandy surface, and the dust that came with it. There was very little traffic, if any, at that time of day, and the visibility was good compared with the day before, although we did leave a large dust cloud in our wake. We had barely gone another fifteen minutes when Mum noticed a car parked in the road up ahead that hadn't pulled into the side.

As we approach it became clear that it was a black

Mercedes Benz, with a white D sticker on the back, which meant it was from Deutschland (Germany) but what also was noticeable there wasn't anybody near the car, in fact there was nothing in any direction for miles. Dad slowly but keeping a safe distance pulled up behind it and stopped leaving our engine running. He wasn't sure but said after straining to look through the back window from our car, that the occupants were asleep.

He then slowly got out of our car and walked towards the Mercedes to see if they needed any assistance, calling out as he did so but also looking back to keep an eye on us, as we eagerly awaited to find out what the problem was.

Dad approached the left-hand side of the car towards the driver's door, peering through its window, then suddenly stepping back, returning spritely, with a worried look on his own face to our car.

With Mum asking if anything was wrong, Dad without reply, immediately put our car into first gear and accelerated away as though he was in a Grand Prix race. He was trying to pass this stationary car as quickly as possible, so we wouldn't witness what he had seen.

Unfortunately, I was sitting behind Dad, so as we went past the car curiosity got the better of me, Dad was saying, no one look at the black car, only look at the road ahead. Dad only had the other side of the road to use, so we were very close to the Mercedes on my side as we passed.

What my curiosity did for me that day, has stuck with me all my life, as I peered from my window at this black Mercedes Benz, and saw what a young boy of nine, should never have seen.

The driver's window was open, and I could clearly see a blonde-haired man leaning back in the front seat, eyes shut. You may ask what's strange about that, but this man had his throat slit nearly from ear to ear so his head looked as though it was about to fall off, if it wasn't for the back of the seat holding it up. I also caught a glimpse of the front of his shirt, which looked soaked in a deep dark colour and I now know that this was his blood, from a brutal attack. Dad continued at a fast pace and the black Mercedes disappeared into the dust cloud we had made in our wake, never to be seen by us again. We drove for about thirty minutes in total silence to be well clear of that awful situation, before Dad pulled over and got out of the car, to give himself time to gather his thoughts. We then all got out and stood at the front of the car, Mum with maps in hand spreading the current one out on the bonnet as Dad had requested, as Alexander and I both stood in silence.

The heat was now beginning to stamp its authority on the day, but even before that took control we were all hot and extremely sticky, due to the adrenalin that had been pumping through our bodies for the past hour, because of the frantic unforeseen situation that had just occurred. Dad then explained to us, I think to give him some sort of relief, that in the black Mercedes there were actually four adults, who he presumed were all German due to their European appearance, the car's plates, and the clothes that they were wearing.

He did not mention that they were male or female, just that they had been brutally attacked and killed; two of them were in the back seat of the car, while the front passenger was slumped over the driver's lap so pushing him up and back into his seat. I then realised with a quick flash back to what I had just witnessed, why I had only seen the driver as we sped past, and why still today at the age of fifty-seven, I can only see that one dead figure in the car, one horrible memory that just can't be erased. Dad said that they were most likely to have been travelling at night, and stopped at an unofficial road block and robbed, for we were now entering the tribal lands area where the Turkish authorities really don't even go themselves, due to this type of occurrence.

After looking at the map and seeing that the route to Sivas

was highly likely to be dangerous for European travellers, Dad and with Mum in agreement decided to change route, head north towards the Black Sea, and the costal town of Samsun, around four hours away. So, at the appropriate junction we headed north, all of us on edge and with most of the day still ahead of us, with the heat now beginning to arrive in earnest. The roads were no better than before but as we reached the town of Corum about an hour later and some sort of recognisable civilisation, we started to relax, if that was at all possible, Dad deciding to stop for a drink and something to eat, in a roadside café to settle everyone's nerves. Dad looked at the map again and worked out that we could reach Ordu on the Black Sea coast before nightfall, so our new destination was set.

Not long after we left Corum the roads started to improve and by the time we reached the next town Merzifon, the roads were back to tarmac all the way to Samsun on the Black Sea, which we were all grateful for as our speed could now increase to a much steadier pace. It was just as well the roads had improved, as we now started to climb into the foothills of the Pontic Mountains that led the way to Samsun. Some of them quite steep and twisty, and although we were now on a good road surface, getting stuck behind one of the local lorries chugging up these hills with its diesel fumes bellowing out of its exhaust, was just as bad as having no visibility from the dust we had previously encountered that day.

We then reached a point, where all you could see for as far as you could see, was the blueness of the Black Sea as it stroked the edge of Turkey with its gentle and placid waves, what a sight with the town of Samsun below and the green hills that surrounded it rolling down to greet it. This was a complete contrast to what I had witnessed early that day, a view to take your mind right away from that awful experience.

Samsun was a busy town and a fishing port, with all its colourful boats lined up along the shore, very much reminding me, of the small boats on Abington Park Lake on a Sunday afternoon back in Northampton.

The Black Sea was as calm as that lake, with hardly a ripple coming from its vastness as we skirted along its edge on our way to our next destination. We passed through many small towns and villages, all going about their daily business. The people I viewed out of my window were smiling and looking happy, some of the children even waved as they headed home from school with their satchels and bags on their backs, and as I waved back I was thinking to myself not all Turkish people can be bad.

Still with the Black Sea at our side we reached Ordu around four o'clock, it was not as big as Samsun but it still had all the well-worn but colourful fishing boats tied up along the beach.

We found a hotel in the middle of this town, next to a large square used as a hub for local buses and in one corner of this square set back was a large mosque, with two very tall minarets stretching skywards, and I was thinking to myself you are going to be waking me up very early again tomorrow morning.

After unpacking the cases in our rooms, and the sleeping arrangements staying the same for the third night running which seems to work well, Dad and Alexander in one room, Mum and me in another, sharing the same bathroom across the hall.

Dad had gone out into the square to fetch some food, while Alexander and I shared a bath to get rid of all the dust that had got into every nook and cranny you could imagine, nicely now cleaned, we sat waiting for Dad in anticipation.

He came back with two large cooked chickens and some flat bread, which we all consumed eagerly, washed down with Coke in one of the bedrooms.

It was decided while eating that we would not go anywhere that evening but relax, and all try and get an early night's sleep, especially after what had turned out to be quite a event and traumatic day.

Day 10: Erzurum on the eastern plateau

I got a good night's sleep, I wasn't even woken by the mosque on the far side of the square, apparently Dad, Mum and Alex also slept really well.

It was around eight o'clock, quite late for this family of crazy travellers as we all dressed, had a quick wash and ventured out into the square. It was very busy, much more so than when we arrived the evening before. There were plenty of buses crammed with people some unloading their passengers and some picking up new ones. As they pulled out of the square the amount of smoke coming out of their exhaust pipes was unbelievable. Each bus continuously sounded their horn as if to say look at me. Dad found a small café down a quieter street, where we all had eggs and bread washed down with rather milky tea. Dad said we have about seven hours to cover today and we would be following the Black Sea coast until we reached the town of Trabzon, then we would head inland and all being well hope to reach the town of Erzurum before the end of the day.

After breakfast we went back to the hotel and loaded the car up as usual, Dad lifting the cases onto the roof rack and covering them with the tarpaulin strapping them down tightly. We left Ordu, heading east along the coast road with the sea to our left, on Alexander's side, and the hills to the right on mine. We passed through small fishing villages every ten miles or so, often with a small café with lots of men just sitting around outside drinking and playing what seemed like cards.

Although the road was twisty it was at least tarmac, with a beautiful view around every corner we turned. Still following the tranquil waters of the Black Sea, it didn't seem long before we reached the town of Trabzon.

Dad filled the car up with petrol, stopping at a nearby restaurant for lunch, Alexander and I got stuck into our usual lamb kebabs and bread — very tasty! Mum and Dad had fish, caught that very morning from the waters of the Black Sea.

Now I can remember those two plates of fish very clearly arriving at our table and what a sight, because these two large fish although cooked still had their heads and tails on. This was really strange to me; I had never seen it before served on a plate like that, all ready to eat. The only fish that we had back home in the late sixties and early seventies was fish fingers, or boil in a bag cod in parsley sauce, maybe on a special occasion Dad went and fetched fish and chips from the local chippy, but a whole fish I just kept staring at it, and I'm sure it was staring straight back at me! Lunch over we moved out of Trabzon, it was at this point we turned and headed inland climbing up a steep valley back into the Pontic Mountain range, leaving the Black sea as a beautiful picture framed through the rear window of the Vitesse.

As we drove further inland the tarmac started to evolve into a gravel road but with very little traffic on it, progress was hardly slowed.

We were heading to Erzurum a town set on a plateau in the east of Turkey no more than five hours drive from Trabzon. Erzurum was one of the original destinations on Dads' route before it was decided to divert towards the Black Sea two days earlier.

We reached Erzurum late afternoon on day 10, after travelling through some very scenic mountainous terrain on the way eventually dropping down onto the plateau where the town of Erzurum nestled. What was noticeable was the considerable drop in temperature as we entered the plateau, very fresh and with quite a strong wind coming from a north-easterly direction, such a contrast from our lunch by the sea.

Not at all what you would expect, but after numerous days of heat and dust, as well as being cooped up in the back of the car, this was very welcoming for all of us, as we glided effortlessly along, windows fully down, into Erzurum the radio cassette cranked up as loud as it could go, as we joined The Seekers in a rendition of *A World of our Own*, in which we actully were.

After finding a quite modern-looking hotel this far east in Turkey and Dad unloading the cases as per usual into our rooms, we settled for a nearby restaurant within walking distance for some supper, consisting of omelettes and fried potatoes and a glass of warm sweet tea without milk, which was really nice. While eating Dad explained that now all looks good and although they had decided to change route, we would be leaving Turkey by tomorrow just a day behind his original estimation.

He told us that we would be entering Iran some time tomorrow, and although it was now late September, he had worked out that we needed to cross the mountain range, between the two countries, before the winter snow sets in, or we wouldn't be going any further! That's the reason we left England when we did, but also right across Asia the weather would be much cooler for us, as opposed to two to three months earlier in the year, and more acceptable for our stay in Pakistan our final destination. I thought, 'well, if the last five days were the cooler option in the car then I definitely would not want to be here any earlier than this'.

As we walked back to the hotel you could really feel the cold from the wind, as the night set in, and you really did need your jumper or something even warmer, but with the clear skies the mountains in the distance with the twilight on their snow-capped peaks, was a sight to behold. What we did not know and never have guessed was what day eleven had in store for us, as we snuggled down for a goodnight sleep in our rooms.

Day 11: A Real Cliff Hanger of a Day

Awoken very sharply by Mum at around six, she told Alexander and me to get dressed quickly and put on trousers instead of the shorts that we had been wearing since leaving home. One glance out of the window told us boys why, there was no sunshine appearing from the east as on the previous few mornings, just a thick grey sky and a large blanket of snow covering the landscape as far as you could see and still coming down at a large rate of knots in great quantities. Dad had shoved everything into the cases in no particular order as though it was a challenge, saying in a loud voice, 'if we don't go now, we don't go at all'. It was all hands to the pumps as we hurriedly carried our items out of the hotel door to the car. The sound of fresh laden snow crunching under our feet, with the large cold wet flakes striking our faces as we struggled towards the car.

Cases on top of the car covered in the tarpaulin and strapped down in record time, this was due to all the practice Dad had over the last ten days.

He then, with the help of Alexander, put the snow chains on each wheel, extracted from the boot of the car, which he had purchased back in Northampton. It seemed like ages before Dad and Alexander joined Mum and myself in the car — totally bedraggled from their ordeal outside, and as Dad started the engine we gingerly moved off, it appeared they were successful in their task.

Following the road signs and sticking to the centre of the road as Dad would judge it, we made our way out of Erzurum at a very slow pace with head and hazard lights on to warn any other totally insane road users who had ventured out that treacherous morning.

This was precisely what Dad didn't want to happen because he knew that when it snows, 'it really snows', in this part of the world. That one day's delay due to our diversion had made all the difference in our timing. With Dad totally concentrating on the road ahead, the nervousness of the situation that we were in was felt throughout the car. We kept ploughing on at a pace we were not accustomed to and what should have taken an hour to the next small town took over two and a half hours.

As daylight started to emerge from the dark greyness that we had awoken to, it appeared the snow was starting to ease, even though we were ascending higher into the mountains. Mum and Dad knew there was no turning back that's for sure, the decision had been made as they continuously looked at each other for reassurance. Our little Triumph Vitesse just kept plodding on up the twisty roads as it had done on many previous occasions on this trip, but without the snow. The chains on the wheels were doing a great job grinding their way through the hazard as if nothing could stop them. Since the last village there were now tyre tracks in the snow, suggesting traffic had ventured out before us on this stretch, so it was easier for Dad to make out roughly where the road was, not at all like the previous two hours or so.

We went through fog as we climbed, or low cloud as it is known on a mountain, and it was very creepy to say the least, I found it scarier than the large quantities of snow that had fallen earlier. The snow was not so intense now to the point where it started to turn into light drizzle, but the cold was still out there due to the altitude we were now reaching.

Visibility was really poor from inside our cocoon, then out of the mist a truck came the other way with no warning at all, using the same tracks in the centre of the road as us. Somehow, we managed to miss each other, maybe due to the lack of speed each vehicle was doing, or the shear concentration and skill of each driver. This made Dad even wearier to the point that our speed climbing up was kept to an absolute minimum, but enough for the car to give us traction to progress. We cleared the mistiness that had engulfed this area through these mountains and started to level out along it's top.

The skies still looked full of snow as we passed another truck travelling in the opposite direction and from our vantage point high up, we could make out the road ahead below us, snow covered as it disappeared down the mountain back into the clouds and beyond from whence it came. We then started our perilous descent from the top of this great white mass. Dad continuously changing gear to slow our progress as each bend approached, then having to pull into the side to allow a trudging lorry that had emerged from beneath the cloud to ascend without slowing its momentum.

Dad said it was a good sign that trucks were coming up, this meant the road ahead must be passable. We then disappeared into the murky cloud ourselves, now even more dense than when we were climbing, very scary indeed, its precipitation was starting to freeze itself to our windscreen.

I'm not sure how far into the cloud bank we had gone at that particular moment, and although the windscreen was wet with slush and the wipers struggling to do their job properly, but what Dad then viewed in front of us made him panic in such a way that he was literally standing on the brakes, as he stretched long and hard out of his seat to stop the car propelling itself forward. It was then everything seemed to go into slow motion as the car just kept sliding forward relentlessly, until it came to a juddering stop.

Now if you were not there this may be hard to believe, but it is a true as night follows day. Because of the freezing mist on the windscreen Dad and even Mum had completely missed the sharp turn to our left, in the road ahead, until it was too late. The car slid while braking for what appeared to be ages but was probably only seconds, maybe less than twenty feet or so, halting front first over the edge of this bend. The front wheels of the car had gone into what only I can describe as thin air, and in so doing the car had literally rested itself on its floor pan, just past the front doors. The weight of the engine was pulling us downwards and the car had now started a rocking motion, maybe from an unforeseen updraft or the full load in the boot pushing us back down again like a counterweight, but only slightly. Without any warning as the car again rocked forward Dad fiercely pushed his driver's seat back against my legs, trapping them hard between the seats, at the same time telling Mum in no uncertain words, to jump in the back with the boys, which she did so without hesitation, cuddling us both immediately. In doing this, the car appeared to stable itself, in its perilous position.

The Triumph Vitesse was a two door car and therefore like most two door cars, would have longer front doors than say a normal four door cars allowing easier access to the rear seats. This posed a problem in our current situation because the car was pivoting just halfway where the door met the central pillar, so if Dad had tried to open it, the doors weight when pushing outward and forward, could easily be a reason to tip the car over into the abyss. Even if he had opened the door successfully, his own weight being removed from the front seats could have also tilted the car in the engines favour,

And today, now knowing the real man that was Hassan Agha, that option would have never ever crossed his mind not in the slightest. Dad turned the engine off which then shut down the fan heater, which in turn made the inside of the car quite eerie, with the only sound coming from the wipers still scrunching themselves against the freezing glass of the windscreen. Then as you looked forward past the wipers every so often, you caught a glimpse of a break in the low cloud, exposing a distant but sunny valley below, making the realisation of where we were exactly at that moment even more terrifying.

I remembered Mum calmly producing a magazine, from where I do not know, but softly she just began to read it to my brother and me, as though it was a bedtime story, trying to make us feel that what just happened moments earlier had not actually happened at all.

For how long we actually hung there, Mum progressing through the book in an even tone, I couldn't say, but after travelling day after day and hour after hour trying as the situation dictated; to stay as still as possible for the four of us seemed like a lifetime. Then my mind immediately harked back to that man, Michael Caine again and *The Italian Job* and the scene at the end of the film showed a bus balancing itself high on a cliff edge with no real outcome. The problem here was this was not Hollywood, so our predicament had to be resolved, and getting out of the car was not an option, just like in the film.

It was now getting to be uncomfortable especially for me, as my legs were still trapped between the seats, and hurting to the extent they were now going numb. Mum told me to slip my shoes off and try to squeeze my legs between the seats, so I then could stand on the seat with my bottom resting on the back shelf. After some persistence I finally managed to achieve this. Dad then managed to fold his driver's seat backwards nearly flat, and crawl towards the rear of the car, which ended in all of us now on the back seat adding more weight to the rear of the car, thus trying to give ourselves as much of an advantage as possible.

I mentioned early on in this book that at one time we truly felt bonded as a family, but at this moment in time we were literally bonded, in fact I was totally squashed on to the rear parcel shelf, Dad's head was pushing hard into the roof lining, while Mum and Alexander were crushed together against the far side of the car.

Again, I'm not sure how long we all were cramped up like that on the small back seat of the Triumph, but we were all still breathing and that's got to be good in anybody's book, (especially mine).

We then heard the sound of a lorry chugging its way up and around the corner, the anticipation that someone was outside swept across that backseat in earnest. The windows were now totally steamed up from our breath, we could not actually see this lorry as it approached with its engine growing louder every second that went by. To our astonishment, this lorry just kept chugging on and passed the rear of the car by feet not as so much to think about stopping for one moment, its engine now decreasing in volume as it trailed away. Dad reassured us all that someone would eventually stop and help us and that we would be fine, as he tried to re- position himself forcing our little car to moan with sounds we were all unfamiliar with, making us all even more nervous.

Time passed with very little movement or conversation from amongst us, it wasn't even an appropriate moment to start playing I spy. Then all of a sudden from out of nowhere, and directly behind us, with hardly a sound, a light projected itself through the back window, as bright as the sunlight that had been seen by the Black Sea two days earlier, no doubt highlighting the outline of our bodies against the hazy glass. This light grew brighter and brighter as it edged ever closer to us, making you wonder if it was some religious phenomenon finally coming to end our predicament once and for all. Lights still ablaze we could hear the sound of rustling coming from under the car, then suddenly the cranking of an engine rumbled into earshot, not long after our little Triumph Vitesse started to move backwards, the rear wheels grinding on the snow chains as it did so, and to our relief the sound of the front wheels doing exactly the same, as we were gently eased away from the edge of what could have been our final fate.

Then the door on Mum's side suddenly opened, and what can only be described as a happy smiley but dirty face appeared through it, hat and scarf protecting the rest of the head from the cold, which rushed through the door at the same time. I have never forgotten the words that echoed from this man's mouth, his breath steaming out of him as he did so, *Merhaba Merhaba* (hello hello). It was if he already knew us and he was just greeting us all on a perfectly normal day in a perfectly normal situation. He wasn't and we weren't, but we were very grateful he did, and I still am today. We all clambered out on to the cold wet slippery road, each of us in turn shaking and patting this unforeseen hero as we did so.

What stood behind us was a huge turquoise lorry with the Mercedes star prominent on its front; adorned with rows of lights all giving off tremendous heat the nearer you approached them. He had noticed our predicament, and slowly glided his truck towards us coming from the same direction as we had. The driver had managed to crawl under our car and attached a small length of rope, the only one he had, to our axle from the front of this lorry, meaning he had to get as close as possible, hence the very bright lights through the rear window.

What we didn't realise but now started to contemplate, is that he was on his own and had no guidance of how close to get to the rear of our car, one slight misjudgement on his behalf, could have easily nudged us over the edge.

Worryingly we probably would have then become just another statistic on some foreign office desk, just like the four unfortunate Germans we left at the side of the road a couple of days previous, or just forgotten about in our own little village as time passed, like my friend John Metcalfe.

While clasping my mothers hand, as I've never clasped it before standing next to the warm lights, I noticed Alexander just standing on the edge where the car had been, he appeared to be in his own little world staring out over the edge, most likely wondering to himself what might have been. Dad checked the car for damage and could only find dents and scrape marks on the bottom of the car where we eventually ended up pivoting; we literally had just dropped off the end of the road. Rope unattached and the car now with its engine

The Kose Mountains and gravel roads of Turkey

again purring as usual as though nothing had happened, we steadily followed this unknown hero and his lorry down what I now know today, as the Kose mountain range. Not sure of the time of day but feeling very hungry as the realisation that we have had no breakfast, due to our quick exit from Erzurum, and that food had never been in the thoughts of any of us due to the intensity of that morning's events.

We pulled into the small town of Agri for refreshments, where we, and the lorry with the kind-hearted Iranian driver, who never told us his name, finally parted company without him accepting any sort of payment whatsoever. He was just one good human doing good to other humans.

Fully refreshed and lucky to do so, Dad took the snow chains off the wheels, as the road ahead was more slush than snow, we headed out of Agri for the Iranian border around two hours' drive away.

We were all very quiet as we made our way through this final part of Turkey, Dad listening to the car for any unusual noises, whilst we all pondered to ourselves what actually had happened that morning.

Today I still wonder why we travelled that day, and in hindsight we should never have set out in those conditions in our little car, (They say it is better to be late in this world than early in the next). But Mum and Dad made that decision without hesitation, and you totally hold your trust in them at that age — you have no choice. The wrong decision could have been going on this epic journey in our little saffron yellow Triumph Vitesse instead using a type of four wheel drive Land Rover, but again I wonder, would it have stopped in time on that exact same corner — who knows? The fact that our little Triumph was weighed down to such extent in its boot and on the roof, pushed those snow chains hard into the ground, not only giving us more traction when needed, but allowing our stopping distance to be reduced sufficiently, that I am here today writing about it.

Finally we reached the border crossing, not unsurprisingly there was very little traffic due to the weather. Timewise we were not too bad, around two in the afternoon, making us about five hours away from Tabriz, the large city which was to be our next stop. Ushered through to Iran without any problems in very quick time, probably the border guards didn't want to venture out into the cold, and who could blame them.

From the hectic events of the morning and the rewarding food we had just had, I must have nodded off soon after, my head resting on my familiar pillow, the now warmer and roomier back seat adding to my comfort.

I awoke as we entered Tabriz just about dusk with its streetlights on and the mosques calling everyone to prayer, although not religious in the slightest you could say ours were answered today high up in the Kose mountain range.

Mum and Dad found another motel where you could park the car right outside and two rooms were acquired for the night. These were the first rooms that had air-conditioning, which was new to Alexander and I but very grateful for, as it was still quite chilly here in Tabriz, as the previous night in Erzurum, but you could put the warm air on to make the room cosy. Whilst my brother and I got washed and ready for bed, Dad had gone out and fetched some food, again warm bread and a large chicken washed down with bottles of water. We all got an early night's rest and hoped that day twelve would not be as eventful as day eleven had been — or anywhere near it!

Day 12: Modern Tehran

Up early again, Dad said we had an eight hour drive ahead of us to reach the capital Tehran. Now Iran was completely different from Turkey on so many levels. It was ruled by the Shah of Iran, known as the King of Kings, and although it was an Islamic state you would not have thought it, as I peered out through our murky car's windows. You could tell this was a very westernised country, the cars were modern, the roads had nice verges, there were trees and plants down the middle of the very wide roads, some even had traffic lights, I can't remember the last time I saw any. But what was most noticeable was the fact a lot of the people, men and women, were just dressed as normally as we would, jeans, t-shirts and flared trousers.

Iran appeared in a much better state than both Yugoslavia and Bulgaria that we had passed through early on in our trip. It did not appear as poor as Turkey, Dad saying that it was due to its rich oil fields in the south of the country and having

been given a great deal of funding from America.

After a long drive, having stopped for food and several comfort breaks, we reached the capital city Tehran. This metropolis was ultra-modern for the middle of Asia. Tall skyscrapers shimmered brightly in the late afternoon sunshine, modern cars, trucks and buses and at the end of a very large open boulevard stood the magnificent Shahyad Tower. This monument had just been completed and was made of gleaming white marble, it was more of a huge arch to me, rather than a tower but it was something to behold.

Mum and Dad agreed to find a motel on the far side of this large city, to make our exit in the morning much simpler. It seemed easier to travel through this capital city as it all appeared to be very calm and organised, compared to Ankara and Istanbul. There were a lot of street sellers away from the centre but it all looked very colourful and interesting to Alexander and Me, as we pointed out to each other look at this, and look at that, as we meandered our way through the streets.

We found a hotel in District Fourteen of this city, not the best we have stayed in considering this modern looking city but on the correct road to leave in the morning.

That was a long day in the car but much ground was covered, Dad said that the distances between the towns and cities would be very long from now on and our timing would have to be judged very carefully, to reach each destination in daylight. We ventured out into the streets after having a wash and freshen up at the hotel. The city appeared to come alive after dark with its bright lights and different smells attacking

Uncle Yaya Khan with the Shah of Iran 'The King of Kings'

your senses. Not too far from the hotel we found a small eatery that you could sit inside.

Very brightly lit with minimal décor and white walls, my brother and I had burger and chips plus a Coke, not very authentic or spicy, but very delicious all the same. All nicely full, we headed back to the hotel for a good night's rest, and while I was being tucked up in bed, I remembered saying to Mum I was just thankful that today had been just a normal kind of day, she replied, we all have much more to give in life, so don't worry whatever will be will be, and with that thought I fell asleep.

Day 13: Eastwards to Mashhad

Up early and in the car before I had time to clear the sleepy dust from my eyes, we made our exit from Tehran on good roads, Mum guiding the way according to the maps in front of her. Dad said we would stop for some breakfast along the way, then lunch but not for long, as he intends to reach a city called Mashhad in the east of Iran. Although Iran seemed modern and what you might call oil rich, it soon became apparent that most of the wealth was spent on and around the capital city. The further east we travelled from Tehran the poorer the country got.

We reached the small town called Garmsar where Dad topped up with fuel; you must at every opportunity fill up where you could. The garage had a small restaurant attached and a fried egg in bread washed down with sweet tea was the order of the day for all.

Back on the road again in no time at all, with snow-capped mountains skirting our left-hand side in the distance and barren flat lands to our right we continued deeper and deeper eastwards.

Traffic consisted of large lorries, not many international

ones now, more local and quite a few old buses. Cars started to get thin on the ground being replaced by small mopeds and donkey carts, this again told you that the wealth in this part of the country was fast diminishing. The sun was shining in a clear a blue sky as the day started to heat up quite nicely to an acceptable level, as we pulled in for more fuel and lunch, in the large town of Damghan.

This was once the oldest city in this part of Iran with its fortress walls, which guarded this eastern plateau, still in existence in places. Now several thousand years later our family, stand viewing what Alexander the Great viewed many centuries ago. These walls that stand today are so high and extremely wide, it was said they drove chariots along the top, and looking at them, I would say it's probably true.

Lamb for lunch with flat bread and an orange Fanta eagerly dispatched, Dad viewing the maps and said we still had a good way to go, so back in the car with the bottle of orange in hand.

The roads were still tarmac, not so wide but very dusty due to the winds blowing across this large open plateau as we still trudged east, the sun now high in the afternoon sky. Although our little Triumph Vitesse was one of the fastest cars developed by Triumph at the time, it was not really making inroads into the distances it was being asked to achieve in daylight hours. Dad then conceding that we would not make our intended destination of Mashhad before nightfall. This got Alexander and me a little anxious, knowing what Dad had told us previously about bandits and not travelling at night in this part of the world. We all started to watch the small clock on the walnut dashboard as the evening light started to fade, rather too quickly for our liking.

Realising that there were very few TIR international lorries travelling this road, meant there was unlikely to be a place where the international drivers would gather for the night and we could park, with the thought of safety in numbers.

Mum's maps showed very little detail in the way of any towns before Mashhad but remembers going through a small town not long after lunch, which also did not show on her map. So we were all hoping that this map supplied in Northampton by the AA would be wrong again, putting us all at our ease.

Headlights fully on as the stars started to twinkle in the clear sky, the distant mountains now fading away into the darkness, as if they had never existed. We passed through the odd small village with very little activity, it seemed travelling after dark was not a done thing around here, and anyway. where would you go? Apart from out into the cold dark wilderness. The time now was about eight-thirty according to the dimly lit clock we had been watching at the front of the car, as we continue to follow the small but straight black road with our headlights. Out this far east there was no large wildlife to worry about hitting in the dark, so our speed was although not the fastest we had achieved that day, quite considerable given the night vision we had. Then all of a sudden and without warning Dad swerves the car violently to our right, forcing Alexander to fall straight over the top of me, as though we were playing rough and tumble, back in our bunk beds in Wootton.

Now I didn't see why we swerved due to Alexander completely swamping me, and by the time I recovered the car was back on track, as though nothing had happened. Mum explaining to us that it was a stray cow stepping onto the road, eyes bright from the lights of the car on her side, which forced Dad to act. Alexander and I just laughed at the position we found ourselves in, I think it was more at just easing the tension that we had both been feeling for the last hour or so, than to what had just occurred.

Then as we cleared the top of a small ridge in the road a concentration of lights appeared in the distance, too many to be anything but a small town or village, as we all stared out of the windscreen, watching it draw nearer and nearer.

We reached this town known as Sabzevar, which did not appear on Mum's map, but we were all grateful that it did appear in real life and was not some sort of mirage. Although from a distance and in the pitch darkness with its lights as a beacon that could be viewed from miles around, Sabzevar looked large but in fact it was quite small, consisting of two or three roads going from east to west, linked together by several small side roads, the local mosque being at the centre of this small outpost.

Dad drove up and down these small streets, which were just dirt tracks, compared to the tarmac on the main street, but no hotel could be found, and it was well past ten o'clock by now.

Dad saw a sign for the police station and stopped to get some information on where we could stay for the night. He returned to us with the news that there was not a hotel in the town, but had spoken to the only policeman on duty who said he would send a message to his superior, and inform him we would be stopping in the town by the mosque for the night. Dad viewed this as the safest option in the circumstances, rather than keep travelling into the unknown.

We parked the car in front of the mosque hoping to settle for the night, Alexander and I head on pillows, covered by a blanket, Mum and Dad trying to nestle down in the front two seats the best they could. It was only a few minutes later that our car was lit up by another cars headlights that had stopped in front of us, not as bright as the lorry in the mountains of Turkey, shining at us through the back window, Dad putting his hand over the top of his eyes to try and see who might be causing this interruption. Then we heard the cries of 'hello, hello, English people, hello'. Dad immediately told Mum to stay in the car as he gingerly opened his door, venturing out into the street to see what ever might greet him.

Apparently, the words uttered in broken English, were the words of the local police chief, he had come to meet us after realising that we were stopping the night in the car in his town. He then had a conversation with Dad, and it was agreed, actually he insisted, we could stop at his house with his family for the night.

We followed him to what only can be described as a large compound within this small town. I stood close to Mum, clutching her leg as this small round man with a large dark moustache introduced himself as Jahmir.

'Welcome to my home', he said, and with that he ushered us through a door and inside to be then greeted by his wife and other members of the family, I did not have a clue how they were all related, but all I can say there were plenty of them.

Jahmir had been at Birmingham University in the late fifties and had learnt some English while he studied for a degree, then returned home to become the head of police for this region. He said it was an honour to have an English family stay in his home, as he had stayed with a family in Birmingham.

We all sat on the floor which was covered in a lovely carpet with many large cushions scattered around for your comfort. Although all of us were very tired and had nearly dropped off to sleep in the car, our senses were awoken when his wife and other members of the family, brought in quite a substantial amount of food. The spiced lamb and steaming hot rice were very welcoming, followed by sweet tea and home-made pastry biscuits. The conversation flowed between Mum, Dad and Jahmir as my eyes started to close from the very long day we had just endured.

Time was now getting on and Dad said we all must get some rest, Jahmir said we could stop in this room, and then beckoned his family members to bring in a *Korsi*. This was a small two-tier metal table, which they placed in the centre of the room, followed by a tray of hot coals which was placed on the lower tier.

His wife then bought a very large heavy blanket and

proceeded to cover the table and the area around it, thus trapping the heat given off by the coals. We collected up some of the cushions and placed them around the edge.

Dad fetched in the cases as Alexander and I had a wash in quite a modern bathroom, considering the house from its first appearance.

We then put our pyjamas on and snuggled down under the now very warm blanket, very cosy, and it wasn't long before I was well on my way to a deep sleep, not knowing if the rest were asleep as well, but knowing this was far better than trying to get your head down in the back of a car outside a mosque, thats for sure.

A stock picture of what a Korsi looks like

Day 14: Mashhad to Afghanistan

Woken early by Mum from under a still heavy but warm blanket, then after clearing the sleepy dust from my eyes, to find an array of foods, which had been placed on the top of the Korsi in front of me. Lots of different breads; some thin and flat some round and one in the shape of a triangle. There was a goats' cheese with a variety of herbs and spices rolled into it, butter, jams and fruit along with the usual hot sweet tea, all good for me, I thought. As we all tucked in sitting up to this table still with the blanket over us, we were then presented by the wife of Jahmir a large bowl, and in it was a dish called Pache. This was a traditional dish eaten at breakfast in this part of the world, and it comes hot just like a soup. Back in England I didn't like it when Dad made porridge for breakfast, and I was made, no forced to eat it, (child cruelty), but I would gladly take some now, instead of the dish which sat before us proudly in the centre of the *Korsi.*

Pache consisted, in this case, of sheep's brains, hooves, eyes and tongue, well you can guess the rest. Mum, Alexander and I flatly refused this, and the look, as well as the smell, put me right off the rest of my breakfast.

Not to offend our hosts Dad bravely accepted some of this Pache, and was even told the eyes were the best part and an honour to have, which made us all squirm even more as he tried one. Breakfast over and not quick enough in my opinion, we said our goodbyes to Jahmir's family. Jahmir said he would give us an escort as far as his jurisdiction would allow and then say his farewells.

As we left Sabzevar Mum noticed these three very large domes set at the side of the road just like large mole hills, very weathered in appearance made of stone and mud standing around thirty feet tall (10 meters). Dad told us these were old ice houses where the locals would store snow in the winter and pack it with straw, then use it as a source of water while

The city of Mashhad in the north east of Iran

it slowly melts out through a small channel and you would find many of these in this part of Iran, they looked very weird but they have been a lifeline for the locals for centuries. Sabzevar behind us and its wonderful hospitality, in fact that's the second time we have been helped by Iranians, what a good society these people live in to do such things, and how different it would be for this kind nation ten years later, when this amazing country would be stricken with turmoil.

After about an hour with a two car escort from the police, one in front and one at the back speeding along at a great rate on a virtually empty road, creating our own dust cloud as we did so we eventually came to a halt in the middle of nowhere. Jahmir who was in the lead car got out and said his farewells and wished us luck on our forward journey, all in his now familiar broken English.

Our aim now was Mashhad, around an hour's drive which was originally yesterday's destination before we ran out of daylight. Dad told us that it is the largest city in this region and very religious, reaching it around late morning would allow us to visit the holy shrine which is well known throughout the Islamic world and one he has always wanted to see himself.

Mashhad again was a beautiful place, not as busy or westernised as the capital Tehran, but totally dominated in its middle by the Holy Shrine with its large golden dome and towers. Standing beyond this and not at all phased by the Holy Shrine, was the largest mosque in the world by dimensions, with a dome just as big but in a vibrant turquoise colour. It was as if they were both vying to be the brightest and the best domed building in the city, but they both looked magnificent set against the crystal-clear blue sky.

We parked the car under some trees so the shade could give some relief from the heat of the day, Dad calling over two boys about Alexander's age, and gave them some money, this was to look after the car while we were visiting the shrine and told them there would be more when we returned. As we headed for the Holy Shrine holding my mothers hand, I glanced over my shoulder back towards our car half expecting to see two lads scarpering off down the road money in hand, but no, they were still sitting where we had left them one at the front and one at the back, I suppose they were just trying to earn a few extra pennies like the rest of the Asian world.

The Holy Shrine was even more dramatic and colourful the closer you approached, set with a large mosaic square in front of its huge arched entrance, walls tiled from top to toe in many colours. We all removed our shoes at its entrance, we then entered this huge carpeted room with pillars as large as any tree trunk I had ever seen, and no wonder they were big, the ceiling that they were holding up was just jaw dropping, glittering gold and silver everywhere you looked, just too much for one person to take in let alone a child. Dad led the way, passing all sorts of different people and whole families praying on the carpets provided, oblivious to this western family walking amongst them. We must have walked the length of the football pitch at the recreation ground back in our little village of Wootton, before we came to another entrance. This led to the Mausoleum of Imam Reza which was directly under the golden dome. He was the eighth Imam of the twelve Imams of the Shiites and is part of the Islam Dad grew up believing in, so this was a special place for him to come and visit.

The tomb was not as extravagant as the building it stood in; to me it looked like a large square shed made out of stone, with holes in it just like some of the new garden blocked walls that started to appear around our village. Inside was his stone grave, but if it hadn't been in such an iconic religious building and instead was in one of the many back gardens in our village, I'm sure it would be where the coalman would have left his weekly delivery.

Time was getting on as my tummy kept reminding me so as we headed back to the car. Another round of lamb kebabs for all was bought from a street seller along with a few bottles of water, just what was needed after being dragged round the largest religious mosque on the planet. We reached the car to find the two boys playing 'keeps' against a wall with stones to pass the time waiting to be rewarded which was duly forthcoming from Dad. The car perfectly in order as we had left it cooling under the trees, and as all of us were now revitalised from our trek around the Holy Shrine, we began our final journey to leave this very embracing and optimistic country.

As we headed east our little car was eating up the tarmac road mile after mile, the landscape began to flatten out as we passed through several small towns, each with its own colourful mosque on the way to the border.

It was mid-afternoon when we reached the border with the sun still beating down giving us no respite from the heat we had been enduring for the past three hours. The traffic wanting to leave Iran and trade with the other side seemed non existent, just a few small local trucks and a couple of what Alexander and I would call hippiemobiles, young men and women still trekking along the Hippie Trail or the old Silk Road as it was formally known, just as we were.

Then it was the realisation of where we heading that had everything to do with the emptiness of this border crossing.

'Welcome to AFGANISTAN' the sign read as we cleared the Iranian border control without any hesitation, the border guards giving us a look from their modern electronic barrier station as though we were totally mad! But they must have seen this hundreds of times before. In front of us was the Afghanistan border control, very basic indeed, two old looking buildings made from mud and bricks with corrugated tin as its roof. The barrier had to be hand operated by a guard that gave you a terrifying stare as we proceeded underneath, only to be stopped by more guards and another barrier.

Trapped in an area filled with armed soldiers looking at you as if you were prey, beside our car was one of those hippiemobiles, armed guards stood around it while the owners were frantically removing what looked like every item from the vehicle, and placing it on the ground before them. Three guards then approached our car and told us to all get out, Alexander and I holding Mum's hands while we stood by the car in the heat, myself needing a drink as my mouth started to dry up from the worry of what was going to happen. Dad as cool as you like started talking in Pashto to one of the guards, this was the same language, I heard him speak for the first time in the lift in Claridge's back in London two years earlier. To me they might as well have been from another planet, with the way they were speaking to each other, so fast and so dramatic with several unsightly hand gestures to get their point across both their voices growing louder as they did so. Eventually a senior officer who was standing further back beckoned my Dad over, and took him inside one of the buildings, and as he did so turned back to Mum saying, as her hands began to shake while holding onto us boys, it will be alright. Standing there alone in a huddle as though we were posing for a picture which was so far from reality one of the guards came closer, machine gun in hand looking us up and down then grunting as he pushed us all aside, Mum scraping her shoe down my shin and onto my foot, as we stumbled together, the side of the car there as a support stopping us tumbling over onto the dusty ground. This brute of a guard with a full beard, bullet holder strapped across his chest was forcing his authority on to what he saw as very vulnerable foreigners, as he ushered us away from the car, so he could peer through its dirty windows, to see anything that may take his fancy.

At that moment another guard came from the building and used his gun as a pointing implement to start guiding us forward, Mum still shaking as Alexander and I gripped her hands even tighter. We moved slowly towards the door that Dad had disappeared through a while ago, Mum releasing Alexander's hand to now push the door fully open. Stepping from the shear sunlight into a darkened room did not allow my eyes to view what was in front of me properly, and probably it was the same for Alexander and Mum. Then came the voice we all knew and loved — Dad's!

'Come in!', he cried, 'meet Amir', and as my eyes slowly adjusted to the room this man rose from behind a desk to greet us all, it was the same distinguished officer that had called Dad in earlier, and as I was introduced to him and shook his hand I notice the very large and prominent moustache on a moon landscape of a face, which I still can recall today. For all Mum's anxious worrying outside in the hot sun, Dad had been sitting under a cooling fan drinking tea. The relief on all our faces was clear to see, but at the same time Mum gave Dad such a glare the likes that had never been seen before by Alexander and me. We boys were given a bottle of Coke each which we duly dispatched in Olympic record time, due to our parched throats, the ones we thought were about to be slit. Dad and Mum drank tea whilst sitting and talking to Amir as if they were long lost friends, catching up with each other swapping stories. After a while, Dad said we must be going as we needed to reach the ancient city of Herat before nightfall.

Thanking Amir for his generous hospitality, we returned to the car, it was completely as we had left it, that brute of a guard now harassing another unfortunate group of foreign people that had entered this cordoned-off zone. Dad told us to get in the car quickly; the engine was running before Mum had time to shut her door. The barrier in front was lifted as our little car edged towards it at a slow pace, not to alarm any of the guards looking on. Alexander then said, 'look at the hippie van!', I stretched over to look out of his window, several guards were trawling through the owners' belongings, just throwing their clothes all over the place, there was even one of the seats from the vehicle on the ground, what a mess, the people looked so distraught.

Eventually clear of the border check point which took over an hour or more to get through, the traffic queuing way back on this side to get into Iran, Mum had a right go at Dad telling him never to leave her in that predicament ever again. Dad in his defence said, that in this part of the world business is done away from the women and children, and after getting to see Amir who was the senior man there, although he seemed perfectly fine to me, not so, Dad had to pay him, so the mauling the hippie van got didn't happen to us. He said this is what goes on, money talks and everyone tries to get it one way or another and he was no different in that respect, and why should he be.

Afghanistan was made up of lots of different provinces and we had entered the country in the Herat province, Dad had paid for us to be allowed into that province along with a little extra for Amir. Due to its tribal nature which had been its basis for hundreds of years, each province of Afghanistan is ruled by a different war lord and his followers.

This now meant that our journey across this old forsaken looking land compared to Iran, we would have to pay a small toll for the privilege of passing through each province, and each payment being different depending on that province. With the debate still going on between Mum and Dad, none of us actually noticed the road surface had changed until about halfway to Herat, the nice tarmac roads of Iran had now dwindled into a dusty concrete road, very flat but continuously bumpy because of the gaps between the concrete sections, every six yards or so (five and a half metres). All you could see from any of our ever-increasingly dirty windows was a very inhabitable barren rocky landscape, with absolutely nothing else in view. Then on the horizon we caught a glimpse of these tall towers, we counted five in total and the nearer we ventured the taller they got, until we went right passed them.

They were made of mud and brick and looked like chimneys, very similar to the brick chimneys we could see near Bedford (Stewartby) on our Sunday afternoon drives in the countryside back home. That's where the similarities ended, the landscape and the weather, green fields, trees and rain in England but here sand, dust and heat, along with very cold nights. These chimneys looked ready to topple over, one had started to lean and could go at any time. Mum noticed they had what appeared to be windows in their structure, one near the top, very strange, then later that night we found out they were minarets, from an old mosque complex hundreds of years old.

Soon after that Herat appeared in the late afternoon sun which by now was starting to drop through the rear window of the Vitesse, but at the same time lighting up the gold and blue mosaic mosque at the end of a very dusty main street,

A typical scene in the streets of Herat

full of horse drawn carts called Tongas, in fact we were the only car on the street, as I looked out at the hustle and bustle of the bazaar. As we approached the mosque, to our right, was a fort or citadel again made of mud, very old and quite derelict, perched quite high compared to the rest of this small city. Hundreds of years previously Herat was a major city on the Silk Road, and another city that Alexander the Great conquered with his army going eastwards. Not far from the mosque we found a hotel, again not the best, but most likely the best Herat had to offer, and it seemed that other foreign travellers thought the same. It was getting quite cold now as the last of the sun's rays disappeared, Dad having to do his daily chore of taking the cases off the top of the car much to the amusement of a small crowd of people watching. The hotel didn't have anywhere to eat so once we were ready it was off out into the street to find some food, Mum first putting on a head scarf before venturing out to show some respect.

Not too far away was a busy bazaar, not too well-lit because Herat had very little electricity, if any, it was either gas light or the sound of a small generator which provided them with the means of power to continue trading. We found a little café style restaurant for some food, we had a huge plate of pilaf put in the middle of the table and four very large naan breads along with some water. The pilaf contained lamb and vegetables along with currants, very different but very nice all the same. There were other travellers enjoying the food at the same time and Dad got talking to them, they were the people who told us about the minarets to the old mosque, they were hoping to reach Nepal and Tibet on their journey. They also told us it took them three hours to get across the border from Iran, the guards searched everything, looking for drugs, but it's a bit ironic when Hashish is openly for sale right outside, here in the street. Dad told these people that all the guards are looking for is a small bribe to keep them happy, or as they would put it a donation and foreign tourists will have money, so why not try a little pressure. Back to the hotel to get some sleep ready for the journey tomorrow, Dad venturing out to get some fuel ready to go to Kandahar our next destination.

We must now leave the old Silk Road, the map shows the original route is nearly a straight line between Herat and the capital Kabul, and there is a road albeit a treacherous one, across unlawful tribal areas. The best route and better road is via Kandahar, but if the going is good it still adds on at least another day and a half to the journey. But at least you can stop in Kandahar the second largest city in Afghanistan to break this arduous trip across such a bleak landscape.

Day 15: Herat to Kandahar and a picnic to boot

Up early before seven dressed and then helping Dad to lug everything to the car before we started this leg of our journey, out of Herat and on to Kandahar, first stopping at a small street sellers stall on the edge of the city to have some fried eggs with large freshly baked naan and a nice glass of *chai* (tea), to set us up for the day ahead. Dad also bought extra bread, some oranges and four of the eggs to take with us along with six bottles of water.

About three hours into our trek, on a fairly straight road, we came to our first of many check points. A little hut absolutely in the middle of nowhere with a man operated barrier, just a pole across a road, stopping to show our passports and our car documents.

We were now entering the province of Farah, Dad paying a small fee for the privilege of doing so, not that there was much to see as we followed the road skirting the lower region of the foothills of the start of the Hindu Kush mountain range, the one we will be following on and off all the way to the capital Kabul. This sandy and uninviting landscape and rocky backdrop with no light pollution at night what so ever, looked just like the moon landscape in pictures I had seen from the space mission of Apollo 11 two years earlier. In fact, the Americans were in Afghanistan at that time, as well as the Soviet Union, so as long as they paid the man at the barrier, I suppose they could do what they wanted to win the space race.

At the start of the Hindu Kush Mountain range Alexander pointed out to us all, what we believed were small structures dotted along the edge of the foothills in the distance. As the land flattened out into this desolate plateau that we were travelling on, you could just make out the construction of tiny, what must have been mud huts that blended into the scenery as if trying to hide under camouflage. I then thought if I was standing where these huts were looking at our car, in its Saffron Yellow and dusty condition we would also appear to be camouflaged against this background. What a good colour to be travelling in the desert, In these unruly tribal lands, it's just, I don't think the makers of the Triumph Vitesse, had this in mind when they chose the colour, but I would bet they would have loved the worldwide publicity:

Triumph Vitesse in saffron yellow the car you can take in the desert if you are as mad as this family!

Another hour passed and another check point on the road, a little more activity going on but still a pole across the road, documents to show as well as the small fee. We had now entered the Nimroz region, and only about fifteen miles on when we came across the very small town called Delaram, where Dad topped up with petrol, at the only station, well there is not going to be a chain of them, not out here, but I wonder if they might have Jeff Astle from the Esso coin collection, you never know. Not long after leaving this town and crossing an old bridge spanning a very dry but wide gully, we stopped at another checkpoint. We had to go through the same process and another fee, it was less than an hour since we had entered the Nimroz province and that was with a fuel stop, and now we were having to go through it all again, this was starting to be tedious and time consuming, but it's the one and only road and those were the rules.

After clearing this checkpoint the land really flattened out, the foothills were nowhere to be seen and the temperature kept rising to a near unbearable heat, even with the windows down. The sign at the side of the road said, 'welcome to Helmand Province', well, there was nothing welcoming that I could see, just the concrete road and the heat haze of the midday sun. There was absolutely nothing in any direction then Mum said, 'according to the map this area is known as the Desert of Death', well Alexander looked at me and said, 'I think the map has got it right for a change'. Very different to when we were in Iran when towns that were there did not show up on the map at all, it makes you wonder where the AA got their information from, they certainly didn't drive this route, I can tell you!

After a while Dad stopped the car to give it a rest putting up the bonnet to give the engine some extra relief, if there was any, and then said, 'let's have lunch'.

Wow, nothing in either direction — not a tree, bush, even

a vehicle in sight — the heat must really be affecting him. This must be a first, a family picnic at the side of the road in a desert and just to make it special the Desert of Death, in the hottest part of the day.

Mum broke out the bread and water bought that morning, then Dad took the four eggs and cracked them onto the roof

Gereskh main street

of the car. They cooked quicker than in any frying pan to the point the edges of the white turned a nice crispy brown, then without hesitation put straight into the naan bread. Well I can say using the roof of a 1970s Triumph Vitesse as a barbecue was very successful to the point where it should have been mentioned in the sales pitch like the radio cassette! 'Triumph Vitesse comes with own BBQ roof', they just didn't tell you that you needed the Desert of Death.

Food consumed, bonnet down and back in the car for some shade not that you could really tell the difference.

Around an hour later and what we all thought was a mirage, in the tremendous heat haze, was actually a green belt, mainly of trees but when you got close there were also some green terraced fields and a small village or town, Mum had this one on her map as Gereshk.

The town consisted of mainly mud houses dominated by an old mud fortress which looked very old and dilapidated. The main street, which was very busy compared to the desolate desert we had just crossed, was lined with what can only be described as shacks on both sides, themselves covered with old worn out sheets or tarpaulins, which extended out on poles to shade the different wares the locals were trying to sell. Dad saw petrol for sale, not in your usual filling station with pumps, but in bottles and containers on a table outside one of these covered shacks. He thought he might top the car up but still had half a tank left, and couldn't be sure what might be in them so gave it a miss, but the locals must use it all the time so it can't be all that bad.

Leaving the town, we crossed a large gulley, full to the brim with water, and plenty of green fields on each side as far as the eye could see, a far cry from the desert we had travelled through today and the one reason people had occupied this area for many centuries. It didn't take long for the sandy, rocky terrain to take back control, as we continued towards Kandahar, the all too familiar concrete road continuing eastwards as though it would never end, our car juddering along on its surface. Then without any surprise to us, and as sure as eggs are fried eggs out here, another checkpoint. We were leaving Helmand province and entering the province of Kandahar, although documents were checked no fee was paid and I thought the guards missed a trick to line their own pockets like Amir did back at the border yesterday.

Kandahar was around two hours further on as the late afternoon sun started to give up its heat to a more acceptable level. About halfway along this stretch of road there was another older abandoned mud fort that stood alone just waiting for the years and the weather to return it back into the sandy earth from whence it came.

With the light fading fast we made our approach into Kandahar another bustling town in the middle of nowhere. As I looked out at this town through my window I started to notice, for the first time, lots of women covered from head to toe in clothes that are called burqas, probably because they were mainly blue in colour, standing out more than the odd black open faced head dress that was popular in Herat. I was told they were women underneath this attire by Dad, then I thought it actually could be anyone, who knows?

Kandahar, Afghanistan's second biggest city today, was just a small town when we gave it our presence in 1971, and not for the first time a town named after Alexander the Great (formerly Iskander, then Kandahar) after he conquered this desolate area. That man, Alexander the Great, annoyed lots of people back in his day and my parents hopes came true, my brother literally followed in his footsteps and has done exactly that, including me on many occasions.

Here in Kandahar, there wasn't an old fortress as a dominant feature that I could see, unlike the other towns we had ventured through in Afghanistan. There were just a couple of old arched gateways that told you this once was

Hippies in Kandahar – hashish on tap

a walled city, along with its usual mosque calling people daily to prayer. Mainly a market town now and a very vibrant one at that, normal citizens going about their daily business, lots of tongas and rickshaws everywhere you looked. Buses packed to the rafters with not only people but goats, baskets of live chickens, colourful painted lorries adorned with fancy trinkets, stacked as high as you like with every conceivable type of goods you could think of. We eventually found another hotel which again had only a few guests, most if not all foreign travellers, and to me at the time that I saw them, around the hotel, looked a bit lost or unsteady, maybe even drunk, but this is a so-called dry country. Asking Dad what was wrong with all these people, men and women, he replied they must have been smoking hashish, which sends their brain into all sorts of confusion and this is mainly why they come on their trips, to buy hashish which is readily available on the streets for very little money.

There's enough trouble with extremely hot days, very cold nights, guards to bribe and all the tribal bandits to worry about, but then to be getting high and out of your mind as well, good luck to them on that I thought! The hotel had a lounge that you could sit in and order food so that's what we did, chicken salad and bread along with bottles of water, we took some back to our rooms. We had to share a bathroom and again not the best accommodation, although quite adequate for one night.

We all slept really well, I think due to the long day and the heat which was so exhausting and prominent throughout.

Day 16: Kandahar to Kabul

Up early and down for breakfast around seven-thirty, warm milk and omelettes for all, car packed and off to Kabul, the capital city of Afghanistan, filling up with petrol as we left Kandahar. The traffic was quite considerable, mainly lorries and buses travelling between the two major cities, the road following a small but running gully of water, the Hindu Kush starting to return to our left, as we headed north east.

A queue of traffic slowed our progress as we crossed another checkpoint and paying a fee to enter the next province from the Kandahar region.

The wind coming from the north was blowing sand across the road to the extent that it looked like snakes, zig zagging their way across in front of us, and in some places leaving small drifts in its wake that the car would bump over, giving us all something to giggle about. The sand and dust were increasing each mile we travelled making it more difficult to overtake the slower lorries and buses travelling in our direction, Dad putting on the headlights so that we could be seen in our 'camouflaged' Triumph Vitesse.

Eventually this small sandstorm abated as we approached another checkpoint, Dad showing our entire documentation, the man writing it all down in a book then paying him the usual fee.

Ghanzi province we had entered this time, another area ruled by another war lord, What I did notice was that one of the buses that had stopped next to us was boarded by armed men, it looked like they were getting a fee off every passenger, not only these people paid for the journey on the bus, they then had to pay a fee for the privilege of travelling in their own country. About an hour after this checkpoint and after passing all different modes of transport along the way we came upon the walled city of Ghanzi.

Mum's maps indicated around three to four hours to Kabul from here, so Dad said we would have lunch once he had filled up the car with fuel, giving us a little time to spend in this town. Our dusty car now parked, we strolled the streets of Ghanzi for some 'fuel' of our own, eventually

Ghanzi and the hard reality of life

sitting under a tree on benches and being served a plate of lamb pilaf and naan bread, that Dad had ordered using his knowledge of Pashto, the local dialect. Alexander and I had Coke, while Mum and Dad drank chai, sitting there quietly watching the world go by. This town was way behind Herat and Kandahar, so much more primitive but just as busy. The people walking past were oblivious to this western family sitting and eating in the middle of their town looking totally out of place, or maybe not, perhaps they were used to it or in the wider scheme of things it didn't matter there were more important things for them to be concerned about.

Most of the women had a burqa on, again mostly blue but now and again you would see a beige coloured one, similar to the daleks in *Doctor Who*, mostly are the same colour, then along comes the odd different one.

Some women were shopping in twos or threes, then you would get some that appeared to be browsing on their own but actually not, if you looked carefully enough their husbands would be five or six steps in front of them, hands clasped tightly behind their back perusing the situation like the male peacocks at Woburn Abbey.

Alexander and I tried to guess who belonged to whom, which was hard due to the fact there was no conversation or eye contact between them, it was so much harder than counting red cars on the M1 motorway. Mum started to join in and we all had a laugh when we got it completely wrong, the only way that you could be sure you were right, was that if the woman had bought some item at one of the many stalls, then the husband would walk back and pay for it. I suppose it was a silly game but being stuck in a car for hours with nothing but dust to look at; this was quite entertaining to say the least.

Game over, just can't remember who won, knowing my brother it was him whether he did or not. Strolling back to the car, the streets were laden with every type of item you could imagine for sale, I tugged on the hand of Mum, which I was holding at that moment, pointing out to her the man walking in front of us at the time. He had a gun strapped over his shoulder as casual as you like, as though it was a fashion accessory, in fact the more you looked around the more men you noticed who had guns, imagine that in Abington Street Northampton on a Saturday afternoon? Dad explained as we reached the car, 'this is real tribal land and very religious, so expect to see more guns and more women covered up', he also suggested that Mum kept her head scarf on at all times so as not to alienate the locals.

Not long out of Ghanzi we came upon two old stone minarets, they looked older than the ones back in Herat, but the columns were not round like chimneys, they had eight sides, very strange. The road from Ghanzi to Kabul was about the same, as previously we had been using to travel through Afghanistan, dust covered, bumpy with two more toll checks, and the odd sporadic colour of green appearing as you crossed another small gully of water. Finally we started

The Kabul River

The many sights of Kabul

to enter a large valley in which Kabul nestled majestically in isolation, posing against the backdrop of the snow-capped mountains of the Hindu Kush, its foothills spreading out and reaching down like some old person's wrinkled and worn hands, stretching around its outer suburbs.

Kabul was like no other city we had the fortune of gracing our eyes on during this trip. As the capital of this vast country there wasn't any real stand out monuments that I had noticed, no real historical architecture, in fact nothing to say, 'look at me, I'm Kabul the capital of Afghanistan'. The one thing it was, was colourful, noisy and very busy, it seemed that everything wanted to be on the streets at the same time. Buses, rickshaws, tongas, lorries, scooters, there were carts pulled by cows, donkeys and even people, everything going everywhere, but not at any great pace, because of all the foot traffic and bicycles crisscrossing in front of each other halting each other's progress.

Then every so often there would be a bottleneck due to the

sheer volume of vehicles and people trying to negotiate past shops that have sprawled their wares out onto the already congested road. 'People were that close to the car they might as well come and sit next to me', I thought, 'we have had four on the back seat this trip already, so space is not a problem'. It took us over an hour to get anywhere near the centre of this city — if there was one.

Eventually following a high concrete wall that formed the sides of a low river now, but suggesting that it would be full of water sometime in the course of a year, maybe when the distant mountain snow melts. It was now getting to be very tedious the amount of time it was taking to move, Mum trying to find us a way through this mayhem by her maps but nothing stood out as a focal point to give us any real guidance, driving through London seemed like a walk in the park compared to this even today in 2020, if only someone had the bright idea of a congestion charge they would have made a real killing. The rule being if you didn't pay, they would kill you —sounds good to me, where's the Afghan version of Ken Livingston when you need him?

Flashing in front of us, and about time too, a very welcoming sign of a large hotel, itself nearly hanging out over the road trying to block your progress, with Dad managing to park the car right outside the front because a tonga had just vacated the space.

Rooms booked on the first floor, shared bathroom again I'm afraid, but you can't have the luxury of an en-suite in Kabul, even if it is the capital city — that just wouldn't be Afghanistan, would it?

We all went down to give Dad a hand to unload the car because of the chaos in the street, passing through the lobby out onto a raised terrace where they served meals, then down some steps to the car. Alexander and Dad lifted the tarpaulin creating a huge cloud of dust gathered from today's journey and as they did so, getting some lengthy verbal abuse from one of the street sellers offering popcorn from his cart, it's a good job Dad didn't teach us Pashto, I might have understood what he was saying. Cases dragged up the stairs and into our rooms, Dad said we would eat in the hotel rather than venture out into the sheer madness that was the streets of Kabul. Dinner was the usual lamb pilaf but with some nice sultanas mixed in, giving it a sweet as well as spicy tang with fresh yogurt to add. The table was overlooking our car and as we sat there out of nowhere two small boys came with buckets of water and sponges and started to clean the car

Dad shouted out not to wash the car, Mum said they were only trying to earn a few pennies, but Dad wanted the car to look the way it did, because tomorrow was the last day of this never to be forgotten journey, and he wanted to show his family what a trial it had been to reach them. Dad had made a phone call from the lobby before dinner to his family in Peshawar, the place he once called home, to tell them of our forthcoming arrival that would be sometime around midday tomorrow at the border crossing all being well.

Food eaten then upstairs to the two bedrooms, this time I was sharing with Dad for a change with both the rooms overlooking the street. Dad opened the window to check on the car and would you believe it those two boys had almost cleaned the car from top to bottom, and what I could see from my vantage point, they had done a reasonable job.

Dad went downstairs and out to the car and all the two boys wanted was a few coins to get some food, which Dad did give them after he watched them finish their chore, he was always such a strict but fair man, but to me he will always be Dad.

Day 17: Journey's End

The last leg, another six hours drive to Peshawar in Pakistan, crossing the border and then navigating the notorious Khyber Pass. Mum got us up around six as the call to prayers sounded across this vast city, itself barely awake from its sleep. Dad really wanted to get out of Kabul before the mayhem in the streets started again so it wouldn't cause us any type of delay.

Filling with fuel and now clear of Kabul we were on the road to Jalalabad, stopping for some freshly squeezed orange juice from a stall at the side of the road for a liquid breakfast.

Jalalabad reached after winding our way around the foothills of the Hindu Kush passing a large turquoise green lake as we went, it looked so serene set against its rocky backdrop. We again had to endure yet another one of those provincial checkpoints, with the now too familiar pole stretching across the road, showing our passports and then paying the toll that was due. Dad told us that Jalalabad was originally a part of the North West Frontier under British rule and that his great grandfather was born here, the family still having some land in this area. Although only three hours since we rose from our beds, albeit uncomfortable ones, Dad

The daily grind in the main street of Jalalabad

said we would have a good lunch now, because the rest of the day would be very long but also tiring for us boys, and the next large town would be over the border in Pakistan and that he couldn't be sure when we would get to eat something substantial next. The town Jalalabad was similar in size as Herat in the west of this country, stalls selling all manner of goods, plenty of horse drawn tongas, it seemed a very normal day for these local people, in a very normal town.

A type of restaurant — if you can call two plastic tables with chairs strewn under a dilapidated lean-to a restaurant — was found for our meal. Mum ordered me a lamb steak with an egg on top, plenty of naan bread to accompany it but no vegetables whatsoever, just what a young boy likes, couldn't have chosen better myself! All nicely fed and returning to the car and from a distance noticed that our camouflaged vehicle had disappeared!

It's not that you couldn't see it, but there stood shinning quite beautifully, was our saffron yellow Triumph Vitesse. I couldn't believe how clean those boys had finally managed to get it until now, not really noticing the condition of the car when we set off this morning due to the light, well the lack of it, and I think I was half asleep anyway.

Back on the road which was busy with buses and all kinds of lorries stacked full to bursting point, it's beyond me how they do it, on some of them you could just make out the colourful cab underneath the load where the driver sat — total madness!

You got the sense we were climbing all the time, twisting one way then the other, the road narrowing in places following a gully which turned into a large gorge the further we went up into this rocky mountain range, lorries belching out fumes as they struggled to even reach walking pace.

It took us ages to pass these old tortoise-like vehicles, one after another bobbing in and out missing the traffic coming in the opposite direction. They were travelling down at much

The lorries of the Khyber Pass

greater speeds, I saw some of the looks on the drivers faces as they passed, it's as if they were praying while grappling with the steering wheel on these old vehicles totally out of control. Alex pointed out in the gorge below lots of old wrecked trucks and even a bus, they must have gone over the edge after an horrendous accident, now I know why the drivers looked like they were praying as this may well have been their final journey.

After about an hour of playing dodgem cars on the mountain passes, which was so far from the dodgem cars at the annual fair which comes to Wootton's recreational ground, the road eventually started to level out, and we began slowly to enter an area of very high activity. We had reached what could be described as a small village, but really it was a long line of shacks each side of the road, selling and storing all manner of goods, so many lorries unloading and loading, some going east and some going west back to Kabul.

This was Torkham where different traders ply their daily business because the border with Pakistan was less than a mile away. Continuing steadily in a queue we approached the Afghanistan border control, eventually showing all our documents the guards on duty taking a routine glance in

Torkam and the loading of goods

the boot of the car, then releasing us very quickly when they were satisfied with everything. We then began to enter what is known across the globe as no man's land, as Alexander and I perched forward in great anticipation, holding onto the backs of the front seats our eyes gazing through the front windscreen as we did so.

It was then the realisation hit home that after nearly seventeen days, eight countries, two continents, over five thousand miles of the most unpredictable travel, in all kinds of weather you could ever imagine, our goal lay just a few hundred yards in front of us. Now to Mum, Alexander and myself this next border crossing got us excited as to what may lay ahead but give a thought to the driver of this vehicle, my Dad. If the three of us were on tenterhooks with anticipation, how he must be feeling? What thoughts must be rushing through his head, it must have been a whirlwind of confusion at this moment, and how did he manage to process it all in the very few yards we had left to travel?

Dad had left this land which now lies before him some twenty-four years earlier at the age of seventeen, not really a man in many people's eyes, but he left all the same, but then was expected to return when he had completed his education in England. He never did as a result of meeting Mum, and in doing so became an outcast, the black sheep of the family, but the realisation that he now could meet his four brothers and only sister, along with the rest of the family, some of them he had never seen before as they were not even born when he left, and also at long last pay his respects to his parents' graves after such a long time. But it never showed for one instance even if he had the feeling of trepidation and a tear in his eye, here he was bringing with him the family he loved and chosen to be with, and nothing, not even his traumatised past was going to distract him from that, that was the Dad I had come to know and love. It also must be taken into consideration about Mum, she was entering the comfort zone of those who may have decided but could do nothing at the time, that she possibly was to blame for all this and prevented my father from returning all those years ago to fulfil his duties as a Muslim boy should. So many scenarios to contemplate, so many questions unanswered. (Again, tell me why we made this trip of a lifetime?)

At this moment it appeared we were trapped in some sort of suspended time zone here in no man's land, there wasn't anything behind us except the barrier of the Afghan border and in front, two huge closed gates with the Pakistani flag embossed on each of them attached to a tower manned by a guard. Where had all the trucks gone that were in front of us in the queue? It's as though they had disappeared in some type of strange and weird twilight zone. We all looked at each other and had no idea why we were now not progressing any further, and for what reasonable reason the gates in our path remained closed. After several minutes the guard in the tower waved his hand and the gates started to open slowly inwards. Well the sight that greeted us was phenomenal and beyond belief, it was as if we were going to put ourselves into some kind of giant bubble and what lay beyond these gates was another world, very similar to when *Doctor Who* opens the tardis doors on some strange and distant planet, or even more surreal than that, just like Dorothy opening the door to the house that had landed abruptly in Munchkinland.

There was a line of guards stretching out along each side of the road; I now know these were the Khyber Rifles very smart and regal, each with a prominent elegant headdress. There were people behind these guards peering intensely to get a glimpse at our car as the gates continued to open, exactly like Alexander and I peered round Grandma Blaney's parlour door to glimpse what cars were on her sideboard, but not like us, this time they only had one choice — yes you guessed it! A saffron yellow Triumph Vitesse without the box, but still shiny and clean thanks to those two boys back in Kabul.

I said at the beginning of this story that I have a good memory and this is still the case, but what I cannot remember for the life of me from that day onwards, while we were in this spellbinding country were all the different names of the supposedly aunties and uncles I had, plus the endless number of cousins first, second, third and beyond. It was easy for them as they only had to remember the names of Alexander and Jason, so to make it easier unless I do know their names, I will just call most of them uncle or auntie and their children. I'm sure it would be the same for most of you put in this position aged nine. This was the North West Frontier and up until 1947, only twenty-four years earlier, was previously ruled by the British Empire as part of India. There was a caste system used under the British Raj, and the best and influential positions in government and the military were allocated to the caste of Brahmins and Kshatriyas, of which most of my father's family were fortunate to be. In the caste system you either have wealth or you don't, and this decides what caste your family falls under.

My great grandparents and grandparents were in very prominent positions, given to them by the British authorities and therefore had a very influential impact on how this tribal area was governed on behalf of the British Empire, but also at the same time feathering their own nests. This made them a key and prominent family of this newly formed country as partition took place in 1947, and they built up this position further to their advantage over the next few years, as the new state of Pakistan evolved, eventually leading to one member of this very large family to becoming the President in 1969, my uncle who we all met back in London, Agha Muhammad Yahya Khan.

Unknown to me and presumably my Mum and my brother, our uncle had placed Pakistan under martial law and his

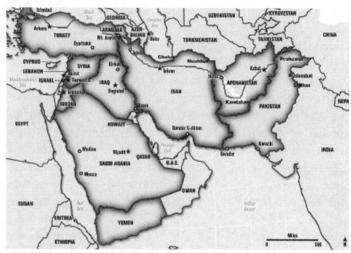

*The Aghas conquered the Middle East 2,300 years
after Alexander the Great*

authority was backed by the military. They say keep your
enemies close, well he didn't have to, he just gave most of the
top jobs to his loyal family where he could and the rest to his
military friends.

All that follows in this story happens in the Khyber and
Punjab regions of Pakistan, which is in the north of this
fascinating but still evolving country, and is where our side
of the family originated from, their influential positions were
allocated to govern on behalf of my uncle and the acting
government. This allowed my uncle, the President, to carry
out most of his duties in Karachi, which is in the South. He
visited the north twice in the period we were there, and we
did meet him, once in Peshawar and again in the new city
of Islamabad.

But these were very troubled times in Pakistan, and he
couldn't afford to spend any length of time with us, which he

stressed he really wanted to, knowing we had now arrived safely from England. None of us realised that in the short time we were to spend in this country, how troubled it would become for our uncle, to such a point it was in fact life changing for him.

Gates fully opened now as the Khyber Rifles band strikes up a tune, anybody would think royalty had arrived the way it was all staged managed, just imagine the Queen arriving at the Khyber Pass, stepping out of a Triumph Vitesse and a saffron yellow one at that — now that would be a sight! Dad slowly moved the car forward, not far though, as a crowd of people surged towards us, Dad immediately jumping out of the car after realising that one of his elder brothers who he had not seen for over two decades, was at the head of this onrushing wave of people.

Eventually embracing each other tightly as they came together just in front of us, the crowd then engulfing them and the car as they all began what I can only describe as a mass celebration, it's as if George Best had scored a seventh goal against Northampton Town — utter jubilation! Mum had noticed, then explained to Alexander and me, as this passionate crowd surrounded the car, that there were no women at all to be seen amongst them as this was the nature of this society.

With the guards beginning to restore some sort of order and forming a human barrier which circled the car we all managed to exit safely.

At first being introduced by Dad to his brother, Agha Mohammad Khan, but understandably not for one instance, would he be letting go of him.

My new uncle, then introduced us to his two eldest sons, my new cousins Zia and Zaka, the youngest son Sabah, remained in Peshawar.

Then the officer of the armed guards came over to us and yes you might have guessed, he was another uncle, head of the Khyber Rifles based at the fort nearby and it was he who had

*Dads' brother Agha Mohammad Khan Zahid and his
two sons, Zia on his left and Zaka to his right*

arranged this musical reception for our arrival. The crowd
probably hadn't a clue who we were but just cheered anyway.
I wouldn't imagine that too much happens here, on this
distant rocky outcrop involving a well-drilled military band
and a Triumph Vitesse. A tray of drinks was ushered quickly
towards us by one of the elegantly dressed guards, which we
all were grateful for. This was then followed by a tray of fresh
fruit, the oranges so refreshing, just right for my dry mouth
and throat. Flowered garlands were then placed around our
necks, as all of us were swept along on this endless wave of
emotion that had gripped this small but momentous reunion
of two brothers in the middle of the notorious Khyber Pass.

Once all the euphoria of this event had died down we set
off in a convoy of four vehicles, two pickup trucks with armed
guards front and back of our car and my Dad's brother's car
with my new cousins in it, all heading towards the home
town of my father. This was to entail the very winding trip
through the famous Khyber Pass on a road that was not
exactly fit for purpose but being used constantly day by day.

Mum then brought to the attention of all of us that we had entered Pakistan without producing any documents to the authorities, Dad said when you are the authority, what's the point of showing the document to yourself, he had a point!

The Khyber Pass was something to behold and very picturesque in its own way, rocky, rugged and steep, the cold melting snow waters from way up high seeping into the gorge basin at every opportunity, sometimes spilling across the road in front of us then continuing down the steep sides, finally entering the Khyber river. The Khyber Pass had been the gateway to India for centuries and now it was our gateway to my father's home city of Peshawar, a city that would lead to an everlasting and unfortunate life changing memory that would change the whole outlook on life for this nine year old boy.

It took nearly two hours to reach the outskirts of Peshawar, even with an escort that cleared the way the best it could, considering all the vehicles on this ever-winding road that had no traffic sense at all. This led us to believe, that with the amount of miles we had just covered in the last seventeen days, in so many different countries and cultures, it was noted by all, that these drivers were the worst we had seen. You started to wonder if for some of them it was their first day behind the wheel, they were that bad. There were so many crashed trucks and buses at the side of the road it had started to become the norm rather than the exception, the only consolation for us was this armed escort in front and the fact this was the first country since we left England, that drove on the same side of the road, (the right) if that really mattered, given everybody was driving all over the place, and which side of the road you were on didn't come into the equation.

Peshawar was a frontier outpost very similar in style to Kabul but much smaller, it consisted of one large old fort mainly in ruins, suggesting this once was a major city and an important gateway to the west or east depending on your journey. It had a very noticeable white-fronted mosque and

The Inter-Continental Hotel, Peshawar

some old colonial buildings that the British had built, one was now the University of Peshawar. It was more about the people than what the city consisted of in a structural form, and it had been this way for centuries, an old city centre sprawling out like a spiders web, the more trading, the more the population grew, all living in basic dwellings.

We were taken to the Inter-Continental Hotel by our escort where the best rooms had been arranged for us to stay by members of the family. Ushered in like royalty this was to be our base for the first few days to get us used to the city, in fact it was over two weeks that we stayed here, but no complaints on that point. This hotel was the end of our journey. I was very glad to see it, day-in day-out of hard travelling non-stop, seventeen days in a 1970 Triumph Vitesse, probably never been contemplated before by mankind — it only took four days to reach the moon — and they had air conditioning, that tells you all you need to know about this journey. We eventually would be taken to Dad's family home, Agha Manzil, the home he grew up in as a boy, a traditional large house in the old part of the city, where we would feel much more comfortable and have time to get to know our newly acquired family. The real reason we had to stop in the only westernised hotel in the whole of the North West Frontier at that time was, Agha Manzil was having a new bathroom built especially for us and it was not quite ready. There was a delay in the supply of the porcelain toilet, not really that common in rural Pakistan in 1971, especially this far north. They were more accustomed to an unsightly hole in the ground, which my brother and I frequently used over the coming months, and naturally we ended up calling it the drop zone. A good night's sleep in one of the plushest rooms with air conditioning, heating and a bathroom attached that we have had since first stepping onto the Asian continent, actually you could say since the start of the trip. In the morning a good hearty breakfast in a clean dining room, another added bonus, before relaxing around this newly opened hotel with Mum and Alexander, while Dad was picked up by his school friend and colleague Hashim Khan, and taken into the city of Peshawar to reminisce after being away for so long.

I think it did us all some good just to be separated a little after that journey, and it was a great feeling just to sit around the swimming pool area, than to be sitting day after day in the back seat of a car being jostled hour after hour. With food and drink readly on tap, rather than having to wait and see if the next town could supply us with any type of refreshment.

CHAPTER 7

Pakistan; a different world

THE FOLLOWING EVENTS are all true, they may be a little out of sequence and the time scale between these events I am a little unsure of, but all none the less true, and for two boys aged fourteen and nine we might just as well have been in the Land of Oz with Dorothy.

We were definitely in our own giant bubble, treated as though we were two long lost princes, but too young to understand it all. Oblivious to the rest of humanity, we didn't even contemplate if there was life outside of our new environment, as we were swept along on a tide of emotion. The tiny village of Wootton we left seventeen days back in England, nearly becoming a forgotten memory at the back of our minds, you just couldn't explain some of the things that actually happened to our school mates, they would just reply by saying, 'yeah right, pull the other one'.

As you read on, you just might think the same, but with privileges we now could exploit, comes the stories that I can tell.

Old habits die hard

The Khyber region had warm days and cold nights, so the heating in the hotel room was very welcome when first awakening. On this particular day I woke to a brilliant blue sky at around seven-thirty, a day trip had been organised by Hashim Khan, Dads' closest friend. He had visited us twice in Northampton in the late sixties, so he wasn't an unfamiliar face to us in this new world of ours. Pick-up time was around nine o'clock, so there was time for all to get a good breakfast down us before leaving. Dad had always told us that Hashim was of royal blood and he was by rights a Prince, but we all took this with a pinch of salt, just about the same amount I put on my nice fried egg that morning. Hashim joined us in the foyer as we all waited for transport to arrive, which was in the form of a minibus, explaining to us that we all would be spending the day going on a shooting expedition into the Kyber Mountains, a very traditional event in these parts stretching back to the days of the Raj.

All in the minibus heading out of Peshawar, dodging rickshaws, tongas and everything else as we went on our way. Around an hour later we reached the Kabul River, which has its source near the capital then winds its way through Afghanistan and the Hindu Kush mountain range, entering Pakistan before reaching the Indus River further on in it's travels.

At the river we met three of Hashim's friends, and they had organised three boats all the same size to take us duck hunting up the Kabul River and in to the mountains, as far as the border with Afghanistan. In total there were only eight of us and I can say for sure Mum, Alexander and myself had never shot a gun before, not even at the fairground, as for Dad, well the nearest that I had known him get close to a gun was watching Randolph Scott in a western on TV. We got in to the first boat, it was big enough for all eight of us and more than half of it's length was in the open, and the other section under a very elaborate canopy for shade. We set off with the engines chugging away quietly and with the other two boats following behind, for the life of me I couldn't see why we needed all three boats and the many local men who were accompanying us, just to go on a trip up the river; it really was a sight to behold. Absolutely nothing like the boating lake in Abington Park Northampton, you would be lucky to get three people in one of those boats, and then the chances of it tipping over and sinking very much favoured the lake.

Not long after setting off one of the crew members offered drinks from a cool box, as we all sat listening to Dad and Hashim tell stories of their school days, as these three boats meandered up this river into the Hindu Kush, the rocky sides getting ever steeper as we went.

The water was so tranquil, colours of green and blue, sometimes turning a bright turquoise where the sun caught it, reminding me very much of the colour of the dome on the Mosque in Mashhad back in Iran. The owners of the boats must know these waters like the back of their hand, as after about an hour we pulled into the side of this ravine slowly cutting the engine and gliding on to a type of sandy beach area, every one of us disembarking. As we did so we were told to keep very quiet as some of the local men from the second boat produced some rather large guns.

Now if I didn't know that this was an organised trip by uncle Hashim, the sight of these men dressed very plainly and in traditional headgear with several guns in their possession wandering up this isolated beach, would send you into a state of shock and make you think, well, this could be it folks!.

Uncle Hashim and his three friends were given guns by these men, then they walked to the edge of the river towards a large area of reeds and bull rushes.

Before you could blink your eyes, a brace of Mallards broke cover from the reed beds to a large crescendo of noise from these guns, echoing around the ravine the likes I had never heard before, it made the shouting of my name, then listening to my own echo that I had done previously on our journey in Austria, sound like a mere whisper. After all the commotion and noise this distant ravine slowly returned to its natural state of tranquillity, as though nothing had happened, then came a splash and the sight of one of the local men, with all his clothes on swimming out into the calm water.

In England, when people go shooting they have a dog to retrieve the prize if the shooter had been successful, here why take a dog when one of the servants can do the same job, I'm just glad he could swim for his sake! Two ducks safely retrieved as the conversation and euphoria centred on these lifeless items, never mind the poor bedraggled soul, totally out of breath, standing just a few yards away.

Back on board to head further into the rugged mountainous region of the North West Frontier the sun disappearing for small periods of time making the boat chilly and slightly dark, as the sides of the ravine seem to close in tightly. Then from these narrow passages the steep sides all of a sudden opened out, allowing endless streams of light to bear down on us, so bright you had to cover your eyes, this light was intensified by the reflection of the clear cold water. Then Uncle Hashim took his gun, and laid himself out overlooking the bow of the boat, as it quietly slipped into another open stretch of water, tall grass like reeds with brown heads adorned both sides of the river waving slightly in the breeze, moving as if it was a crowd of people all coming down to the water's edge to drink. Again a crack of a gun, even though it was half expected it still made Mum and I jump at the sound, the echo again ever decreasing as Hashim stood up pointing to the driver of the boat which direction to retrieve another large but lifeless duck from the water. As he stood and admired his latest achievement, he declared that it was time for lunch. That left me wondering if that meant duck was on the menu, pellets included, and I didn't have long to find out, as all three boats grounded themselves onto another sandy outcrop. I now know why there were three boats and plenty of local bodies. We all stood and watched them unload chairs and a table, covering it with a cloth then followed by two large parasols. It looked as if we were in a fancy restaurant in Northampton.

As Alexander and I played skimming stones across this flat stretch of water while waiting for lunch, we heard the sound of a flute like instrument, whistling its way down from upon high, and there in the distance, a shepherd boy tending to his flock, keeping himself occupied by playing sweet music that drifted away just like the river. Hashim told us that they play music to keep the snow leopard away that might steal his goats, as they are very valuable to the family, he said if you look hard enough you will see one, but we never did.

Lunch! Well for eight people there was enough for eighteen and more, no duck though thank goodness, they were left on the boat. It was a buffet for a King, cold meats, lamb, chicken and even beef, which I had totally forgot about since leaving England. Breads, samosas and tasty cold fried vegetables in batter, that's how to do veggies, followed by different pastries and cakes, you just didn't know what to have next, what an array of fabulous food. There were four waiters to tend to your every need, one just waved a fan about, I think it was just to keep any flies off, but the small breeze was welcoming all the same, all this food was accompanied by cold drinks or hot chai, both if you wanted. Uncle Hashim said this is how the British society went shooting when it was a ruling empire, and the elite still do this today, he said it's just as well, old habits die hard.

I thought, 'good job too', if this is what duck shooting is all about then I would like to go more often and the sooner the better. The afternoon was relaxing, I paddled in the cold-water holding hands with Mum, Alexander didn't want to take his socks of in case there were any nasty bugs about but there wasn't, he went with Dad a little further up the beach, where the men were shooting at cans with an air pistol for fun. I think we all knew any ducks would be long gone by now. It was so enjoyable just letting time go by as a family, nothing to rush for.

We took tea in the late afternoon, with more cakes, as if we hadn't already had enough, then set off back down the river to meet our transport, leaving all those men to clear and pack away everything back onto the remaining boats. Hashim said that they would share all what was left between them and take it home so their families would eat well tonight.

As the minibus dropped us back at the hotel, we all really thanked Hashim Khan, and said what a great day we all had, and it was a great day.

Agha Manzil

As mentioned previously our time at the Inter-Continental Hotel was governed by the completion of the western style bathroom at my father's family home, but Dad couldn't wait that long to show us where he grew up, and where we would be stopping in the near future. It would also give us the chance to meet the rest of his brother's family so after another good breakfast we ventured out of the hotel's grounds, towards the old city of Peshawar.

The streets of Peshawar

1935, men of the family outside Agha Manzil,
my father bottom right, his father centre middle

Our little saffron yellow Triumph Vitesse battling with all the
hustle and bustle that the streets of Peshawar could throw at it,
just as it had done in Kabul, but this time without the weight of
the suitcases strapped to the roof, how pleased Dad must have
been not to do that daily but necessary chore yet again.

Although these streets were much narrower with fewer
cars, buses or trucks, it was no less busy, they were full with
noisy little scooter taxis known as tuk-tuks and horse drawn
tongas, and there also appeared to be many more people
hurrying about on foot in all sorts of directions.

After winding our way through these streets, we arrived at
the front of what was my former grandparents home, setback
from the road, a pillar wall with a railing fence to one side
enclosing a small park-like area with mature trees, in front
of us stood a large old double wooden door, which graced an
even larger brick and stoned dwelling. Looking up it was as

if I was in London all over again where most of the buildings seem to touch the sky, but this was Peshawar, and this was the only building of any height that I could see.

After a second glance at the large wooden door, the size of which would make you think that a family of giants lived beyond, a sign that I recognised immediately from the first moment I could read comfortably. Manzil, the same name that adorned our bungalow in our little cul-de-sac back in Wootton, but instead of having the number 18 accompanying this sign, it only had the words which read 'Agha Manzil'.

Although Dad, in his wisdom, decided to turn his back on the family for a more western life and not return home in all those years, he never forgot his roots. Naming his own house after his family home here in Pakistan, and the one he was born in, maybe it was just his way of remembering the childhood he had with his parents, trying to keep hold of those precious memories, even though he was a black sheep.

Holding Mum's hand we all followed Dad up the three large stone steps that led to the wooden door, which he pushed open with apparent ease, exposing an opening very dark and cold, as if you were about to enter some sort of ancient cave, it felt old eerie and damp not at all like anything I expected to see or feel. The two old wooden doors stood proud each side of this cavernous entrance leading to where, I do not know, but ahead a shaft of daylight appearing to get brighter, as we proceeded towards it, the sound of the city street, decreased in volume behind us as we did so.

Stepping into the light streaming down from above it appeared we had entered a courtyard within the building, with an old dilapidated fountain in the centre being the focal point some time in the past. Looking skywards I could make out two floors, with old wooden, but once colourful and fancy, railings encircling a walkway that continued around both floors. Beyond this appeared to be rooms with intricate glass windows, but everything was dull and dark covered in dust and grime as though no one had lived here for hundreds of years, it was like some kind of ancient civilisation had disappeared forever, telling the last one out to shut the door.

Mum broke the silence saying, 'Hassan, this surely can't be where you expect us to stay', and at that precise moment, as if it was stage managed, across the courtyard another large but concealed door flung open. An array of people came flooding down to meet us led by Muhammad Khan Zahid, Dads' brother. Well all was explained over the next couple of hours, which of course involved lots of tasty food and the usual sweet tea.

When Dad lived here with his parents, sister and brothers back in the 1930s and 40s and before that my great grand parents lived in this place. The front part of the house was used by all the men of the family, Dad having a bedroom with one of his brothers on the second floor. At the rear of the house, where we are now sitting, was a most beautiful second courtyard three times as big as the outer one, with enough room to have orange trees within it. The trees gave some shade from the penetrating sun that was beaming down on this joyous gathering. Here again there were two floors all having colourful elaborate wooden and glass doors overlooking this courtyard but with no visible walkway. Everything was clean and bright such a contrast to what I had witnessed earlier, when entering this house and the sight I had really expected to see.

Back when my father lived in this house, this part was for the women of the family, set back from the exposure of the prying eyes of the street as religion would dictate.

This second annex included bedrooms for all the women, several lounging rooms on the ground floor, to while away their days, and a kitchen on the roof that was manned by several servants with their sleeping quarters up there as well. This arrangement was to keep them away from the luxury of the rest of the house and its occupants only to be summoned when required. Quite the opposite from the British line of thought, where a typical period London house had the servant's quarters deep down in the basement.

Today as we sit here, the men still stay in this house and in these bedrooms, I see around me. The women of the family now reside in a newer house around the corner about two minutes' walk, known as Agha Manzil 2, but the principle is the same, men and women in different quarters, although they mix freely in each of the houses throughout the day. The day appeared to stretch itself out into early evening without us realising, as Dad's brother Mohammad Khan, who met us at the border and now lives in the family home of Agha Manzil, introduced us to his wife, Nazakat and all their family. We had met his sons; Zia aged twenty-four and Zaka aged twenty-three, on our first day, they spoke a reasonable amount of English as they were educated at Peshawar University, Sabah aged seventeen, his third son, was still there studying.

As the day went on, we got to know his daughters Rukhsana aged twenty-six, Irfana aged twenty-one we called her 'iffy', oh and not to forget little Imrana aged eighteen, who all lived in these two houses as well. The girls were so much fun and never seemed to stop laughing and giggling every time you looked at them, so innocent in their own little world they called home. Understandably their English did not appear to be up to the boys standard, as education was not a priority for women in a Muslim country for many years to come, but the family did send them to the best girls school that Peshawar could offer, which was more than most families could do.

Alexander and I had so much fun with all our new cousins while we stopped in Agha Manzil; they gave us all the time in the world even though they were much older than us.

Good for You

A family picnic was arranged, a day out where we were to meet Dad's oldest brother Khanan Khan, now I'm not quite sure if this elderly gentleman that we met that day was his step brother or an adopted brother, as my grandfather may have had two wives before my father was born, all the same he was truly respected and looked up to by all who attended that day including my father.

We arrived at a beautiful spot on the banks of the Shah Alam River, more of a creek really, but not too far from the city of Peshawar, all of us clambering out of two mini buses, one from Agha Manzil and the other from Agha Manzil 2.

There were a lot of people there already and again chairs were set around several tables, not as elaborate as the duck hunting trip, but what I could make out there was about the same amount of food. There must have been at least forty of us if not more, the ages ranging from a baby to, well, very old looking people very much in need of the chairs provided.

A picture from part of the family picnic

Most, if not all were family aunties, uncles and cousins all just enjoying this family gathering, some getting the chance to meet us for the first time. After we had eaten, we all took part in games; men, women and children, not the old ones mind, they never moved from the comfort of those chairs. The laughter was so captivating and endless, and it was inevitable we would eventually end up playing the national pastime of cricket, as everyone in this country really enjoys it. I lost count how many times the ball went into the creek, but it was very shallow which was fortunate.

I noticed that the boy who was prompted to retrieve it every time was not much older than me, he had white hair, and then it became apparently clear, that his eyesight was not good at all as he struggled to see the ball floating in the shallows, and had to be guided by some of the girls, but he was enjoying himself just like the rest of us.

Mum explained to me later when my curiosity got the better of me, and was told this boy was born like that, and is commonly known as an albino child, he was adopted by my father's oldest brother and he embraces his disability rather than shy away from it, 'good for you', I thought, 'why shouldn't he?' But in a hot, sun-drenched, third world country, it must be very hard for him indeed.

Eventually sitting down and having a well-earned drink after our fun and games we were introduced to a cousin called Dolce Mohammad, and were led to believe he was a son or very close relation to my father's eldest brother. He could speak very good English and had been educated at the university in Peshawar, but the surprising thing about him to me was, he must have been the largest person I had ever seen in my entire nine years on this planet, and as we sat chatting he was devouring a huge plate of chicken legs, followed by bottle after bottle of Coca Cola.

It was a few weeks later that we saw Dolce Mohummad again, not quite in the flesh, but being carried by at least ten, if not more, close members of the family or the ones that were capable of doing so, shoulder high, followed by the rest of the men of the family including Dad, Alexander and myself, through the streets of Peshawar to a burial ground somewhere in the city, how strange life can be.

Did an Angel come?

Dad had three brothers, two lived in Peshawar, the third with his family in Islamabad, now the capital city of Pakistan, and where all the important government buildings are based. It was over a four hour drive south from Peshawar on roads you would be putting your life at risk every time you travelled, not at all for the fear of bandits as in Afghanistan but for the way people decided to drive, didn't the British teach them anything?

This was a very new city just being born, as you might say, with all the buildings built in the same white colour, laid out on a grid system very similar in construction to Milton Keynes in England, without all the roundabouts. It was set on the outskirts of the hectic city of Rawalpindi the former capital of the Punjab.

Dad's brother Baba Khan served there as a High Court Judge, just as his father and my grandfather had done many years earlier, for the British Raj in the North West Frontier and Punjab region of India. He really looked the part, dressed in his robes every morning when going to the courthouse, a well-manicured moustache the likes you would only see in old books sat firmly on a well-rounded face.

He was a well-educated man and lived in a large new bungalow, white of course, set within a lush garden compound with high electric gates, and high walls, how very modern for 1971. It was more for his protection as armed guards stood day and night in a sentry box at the gate. Unfortunately, this

*Anni and Nanni with me outside
the New High Court in Islamabad*

level of protection comes with the high-profile job especially
in tribal Pakistan. We stopped there for more than two weeks
and had a really nice time with his family, my Auntie Begum
his wife, Annie aged eighteen and Nanni aged fifteen, their
two daughters.

While having dinner one evening sat around an oval glass table
on high backed chairs, so different from sitting on the carpet
floors of Agha Manzil, my uncle told us of the many foreign
travellers who were on the so called 'Hippie Trail' across
Asia, and he had the unfortunate task of having sentenced a
number of them to prison over the past two to three years. Not
for anything else but drug related crimes, mainly the quantity
that they had in their possession when stopped at the border.
These foreigners were both men and women and were sent to
the district jail in Rawalpindi where they remained. Mum got
very concerned about this and asked about the women, how
many, and what were there nationalities. Uncle Baba said

Dad's brother the Judge (Baba Khan) relaxing in his garden

Baba Khan, with Anni and Nanni, his Daughters

he will call Malik then immediately went to the phone. The call was to another family member, yes, that's right another uncle who conveniently was the current Inspector General of Prisons of the Punjab. Is there any member of this family not in a prominent position? It appears not!

The information came back that there were five foreign women in the jail, two Canadians, one Irish and two Dutch serving different prison terms between them.

Mum asked if their governments were doing anything to help but my uncle didn't know and thought not, and as Alexander and I went off to bed, the discussion went on well into the night. Two days later it had been arranged that Mum could go and see these women and because I was classed as a child in the eyes of the Islamic religion, I could go along too. Why me — when I could be going out for the day on a nice picnic with Dad, Alexander and the two girls?

Mum and I were picked up at nine in the morning prompt by an official prison Jeep, an armed guard sat in the front with the driver, and there was another jeep full of men with rifles,

The district jail, Rawalpindi

to escort us through the streets. The envy on my brothers face when he saw all this, made up for all yesterday's ribbings about spending a day out with Dad and the girls, anyway I thought who wants to go on yet another picnic with girls when I could be sat in a jeep with soldiers. The District Jail was about an hour away which felt so much quicker than that, especially when the traffic is stopped for your benefit and you embrace the thought of everyone looking to see who is in these vehicles, well I can tell them — it's only me! The two Jeeps never stopped, entering the jail gates at a constant speed not really allowing me to view the outside, of what was regarded as a place not to visit in any circumstances by the local population.

The brightness of the day had come into view as we dismounted from the Jeep to be greeted by Uncle Malik, the Inspector General who had travelled up from Lahore to oversee the visit, hence the two-day delay. I really think he just wanted to meet Mum, a western woman, and to show willingness from his side of the family as he couldn't do enough for us, putting on a real charm offensive. After taking hold of Mum's hand and leading us to inspect a guard of honour, I followed Mum up and down the two rows of men standing to attention, very surreal indeed. Malik then ushered us into a room set out with refreshments. The usual cold drinks, sweet cakes and *chai* poured from a pot into small glasses from a great height, quite a novelty act and one that impressed me anyway. Mum discussed with Malik and another gentleman, in uniform, who I presumed was in charge of this prison, and it was suggested by him that the foreign women be brought to this room one by one for everybody's safety, and then Mum could talk to them. Mum was having none of that and immediately demanded to see them in the cells where she could witness the conditions, they had to endure raising her voice as she did so.

I had known Mum to raise her voice at Alexander and me when we had stepped out of line on more than one occasion and probably deservedly so, but it didn't take long for Uncle Malik to agree with a western women's way of thinking. I thought just as well, as I can also vividly remembering her one day, grabbing hold of seventeen year old Adrian Gable from the next street to ours around the throat, and ramming him hard up against our garage wall for some reason, just a few years back turning the air blue as she did so. They say you can take the girl out of Ireland, but you can't take Ireland out of the girl.

All of us now heading across a courtyard flanked by six guards with rather large sticks in their hands which I now know are called *lathi*, we enter an old building through a locked gate. The sound of voices echoing from beyond as though we were in a covered street market getting even louder, as we then walked through another locked gate. The crescendo of noise paled into insignificance compared to the smell that hit you with some force, it was literally indescribable. Mum showing no sign of discomfort as she was asked again if it would be better to see the women back at the office, and for once I had to agree with them, even though I might get rammed up against a wall for doing so. Let's continue she proclaimed, then one of the guards hit his *lathi* against the metal bars of the first cell to our left and the whole corridor of cells fell into a deafening silence.

We walked slowly forward as a group, I was holding Mum's left hand a little bit tighter than usual, the smell now seemed more pungent in a near silent environment. The only noise coming from a prison guard who was running his *lathi* along the bars as we walked, creating the same sound as the lollipop sticks that we would put between the spokes of our bicycles back in Wootton to look and sound cool, there was nothing cool about this place I can tell you, nothing cool at all. Glancing to my left into the jail cells, very similar to the ones I would see watching a cowboy film with my Dad on a Saturday afternoon that usually had one or two baddies locked up in them. Here, you could sense these were well crammed, maybe between ten and twenty women in each one and around eight cells in total, the sunlight catching their bedraggled faces from the windows opposite, as we continued. We reached the last cell where the foreign women prisoners were kept. This cell was so much smaller and darker than the previous cells, but after walking past them all, I would swap any one of them, for any of the hotel rooms I complained about on our epic journey to this country.

Uncle Malik and the prison guards stood back as Mum stepped forward, my hand still clutching hers but at the same time half standing behind her leg peering round to see what was beyond these bars, again just like watching *Doctor Who* from behind a cushion on the settee back home. Stepping forward, two Canadian women engaged in conversation, their accents very strong indeed while explaining their predicament, Mum listening with great intensity, myself just continuing to smell that awful smell.

Then two more women approached looking rather worse for wear, clothes dirty and ripped, one of them showing us the bruises on her legs and arms, believed to be from a *lathi*. As the conversation continued with Mum, her voice was choking on her own words, as she replied to the plight of these women, not being able to see for myself but imagining her eyes welling up in the process.

The sun had now moved round in the day's sky, glistening on to one of the cleaner windows that sat up high to our right, sending a shimmer of light across Mum's face as though it was choreographed in some sort of way. 'Are you an angel', a fifth voice said, coming from the back of the cell in an Irish tone, 'we don't get to talk to many angels in here'. Mum beckoned her forward, a young woman with very dirty hair emerged from the shadows.

Mum explained that she was Irish too, born in the county of Louth, a Catholic girl going to a school overseen by nuns, then telling these young woman, after now seeing and speaking to them all, she would do whatever she could to help them. Looking very stern faced at the confused Uncle Malik as she did so, maybe not a good idea to come all the way from Lahore after all.

Mum asked for fresh water and fruit to be brought at once for these women which was well received by them all, then being told that their toilet was a bucket in the corner, emptied every couple of days. Mum gave up her hand cream and tissues from inside her handbag, the guards looking on quite unperturbed. Holding their hands for the last time after releasing mine, the look on the women's faces was of despair, the look on Mum's face was one of anger but hope. As we exited the building back to the main office, Mum talking to Uncle Malik in a slightly raised voice as she did so. I was holding on to her the best I could, being dragged by her fast pace and lack of concern for me, but undoubted concern for those unfortunate women we had just left. Maybe an angel did come that day, who knows? It is said we all have a purpose in life and maybe this was my Mum's, well if it was, it was an apt one.

Returning back to Islamabad, a lot of discussions I believe were had about the plight of these women, not that they involved a nine-year-old boy, far from it, to me it was one smelly experience of a day out. A few days later after Dads' brother, the judge, had spoken to my uncle the President and as he was having so many other political problems at the time, decided it would be seen as the appropriate thing to do to release them all. So the papers were signed, and all the women were sent without delay to their respective embassies. We never knew their names and we all hoped they would lead a normal life from now on if possible, especially after that harrowing experience. Mum, well she just kept on being Mum!

Blood, Sweat but no Tears

Dad's sister Gulner was closer to him than all of his brothers, most likely due to the fact she looked after him a great deal when he was a boy, which would be an elder sister's duty in a Muslim family. We met her in the first few days that we arrived, she having travelled up from the Indian border town of Sialkot to Peshawar with her family, embracing my father as if she also would never let go. Accompanying her was Abid, her husband, a General in the Army, along with their children; Raza aged twenty-two, Shakeela aged twenty, Saira aged seventeen, Hashim aged thirteen and Qasim the same age as me, nine.

The second time we saw them all was when we were called back from Islamabad at very short notice along with Dad's brother, the judge, and his family, a relaxing time unfortunately interrupted. The reason being Khanan Khan, Dads' elder brother had passed away in the night, from what was believed to be a heart attack.

It was just over three weeks since we had buried Dolce Mohammad, they say he never got over his son's death, but a good innings was had by him, as the average life expectancy for a typical male in Pakistan at this time was fifty-two, as most succumbed to heart disease, unless unfortunately you were murdered.

Up at five in the morning and all in two cars for the long journey heading for Peshawar, the early start was because that here in Pakistan and throughout the Islamic world and warmer countries in general, they buried their dead on the same day for obvious reasons. Later that afternoon all the men gathered at Agha Manzil 2, and after the women had washed and prepared the body as well as paying their last respects, I watched as the men took my uncle's body. Then in an orderly procession, leaving the women behind, it was carried shoulder high through the streets to the graveyard where they laid him to rest under a marble tomb stone.

We stopped at Agha Manzil for a period of time after that, Alexander and I spending the days with our cousins going between the two houses on our own, stopping off at the chemist shop opposite owned by one of Dad's friends, to say 'hello', knowing a supply of orange bubble gum would be forthcoming from him as he greeted us. We all played cricket in the park next to the house and lots of games of hide and seek all over Agha Manzil, one time Imrana had shown me a secret room behind the door of a large bookcase, very much like a priest hole they used in England in the sixteenth century — it was very dark and eerie, Alexander never found us. I would venture to the roof to see the servants as they carried out their daily chores, the cook often giving me mangos or oranges to eat. Zaka brought me two doves to look after which were kept on the roof in a cage, and I used this quite often as a great excuse to see if the cook had any more treats for me.

The girls taught me how to count in Urdu and a few sentences and words to say, how they laughed as I try to pronounce them correctly, I think most of them were swear words, and I was just being used for their daily amusement.

Alexander and I were both treated as young adults rather than two boys going out with Zia and Zaka on the backs of their scooters around Peshawar, dodging all the traffic as we did so, going to the river or the park by the university, then at night zipping off to watch the latest Bollywood film that had come to the only cinema in Peshawar.

To me the music was ok but I did not have a clue what the films were about or what they were saying, you just couldn't get much further away from the good old cockney voice of Michael Caine if you tried.

Amongst all this fun day after day, there was of course the religious aspect, the local mosque calling out for you to attend

The cinema house Peshawar

prayers, with each family member doing so without the slightest hesitation, the women and men praying separately. One of the most, you might say shocking but unbelievable rituals I was fortunate or maybe unfortunate, depending on your point of view, was witnessed from the balcony of Agha Manzil 2 with the women of the household. This was the religious ceremony that Shia Muslims know as the *Day of Ashura*, which mourns the death of Imam Hussein in 680 AD.

Crowds gather in the sun-drenched street below. All the men, by the way, and some of our own family members chanting religious texts slowly beating their chests and the tops of their heads for well over ten minutes. Then as the chanting grew louder, some removed their shirts while still beating their chests more vigorously, it appeared as if some of them were actually going into some sort of hypnotic trance.

While in this state, and the chanting still as loud as any football crowd echoing down this narrow street, they were then being handed very sharp blades, about six or seven in total all glistening in the sun light, these were attached to chains about a foot long which in turn were fixed to a wooden

Family photograph of the day of Ashura

handle. Then all of a sudden they began to lash themselves ferociously on their backs one side then another — time after time until they either collapsed on the dusty street floor or were stopped by some of the crowd because of the harm they were doing to themselves.

Below we saw Zia and Zaka being ushered into Agha Manzil 2, which triggered all the family, including myself to rush downstairs. I was then greeted with such a sight it was hard to understand, both of them were laid out on the floor face down, you might wonder what's unusual about that? Nothing — apart from their backs were torn to shreds from the beating they had just taken. The pain must have been excruciating to the point that they both passed out because all I could see was blood and sweat — but no tears, not even cries of pain, as the women tended to their horrific wounds.

It was many days later, perhaps weeks before they had fully recovered, leaving scars on their backs some of which would make your tummy curdle and all in the name of religion, imagine doing something like that at a harvest festival in your local village church, not sure the rector would approve.

A Fit of Laughter

During this great adventure Dad wanted to take us to see where he went to school, this was in the hill town of Shimla, but that was not possible because of the worsening situation between Pakistan and India. All border crossings were closed as the hostilities grew. His school was in the foothills of the Himalayan Mountains that had been part of India since 1947, after partition took place when the British divided India up to form two separate countries.

Instead to get some idea of what Shimla was like, and to give us all a break from the hectic city of Peshawar, Dad decided to take us to Murree for a week, a hill town in the foothills of the Kashmir Mountains which had very similar characteristics to Shimla, and was the original summer capital of British India.

A very familiar picture of our little saffron yellow Triumph Vitesse heading into the hills of Kashmir, only this time without the roof rack, twisting and turning as we climbed through the forest that covered this area as far as the eye could see, traces of snow that seemed to last forever adorn the side of the road as the temperature in this part of the country is so much cooler but the sun still shines as brightly as ever.

In Murree the only hotel of any stature was an old colonial building on the main street, very grand from the outside but not that exciting once you stepped through the front door, slowly falling into disrepair since the British left long ago..

Murree was originally the summer capital of British India and a sanatorium for the British soldiers in the middle of the nineteenth century. It became popular with the English gentry of the Empire as an escape from the ever suppressing heat of the Indian plains, before Shimla took over that role and became more of an elite and viable attraction.

The first night we stayed we were all quite cold, the beds felt damp from the mountain air, the rooms not at all warm, Dad insisting on more blankets to be provided the next day.

After breakfast, a walk round this town and on the road known as the Mall, basically the one and only street of any substance in the place, but if you never knew where you were, you could have mistaken this place for an old English village. There was a small traditional looking church made of stone which stood proud on the hillside along with houses that seemed that they were plucked straight out of England. We stopped at the post office, climbing many steps to it's door, Mum sending a postcard home to grandma telling her

The Kashmir hills of Murree

As you can see, nothing like the Virginian

we were all well. We wandered to the edge of the village where they were giving you the chance to have a ride on a horse, Dad insisting on me sitting on the white one just like *The Virginian*, one of his favourite TV shows back home, it's a cowboy series of course.

Well, I had never been on a horse before, I tell a lie, I have ridden the horses on the carrousel at the village fair, but I suppose they don't count.

This was no small horse I can tell you, even though I'm not that tall myself, totally white apart from the brown and well-worn saddle that I was hoisted onto by Dad, Mum standing with camera in hand ready to take a photograph. Mum had all the time in the world as this horse might as well have been dead, it just didn't move, not even its head, to look round to see what all the fuss was about, as I kept shouting as loud as I could giddy up but no joy as Mum clicked the camera. Then suddenly as though the rope had lifted at the start of the Grand National the horse bolted with me on board, hoofs sparking on the tarmac road as we flew up the hill, Mum and Dad in tow. I think I went as white as the horse — not having a clue what to do but hold on for dear life.

Not remembering how we stopped, but stop we did, my hands tightly clasped around it's neck, the horse's white mane across my face, as Dad lifted me off telling me to let go as he did so, but not wanting to for the fear of what might happen. Down on the ground with Mum cuddling me tight and checking I was all right, all I could hear was Alexander laughing out loud from down the hill, as if he were watching the clowns at the circus. His laugh getting even louder as he approached us, me not seeing the funny side of it at all, and certainly not when I found out that unknown to me, Alexander in his wisdom had given the horse such a slap with a stick that it couldn't fail to move the way it did.

No one was hurt, in fact the only one that could have been was me, and eventually we all stood around and had a really good fit of laughter at my expense, laughter that would not be heard again in this family — not ever.

Back to the hotel where we had dinner, then retiring to our rooms, which were still cold and had that damp feel about them. How I longed for the warmth of Agha Manzil, where we would bed down for the night in the lounge area all snuggled up under the *korsi*, the warm coals giving up their heat to us for hours.

Our second day in Murree, Mum was not feeling too well after the cold night, my asthma not great due to the damp, and the one street they call the Mall not offering to much in the way of entertainment, unless you want a go on a runaway horse. (Been there, done that) Dad sensed the uneasy atmosphere amongst us and decided there and then we would return to Peshawar without hesitation, a decision I am very glad he made in more ways than one.

Heads or Tails?

Now firmly back in the warmth of Agha Manzil, cook giving us a nice lamb curry and naan to make us all feel fine, although Mum was still not feeling too good herself, retiring early for bed, kissing me and Alexander before leaving the room. Looking back as she said goodnight her expression different than usual, so very different, it's as if she knew something. You could just tell just for a split second, it was a reassuring look back at her boys, a look only a mother could give.

Both Alexander and I stayed on the second floor in the lounge area under the *korsi* for the night along with our cousins Sabath and Imrana. An undisturbed and warm sleep, which I had wished for a day earlier was achieved, woken only by one of the servants who had brought scrambled eggs, bread and hot *chai* laid out on the *korsi*. While we were all having breakfast, a commotion echoed up from the courtyard below, not enough to drag you away from a hearty breakfast but a commotion all the same.

Dad came to see Alexander and me and said I was to go with Zia, and Alexander was to go to Agha Manzil 2 as soon as we had breakfast, speaking in Urdu to Sabath and Imrana. I could not understand what he was telling them, but their faces changed so dramatically to what Dad had said to them, that a sense of worry had entered the room to be felt by both Alexander and I. Dad or Mum nowhere to be seen, Zia the eldest of my cousins took me out to one of the cars and as we did so passing Dad's friend the chemist on the steps of Agha Manzil, he patted me on the head as he did so, I was half expecting some orange bubble gum but there was none forthcoming, just a very concerning smile.

In the car with Zia our destination was the Inter-Continental Hotel on the edge of Peshawar where a room was booked for me, very odd I thought, just me but I wasn't going to complain, as the room was on the top floor, and as I had written earlier the plushest hotel that we had stopped in since leaving home.

Zia stopped with me for most of the day watching TV, sending down for food and drinks whenever required. Dad came late afternoon with a man I had never seen before who turned out to be a doctor, 'strange', I thought, 'I don't feel ill and I'm sure I don't look ill', he then began to examine me, taking my temperature several times over the period of one hour then discussing with Dad his conclusions. Dad said I was to stop with Zia in the hotel for the night and tomorrow all of us would go to Peshawar Hospital. I asked Dad what was wrong with me, he said, 'nothing wrong, it's just a precaution, everything is fine', then as if on cue a large burger and chips were delivered by room service, 'nice one,' I thought.

The following day Dad came about mid-morning, Zia and I went on the short journey to the hospital, entering a very busy hall with all sorts of different people, some making more noise than others as they waited to be seen.

Fortunately, we did not have that problem, as we were sent straight through into a private room meeting the doctor who had seen me the day before.

First, I had to remove my top as again he checked my torso, then my temperature twice in ten minutes while I stood there, getting quite cold as he did so. We then moved on to a second adjoining room where I was at least allowed to put my vest back on after complaining to Dad. A short while later a nurse then entered the room with a tray holding it at a height that I could clearly recognise it's contents, and from my last visit to a doctor figured out it was going to be some type of injection. I then asked Dad what was this all about and without holding back any longer, sat me on this old wooden chair, its cold back touching my shoulders sending a shiver down my spine, as he explained the situation.

He said without mincing his words, 'I'm afraid that your mother has contracted smallpox'. Bang!, that hit me like the stick that Alexander had used to hit the horse, sending the second but more emphatic shiver down my spine. 'That really can't be' I said, 'will she be alright?' Dad reassured me Mum would be fine, but because of Mum contracting the disease I may have to have a smallpox injection. I then remembered what our own Dr McFarland said to us, that Mum and I could not have this injection because of her eczema and my asthma, and that it could be very harmful to us to the point our immune system could easily and quickly breakdown, eventually leading to the loss of life. Now, take the time to contemplate the dilemma and pressure Dad must have been under, does he allow or not allow an injection, which could or could not save his youngest child. Maybe it would be easier to flip a coin and call 'heads or tails', letting fate decide but wouldn't that be the case anyway, whichever way he chooses.

What would any father do in that situation what indeed? You just wouldn't want to be in his shoes at any time in your life, would you? But in it he was.

This judgement call had to be made by him and him alone, with Mum gravely ill, only the closest family members are allowed to make a decision of this magnitude in Pakistan. The doctor cannot overrule in any way, only give advice and wait for the final say from Dad. Me, I was still cold not only from sitting there in my vest but from the spine-chilling thought of which way this penny would drop to the point that goose bumps had now appeared. The only way, and still today as I write this, that I could in anyway gauge this lifechanging dilemma from my father's point of view, was to understand that he already had first-hand experience by being with my mother over the past two days, and he could process and finally assess what it was like to have to witness somebody suffering who had not had the injection. Maybe Mum and Dad deliberated between themselves, deciding which of the two options gave me the greatest chance of survival.

As my goose bumps got bigger, Dad instructed the doctor

to proceed, who then asked me to turn my head to the wall in his broken English while the nurse prepared my left arm to receive the six needle punch, very similar in stature to a cigarette lighter in a car.

As I turned and looked at the wall for some sort of comfort from the expecting pain that I was about to receive, my eyes were attracted to the large poster that graced the wall, which my mind lets me still see very clearly even today.

Was it there on purpose? Did anyone else see in the room, what a nine-year old boy put in this predicament was made to stare at, or was it just a misjudgement or a fluke? What it did explain without a word being said is why two days earlier Mum gave us a look only a mother could give to her boys.

In graphic pictures, one after another, for the whole length of the poster set out to shock whoever might glance its way, or maybe it was just a way of getting the information across to what actually was a very illiterate society then, who knows? The poster pictures showed without holding back the full extent of what smallpox can do to the human body, leaving nothing to your imagination.

While totally transfixed to that wall, I never did feel those six needles penetrate my upper arm but what I did manage to process from that poster is that, I believe and always have that the decision my mother and father must have made together over whether their youngest child should have this smallpox injection, was totally the correct one. As time has proved, with the scar still visible on my upper arm as I sit here writing this book to all those who wish to read it.

Great Timing

I spent another seven days back at the Inter-Continental Hotel rather than in the hospital in case I might contract anything else, as Pakistan was still a third world country and the hospitals have a lot to be desired. I stayed mainly in the room with cousins Zia and his brother Zaka, who without any hesitation or question took it in turns to keep me company and were pleased to do so.

Dad visited at least twice daily while still looking after Mum, as well as seeing Alexander, the doctor calling once a day to monitor whether I had smallpox or the fact that the injection had some kind of reaction to my immune system, as predicted by the English doctor. None of these symptoms materialised and I eventually returned to the family, I stopped at Agha Manzil 2. Alexander being told under no circumstances to go back to Agha Manzil until given the all clear, and Dad continuing to update us saying Mum was doing better than the day before.

There are only so many games you can play cooped up in a smaller house than you were used to, although for me bigger than the hotel room. So when one of our uncles, how he was exactly related I'm not sure, asked Alexander and me whether we would like to go and see the tank factory in Taxila, an area just north of the city of Rawalpindi, our eyes lit up like fireworks in the night sky. It was a three-hour drive at best from Peshawar, so it was agreed with Dad that we would stop for a few days with his brother, Agha Khan Baba Khan Zahid the Judge and his family, giving us a break from Peshawar. This then meant Dad could solely concentrate on getting Mum better without worrying about us boys; also, it would give us more time to look round the factory as it was only an hour's drive from their house.

We travelled down on December the third, spending the afternoon and evening with our auntie and two cousins Annie and Nanni, Uncle Baba was called away to his office on serious government issues that were now escalating in the country at that time. The next day, December the fourth which had been arranged by our uncle, a car came to pick Alexander and myself up, yes — with a chauffeur in a military uniform! But not nearly as exciting as last time I was here, being picked up by armed guards in a jeep, and I made doubly sure that my brother hadn't forgotten about it several times, while travelling the hour long journey to Taxila. We arrived to what can only be described as a vast area controlled by the army, each car or truck being vetted as it entered through to this vast complex set within a large valley. Soldiers with dogs checking paperwork. Another soldier going round holding a pole with a large mirror attached to view underneath each vehicle looking for bombs. This really was a top official area, with different types of factories and buildings all with armed guards patrolling. Alexander pointing out the large gun emplacements dotted every so often protected by hundreds of sandbags.

After travelling about five minutes from the initial gates we were then checked again as we entered the heavy munitions area which included the tank factory. As the car pulled up in front of some buildings we were met by an officer, flanked each side by armed guards in very smart uniforms, and were told that he was the brother of the uncle who suggested this trip in the first place, and it was an honour for him to show us around.

Then before anything else, cold drinks were brought to us on a tray along with some sweet cakes, very welcome indeed. We all sat under the shade of a tree in the car park area as we tried to answer the many questions that this man wanted to know about us and England.

It was nice and relaxing being shown around this huge factory by this man, treating us like adults, going into great detail of how a tank is made from start to finish over a period of a couple of weeks. He was very passionate about it all, but what a young boy really wants to see is a tank, in other words a finished one. Well I got my wish, at the far end of this endless line of different size chunks of metal — there it was, the only thing missing was it's tracks so it wasn't going to go too far, but it was a tank none the less.

Both Alexander and I thought that was it, the making of a tank; start to finish one end of a long factory to the other — not so, as we stepped out through a door back into the daylight, our eyes ajusting to the brightness as we did so, to be overwhelmed by a row of brand new completely finished tanks. These tanks were all underneath what can only be described as an extra-large bicycle shed with a tin roof, for what I presumed was to keep the sunlight off, how wrong I was, as the real reason was explained to me in graphic detail within less than an hour.

We then ventured further round to be shown an old grey French tank, which had large brown leather plates, stretching round and down from its turret like a girl's skirt, we were told this tank was a version of an AMX 13, whatever that was. As we viewed this elegant grey old lady, skirt up way too high for an Islamic country, not that it would bother her being French. We then heard the distant rumble of another tank as it crept from around the far corner of the building trundling down to meet us, our eyes transfixed as it did so.

We stood back as its engine snorted out diesel fumes, twice the amount any of the lorries managed, climbing the many steep inclines of the Hindu Kush on our trip here. Alexander and I were then given the opportunity to ride in this tank, which would have been every boy's wish had they been standing there, and one we would definitely not be declining in any way shape or form. This tank was a type M47 Patton, American built and used by the Pakistan army over the past ten years.

Alexander being taller than me due to our five year difference in age, was told to climb in and sit in one of the driver's positions low down at the front of this huge giant, his head barely protruding above its metal body, his feet just about managing to reach the pedals. I was then lifted up on to its body eventually climbing to the peak of its turret, where a soldier already there helped me in, showing me inside and how live shells would be put into the gun before firing. Alexander at this time was being shown how to work the controls, consisting of levers and pedals by the second driver, who also was at the front, low down but on the other side of this beast of a tank. So now, with me perched half out of the turret by standing on a fold-down seat and being held by the soldier alongside me we were all ready to go. I could see Alexander below and he had a funny leather type cap on his head with a microphone and earpiece attached, this was so he could talk to the driver on the other side of the large protruding gun barrel.

Then the engine grew louder as we began to move, gathering speed, this huge piece of metal making noises from every corner of its body, mostly due to its tremendous weight of around forty-eight tonnes pushing down on to the concrete road. The faster we went, the initial shuddering, which I can tell you nearly took your teeth out, got better to the point that this old beast seemed to be gliding majestically across the ground at great speed, although its top speed was only about thirty-five miles per hour, it just felt much faster from my prominent postion.

As we reached the end of this long factory, Alexander had to steer this brute round the corner, explaining to me later he really had to pull on the lever as hard as he could to get round without breaking the tank's momentum, his arms beginning to really ache after several corners. To me this was so exhilarating, the chance to sit high on a tank moving at its maximum speed, it was the best fair ride I had ever been on, and one you would never likely to see back at Wootton's recreation ground, not ever. We then began the short trip along to the next corner feeling the crunching of the tracks, as we turned grinding themselves hard into the road.

We went around this factory at least three times, I was totally enjoying myself — what a day to remember for two boys! What a day indeed as we turned the next corner, four men in uniforms running out in front of us waving their arms franticly to try and stop this metal monster. Stop we did, as they commonly say, 'on a sixpence', throwing me forward at such a rate I nearly ended up headfirst downwards on top of Alexander, but for the soldier next to me. As I just about gathered my composure two of these men had climbed onto the tank shouting to this soldier next to me, I know not what, but I think they got their message across pretty quickly and precisely.

Everything seemed to happen all at once, I could see Alexander was already out of the tank and nearly on the ground. I was literally lifted straight out of the turret by one man, then passed down to another standing on the body of the tank, and without hesitation like someone was passing a rugby ball between team mates, I was thrown off the tank and caught by a third man. He immediately took off carrying me under his arm, my head dangling to one side, being shook as if for the second time today my teeth were going to drop out, at the same time catching sight of my brother in hot pursuit. For a moment it was as if everything then went into slow motion, as I heard the screeching sound of what was a jet engine and from the angle that I was being carried looking partly skywards, I glimpsed for a split second the silhouette of an aircraft just above the factory roof against the bright blue sky, followed by an almighty explosion, that my delicate ears had never heard before in my life.

This man that I had suddenly become attached to, not of my choosing you must understand, did not break stride until he had thrown himself and me into a small tin shelter dug into the ground surrounded by sand bags, Alexander managing to land on top of us somehow, as again the roar of more jet engines could be heard above our heads, followed again by the sounds of explosions that cracked right through your ears and down to your toes, as the ground shook from their aftermath.

There were six soldiers, Alexander and me in this tiny shelter sitting patiently but quietly, listening out for the sound of more jet engines, but thankfully that sound did not repeat itself again, not that day anyway. To give you an insight to what and why this had occurred I will endeavour to explain.

Pakistan and India had been at loggerheads since Partition in 1947 and had fought a war in 1965, this latest skirmish escalated in East Pakistan, culminating in my uncle the President of Pakistan reluctantly deciding on the evening of December the third, to pre-empt an attack and bomb several Indian airfields. This in turn provoked India into declaring war on Pakistan, thus resulting in retaliating air strikes the very next day, December the fourth, the day we had arranged with our uncle conveniently to visit one of Pakistan's most heavily controlled military areas — great timing wouldn't you say?

These three Indian Air Force jets had only one attempt at hitting something substantial like the tank factory or even the nearby ammunition factory, but they failed in their quest, only managing to hit a car park area and some outbuildings.

One of the reasons given as to why they were not successful was because they had no ground troops to give them true coordinates to guide them in, which has been proven in previous wars like Vietnam. I can understand now why all those tanks were under large covers, although it took an air strike to do so, from the air that's what they looked like, bicycle sheds. How surreal did this place feel because as little as just over two hours ago Alexander and I went from sitting in that very car park area under a tree drinking *chai* and eating cakes, to being thrown very abruptly into a bomb shelter in the middle of a war zone, you just could not write this stuff — well I am actually! We were kept in the shelter until everybody was certain that the raid was over. Our car was brought as close as possible to us and as I left the security of the shelter and headed to the car, I could hear the engine of our tank still purring, unperturbed by the whole situation.

We stopped in Islamabad for the next five days

contemplating the war, now escalating further to the point our Uncle Abid, Dads' sisters' husband and General, who oversaw many divisions in the Sialkot region of Pakistan, had orders to invade India.

Dad decided to call us back to Peshawar as it was deemed to be much safer, arriving back telling Dad our exploits in Taxila, as though it was a fun day out at some amusement park, not quite understanding the serious nature and ultimate consequences that day could have had on our family. It was around December the tenth that the air raid sirens went off, again this time in Peshawar. Indian jets targeting the airport as many of the Pakistani Air Force planes had moved there for safety, again because it was so far from the Indian border, but obviously not far enough.

Not too much damage recorded, mainly holes in the airport's runway and to some of the surrounding access roads. Zia and Zaka taking myself and Alexander out on their scooters to have a look, along with many of the male population of Peshawar, eventually finding some huge craters in the tarmac road blackened with scorch marks. As I stood by one of these craters along with the many people who had ventured out, I thought it only takes that jet I glimpsed to return and it would have an easy target of all these men just standing in one place, that's if it could manage to hit its intended target, mind you.

Returning to the city Dad told Alexander and I that we could tell our story of the tank factory to Mum, but when we arrived at Agha Manzil what you thought would be a usual type of encounter, seeing Mum sitting up in bed while the two of us sat on its edge excitedly, explaining our brief meeting with the Indian Air Force, was so very distant from that.

We could not go into the bedroom and see her in person but only tell our story looking up from the courtyard at the slightly raised ground floor window, open with an orange net curtain blowing in the breeze, raising our voices so to be heard from a distance, not knowing when to pause, or to gauge the reaction on her face, when we reached an exciting part in our saga. It was very strange indeed, there was no comment or reply throughout, no recognisable sound at all returning from the window, we never once heard our mother's voice, just Dad saying that Mum's very tired now so it's time to stop, and with that he slowly closed the window.

I have often wondered that the tale Alexander and I told that day to our mother was totally insignificant, and that we both could have just been reading out loud from some story book, because really all our mother wanted was to hear the familiar sound of her children's voices once more.

Sixteenth of December 1971

This date was the exact day that the fourteen day war ceased between Pakistan and India, to the great relief of the millions of people across these two great nations and one that many believe was the real date that East Pakistan became the new country known as Bangladesh, a date millions won't forget, a date that went down in history. The sixteenth of December 1971 was also a date that went down in our family history for my Dad, Alexander and I and one we will never, ever forget, but for very different reasons indeed.

Standing comfortably numb in the late afternoon sun next to Dad, Alexander standing on the other side, as we watch an anonymous man lay the last white marble stone on to a pristine marble tomb, the canopy of the tree in close proximity slowly rippling shadowy patterns across its top like serene waves on some vast lake. For on this white marble tomb that stood before us was etched in black with that exact date: 16 December 1971. And above it these three telling words: EILEEN BRIGID AGHA (My mother's name.)

Now I could write in great detail the story of this day, but it's not a story that I or you would want to write, there is no tank factory being bombed or armed guards travelling in a Jeep at speed, not even a large white horse bolting up the middle of the road and there is definitely no happy ending.

Mum passed away in the early hours of the sixteenth of December 1971. Dad was red-faced and distraught telling my brother and me around breakfast time, Alexander cried intently on hearing this unforeseen and mind-numbing news. Understandably, being much older than me and therefore having known Mum five years longer may have made a difference, but we both loved her in the precious years we were very fortunate to have had with her through the good times and the bad. I never cried, not once, not at any time throughout this tragic day, and well beyond, I just stood and watched as the day unfolded. I'm not sure but I think maybe it's that nothing really sunk into me what had actually just happened.

From the moment I was told this was all too familiar to be anything other than different, which of course different it was. I had been through this process twice before in the last six weeks maybe they were both dress rehearsals for the main event happening today — who knows? It was just one continuous blur of a day as all the different generations of family arrived, crying and wailing. Every auntie trying to cuddle me at every possible opportunity, heaping their grief onto me even further. The now familiar procession through the packed streets behind a body carried aloft by the men of the family, although this time I was so much closer to the front of it all. The wooden gate below an arch which led to the small enclosed graveyard, became another place I was also all too familiar with. This now was my third visit, but instead of being one of the first to leave, Dad, Alexander and I were the last to leave as this day, finally, gave itself up to the night. 'What was this feeling of nothing', I really can't begin to explain, was it the fact that I hadn't had any physical contact with Mum, or even spoken to her since our return from our trip to the hill town of Murree at least four weeks ago? A long time for a child to be away from it's mother, or a mother to be away from her child. Was it that everything else seemed more important to a nine year old boy than the condition of his mother's health? Or that Dad's updates were worded in such a way that they were intended to divert any concerns that I may have had on to something less important than the real situation that was unfolding? Could it possibly be that because of the length of time I had been spending with all the different ages of other female members of the family, that I had already accepted that she was no longer to be a part of my life? I really don't know, and I really cannot explain even today, it just seemed to evolve in that particular way over that day, hard to believe but true.

As the days passed and as many people have written before, one day rolls into another which is true, nothing much happened apart from the emptiness that everyone was feeling.

Christmas Day came and went, not that it's celebrated in an Islamic world anyway, and it was definitely not celebrated by Dad, Alexander and I and not for many years after that, it just didn't seem right, putting up a Christmas tree and decorating with an angel on top. The only angel I wanted to see at Christmas was the one that had visited the district jail in the city of Rawalpindi two months earlier, a real angel to me — one never to be forgotten.

Dad had been in touch with the Pakistan High Commissioner in London and explained to him about Mum's unforeseen death, asking him to contact my grandparents, but they were away for a few days in Welwyn Garden City, visiting Grandads' sisters a week before Christmas, so the initial contact was delayed for a few more days until they returned.

Grandad Blaney was one of eighteen children born into

A WOOTTON woman has died from smallpox in a West Pakistan hospital after spending several days in an evacuation centre.

She had been vaccinated against the disease, and her parents feel that it was probably the conditions at the evacuation centre midway through the Indo-Pakistani war that caused her to become infected.

She was Mrs. Eileen Ahga, of 18, Springfield, Wootton, who was visiting the country with her West Pakistani husband, Hassan, and their two children when war broke out.

Evacuated

The family were forced to evacuate the city of Peshawar when it came under heavy Indian bombing, and move to a camp at Rawalpindi where she became infected with the disease.

Mrs. Ahga, who was 33, was moved back to Peshawar where she died in hospital on December 16.

Her parents, Mr. and Mrs.

Ambrose Blaney, of 23, Towcester Road, Blisworth, who had lived through a nightmare worrying for their daughter and her family's health, and who thought they would be safe when they heard about the surrender, returned from holiday in Hertfordshire on Tuesday night to receive the news from the police.

"When the police told us she had died, we immediately thought it must have been the bombing," Mrs. Mabel Blaney told the Chronicle and Echo today.

"We had feared for the worst. But we could not believe it when we learnt that it was smallpox."

Mrs. Blaney said that her daughter had been vaccinated before leaving England.

Eileen's husband, whose uncle is the former West Pakistan President Yahya Khan, notified the Pakistani Embassy in London about his wife's death just before Christmas. But he asked them to wait until Tuesday before cabling N o r t h a m p t o n s h i r e police so that the news would not spoil the Blaney's Christ-

mas holiday.

Eileen and Hassan, (35), were taking a six-month holiday with their two sons, Alexander (14) and Jason (9). It was Hassan's first visit home after 17 years in this country.

They left Wootton on October 20 and drove to Pakistan, sending postcards to Blisworth from the countries they visited en route. But the last the Blaneys heard from their daughter was when she wrote from Peshawar saying that the family were to be evacuated.

"Because Hassan's uncle was the president, and his brothers and sisters were in the army or married to army officers, they were given 'top brass' attention out there," said Mrs. Blaney.

"But still we were always afraid while the fighting was going on," she said. "We watched the news on television every night, thinking that we might see Eileen, or Hassan, or one of the boys in the films of the evacuation.

"The night they flew some refugees into Luton, we sat up until midnight waiting for the phone to ring to tell us to

go and pick them up." she said. "But they weren't on the plane."

"When we heard the war was over I was so happy," said Mrs. Blaney. "I thought they would be safer then."

Eileen had been working at Barclays Bank in Northampton when the couple decided to visit West Pakistan. They were due to return in May.

"I don't know whether Hassan and the children will come back now," said Mrs. Blaney. "Perhaps they will stay there. It is his homeland."

'Never dreamt'

Mrs. Blaney said that although Hassan's family were so involved in the war, her son-in-law had no strong views about the troubles between India and Pakistan.

"When they left," she said, "Hassan never dreamt there would be a war. He said to me 'Don't worry, mother. There won't be any trouble. It's all talk.'"

Eileen and Hassan had been married for 15 years. They met when they were studying together at the Northampton College of Technology.

Extract from the Northampton Chronicle & Echo

a Catholic family in Ireland and he had two favourite sisters who brought him up as a child. He named his first child, my mother, after both of these sisters, Eileen who he and Gran were visiting would you believe, and Brigid who also was visiting from Ireland, so all three were together in one place exactly at the same time as Mum's passing.

Communication was not like the digital world we live in today and back then things were very often lost in translation regarding a certain situation, particularly if you had to deal with the loss of your daughter on the other side of the world, this would be so very confusing at the best of times.

Above is the article that the local newspaper *Northampton Chronicle & Echo* ran quite some time after the event of sixteenth of December 1971 which highlights how Grandma and Grandad viewed this terrible event that had happened on the other side of the world, from the comfort of their front room. It varies on many counts from what actually happened, and as I explained at the start of this story, just shows how things over a period of time can be distorted from the truth, even in a very short period of time as this happened to be, and the main reason I sat down to write our intriguing family story.

You may note that Grandma thought Mum and I had all the required vaccinations, which I know was not true, but maybe Mum bent the truth a little to not worry them, maybe an angel is not an angel after all — you decide:

A Wootton woman has died from contracting smallpox in a West Pakistan hospital after spending several days in an evacuation centre.

She had been vaccinated against the disease and her parents feel that it was probably the conditions at the evacuation centre midway through the Indo-Pakistan war that caused her to become infected.

She was Mrs Eileen Agha of 18 Springfield, Wootton and was visiting the country with her West Pakistani husband, Hassan, and their two children Alexander and Jason when war broke out between Indian and Pakistan.

The family were forced to evacuate the city of Peshawar when it came under heavy Indian bombing and moved to a camp at Rawalpindi where she became infected with the disease. Mrs Agha, who was 33, was moved back to Peshawar where she died in hospital on December 16.

Her parents Mr and Mrs Ambrose Blaney of 23 Towcester Road, Blisworth, who had lived through a nightmare worrying for their daughter and her family's health, and who thought they would be safe when they heard about the surrender, returned from holiday in Hertfordshire on Tuesday night to receive the news from the police. When the police told us she had died, we immediately thought it must have been the bombing, Mrs Mabel Blaney told the Chronicle and Echo today, 'we had feared the worst, but we could not believe it when we learnt that it was smallpox'.

Mrs, Blaney said that her daughter had been vaccinated before leaving England.

Eileen's husband, whose uncle is the former West Pakistan President Yahya Khan, notified the Pakistani Embassy in London about his wife's death just before Christmas, but he asked them to wait until Tuesday before cabling Northamptonshire police so that the news would not spoil the Blaney's Christmas holiday.

Eileen and Hassan (35), were taking a six-month holiday with their two sons Alexander (14) and Jason (9). It was Hassan's first visit home after 17 years in this country.

They left Wootton on October 20th and drove to Pakistan, sending postcards to Blisworth from countries they visited en route.

But the last the Blaney's heard from their daughter was when she wrote from Peshawar saying that the family were to be evacuated.

Because Hassan's uncle was the president, and his brothers and sisters were in the army or married to army officers they were given top brass attention out there said Mrs Blaney. 'But still we were always afraid while the fighting was going on', she said, 'we watched the news on television every night thinking that we might see Eileen, or Hassan, or one of the boys in the films of the evacuation'.

'The night they flew some refugees into Luton, we sat up until midnight waiting for the phone to ring to tell us to go and pick them up', she said 'But they weren't on the plane'.

'When we heard the war was over I was so happy', said Mrs Blaney, 'I thought they would be safer then'.

Eileen had been working at Barclays Bank in Northampton when the couple decided to visit West Pakistan; they were due to return in May. 'I don't know whether Hassan and the children will come back now', said Mrs Blaney, 'Perhaps they will stay there, it is his homeland'.

NEVER DREAMT

Mrs Blaney said that although Hassan's family were so involved in the war, her son-in-law had no strong views about the troubles, between India and Pakistan.

'When they left' she said, 'Hassan never dreamt there would be a war', he said to me 'Don't worry mother there won't be any trouble it's all talk'.

Eileen and Hassan had been married for 15 years. They met when they were studying together at the Northampton College of Technology.

NORTHAMPTON CHRONICLE & ECHO, JANUARY 1972

A Day to Remember

It was now early January 1972, a new year that I didn't really want, but they say time waits for no man, but I'm a child and I want last year back for obvious reasons, a year we all laughed together as one happy family.

I had just woken from my sleep, Alexander was already up badgering cook about what was for breakfast as I made my way down to the courtyard, the morning sun was just announcing itself by streaming in through the glass covered roof putting down a warm glow that made your eyes squint, but at the same time made you feel calm and relaxed.

As Alexander and I both sat at the table in the courtyard of Agha Manzil 2 awaiting cooks breakfast surprise, it was always a surprise even to the cook, but very edible all the same, we were visited by Uncle Hyat, an uncle we had met before on many family gatherings. He was given the nickname of Yul Brynner by some of the family members due to his large bald head, but I think the likeness stopped there. Uncle Hyat was also put in a position of authority by the President and given the prestige title of Chief of Railway Police for the whole of Northern Pakistan, from Lahore in the south to Peshawar in the north and as far west as Quetta, then right across eastwards to Islamabad and beyond. A huge area as square miles go, but in fact there were only six different rail lines, consisting of a single laid track between major cities with passing bays along its route, a legacy left behind from the British Empire, along with its very ancient rolling stock. They had to be continually maintained with parts that did not exist anymore, but that didn't stop the local craftsmen fabricating their own in their little back street workshops, quite a resilient bunch — wouldn't you say?

The reason he visited Alexander and myself was to try to get us away from Peshawar and the constant thought of our mother's passing, and with Dad in agreement, it was then arranged for us to meet him that evening at the railway station. At around six o'clock we met Uncle Hyat along with three railway policemen in uniform as agreed. Dad also came with us and we were led around the back of the station along some tracks towards a large shed. These tracks went right under its door leading you in no doubt whatsoever, that what lay beyond these large doors was something to do with a train.

As the guards struggled but eventually slid the doors open, we were not wrong, although it was no engine that greeted us, but just two carriages all very clean, twinkling in the twilight of the evening sun. These two carriages were from the 1900s and used by the elite of the British authorities to travel around India between major cities.

The front carriage was pure luxury with a lounge, dining area, sleeping quarters, and bathroom facilities. The second and smaller of the two had a kitchen, storeroom, a bathroom and a place for the guards and servants to sleep in. Both carriages were painted in a dark rich green, with gold letters and numbers in various places along both sides, each of them originally coming from England.

Once inside the smell of an evening meal could be detected wafting down the carriage from the dining table, itself all nicely set out with gleaming cutlery surrounded by four matching leather backed chairs awaiting our imminent arrival. All four of us sat down to a tasty offering of lamb curry served by the cook from the kitchen, two police guards stood outside, one at each end of the carriage and the third at the entrance to the shed keeping watch.

Unbeknown to me or Alexander, Dad had a change of clothes from the house along with all the other necessary items so that we both could sleep the night on the carriage, and in the morning we would have breakfast while being taken to Rawalpindi by one of the engines. Uncle Hyat then said 'happy birthday for tomorrow Jason, this is all for you'.

I was totally stunned, not by the fact we were going to be travelling on a train for my birthday, but the fact that I had totally forgot it was my birthday, with all that had gone on in the past three weeks. It just did not enter my head, or even Alexander's come to think of it, nobody mentioned it at all, perhaps it was Mum who usually told me, I just don't remember at all how I was told in the past, it just came once a year like everybody else's. It was the eleventh of January tomorrow and that was my birthday and I had reached the age of ten, a milestone of being in double figures, one to look forward to as a child but one I had understandably totally forgotten about.

After dinner we all went and sat in the lounge area of this carriage. Uncle Hyat producing a large bottle of Johnnie Walker Red Label for him and Dad from a very concealed drinks cabinet, one that was deliberately built into the carriage by the British and no doubt used on many occasion in the past, but very discreetly in an Islamic world. Alexander and I had Coke but with a nice drop of whisky added, well it was my birthday tomorrow after all, and if nothing else it would help us to go to sleep tonight. Uncle Hyat explained to us that two of the guards and the cook, all English speaking, would be stopping the night inside the second carriage and would stay with us on the journey tomorrow, Uncle Hyat keeping in touch with them at all times. Saying goodnight to Dad and settling down in bed talking with Alexander, trying to speculate who over the many years had slept here before us, it wasn't long before we both dropped off to sleep, nice and warm in these colonial beds. Only to be woken in what we thought was the middle of the night, due to the lack of light coming through the thin curtain that covered the window by an almighty thud, and the clanking of metal as these two carriages lurched backwards. It wasn't the middle of the night at all, although dark I had totally forgotten that we were parked in a shed, the now forward movement of the carriage eventually exposing us to the morning light, as it popped itself out of it's night shelter being pulled by a very large steam engine and coal tender slowly towards the station of Peshawar.

Alexander and 1 dressing quickly, so as not to miss a minute of this fantastic day, all the rushing about to get ready was not that necessary as after our carriage had clicked itself over several points on the track while we looked intently out of the windows, we came to a stop about five hundred feet from where we had started, prompting the cook to ask us what would we like for breakfast.

Alexander and I both sat at the dining table, freshly squeezed orange and mango juice readily available to us while we waited for the lamb kofta and scrambled eggs that we had ordered to arrive, the sound of our train's engine letting out steam on regular intervals added real nostalgia to the whole situation. Whilst eating our breakfast the train then began to move very slowly and entered the platform area of Peshawar station. This was a very strange experience indeed, for as we travelled the entire length of the platform tucking into our scrambled eggs with silver cutlery, we were being watched by the many different ages of unknown faces that peered through the windows, it was as if we were in some kind of moving zoo, both of us being the attraction of the day, and at the same time the situation being totally surreal.

The concept of those people on the platform staring through the windows and Alexander and I inside this carriage consuming whatever we wanted for breakfast really brought home to me the have's and the have-not's. A scenario that has gone on for centuries in the world and one that I cannot ever see changing. For a moment Alexander and I chuckled to ourselves at the thought of all these people trying to get onto this one carriage, there must have been at least two or three hundred people on that platform, if not more. Our train

All aboard!

then came to a halt just a few feet past the end of the platform that had been hidden from view by all those people. Alexander and I finished our breakfast then passed through the servant's carriage and stood on a small veranda that was attached to the back, along with one of the police guards travelling with us.

We were now looking back to the platform as it's occupants were jostling frantically for the best position as a second train, bellowing out black smoke from its funnel, pulled into the station, some climbing on board before it had time to eventually stop only feet from where we were standing, it's enormous figure blocking out the days sun, casting a shadow over the three of us as if night had suddenly descended.

Above the noise of the engine letting out steam while it was stationary, you could hear the cries of the people as they swarmed on to the train like ants. Alexander and I both holding on tightly to a handrail while stretching out from the side of the veranda to watch the mayhem that was going on in front of our eyes by the simple introduction of a train into a station. Within minutes (and that's being rather generous), the platform was almost empty and the carriages of the train were barely visible due to the amount of people either sitting on its roof or literally hanging on to its sides by the rails that guarded the windows. I said to my brother, 'if that's what it looks like outside, imagine how the inside looks, it must be crammed solid', apparently this was quite the norm as it was the only train of the day leaving Peshawar going south.

Once the second train was ready, our train, and it's not often you can say that it is actually your train, so I will say it again — our train — moved forward, gathering speed as it headed towards Rawalpindi. Leaving the second train in our wake, it didn't take long for us to reach maximum speed, as we had a clear track ahead of us on this three-hour journey. Along the way several road crossings were closed by employees of the railway, each crossing being done by hand. As we crossed the main highway from Peshawar to Rawalpindi, some scooter drivers, not wanting to wait, or they just thought it was a game of roulette they could play, by taking their life in their own hands as they attempted to cross before the train had reached them. Some succeeded but we then watched one man who had to abort his attempt and drop his scooter just short of the train track, more than likely misjudging our speed due to the fact our engine only had two light carriages, rather than the usual ten or twelve that the train somewhere behind us was pulling at a much slower speed.

We passed through a few stations, their platforms again crowded with people in anticipation of the following train, Alexander and I wondering how on earth are they going to get on, but somehow, they always do.

Sitting back in the old leather seats, Coke in hand with an array of crisps and treats on the table gazing out of the window suddenly realising today was my birthday. I have

Attock Kurd Station (stock photograph)

for the last nine years been celebrating with my close family but today not really celebrating but enjoying with my brother Alexander, the close family thing was to be no more, one that from now I just had to accept and get used to.

Our train, or my train to be precise, after all it was my birthday, came to a halt at Attock Kurd station, a place built by the British in the 1880s. It looked so out of place here in the Punjab more fitting to a rural country village in the middle of the Cotswolds, built of stone but with a tiled roof instead of a thatch.

The train had stopped here to let another train coming from the south to pass, as there were two lines at this point on the journey, one of our police guards said we could get off while we waited. Stepping down from the carriage we were greeted by the station master who had a moustache that told you he was definitely in charge of this place, dead straight under his nose and curled up at the ends — a real show stopper. He explained that he knew we were coming as he had received a message

Attock bridge, road crossing under the rail crossing

Attock bridge, west side fortress and rail track

from our uncle, offering Alexander and I a small tour of this fascinating place while we waited in the middle of nowhere.

The station master was so enthusiastic and utterly delighted that someone had decided to stop at his station and take a real interest in its idyllic location. What was noticeable as we stood admiring this quaint structure in all it's surroundings was the platform, extremely long, built on a curve heading left at the end, not that our train took much of it up mind you. It appeared this wasn't a station many passengers used, but as we walked forward around the curve it revealed why this station was built in the first place.

Attock Bridge, the main crossing of the Indus River, an iron bridge built by the British again in the 1880s, which had a railway line on the top and a road running below on a second level, one we had crossed many a time by car travelling between Islamabad and Peshawar. On some of our trips having to wait ten minutes or more to cross as it was only a single track, giving way to the opposite traffic, which often consisted of a bullock and cart.

At each end of this enormous piece of metalwork there were two stone fortresses built to protect the bridge from tribal attack. The station master said that Alexander and I could explore the fort that was on this side of the bridge, and in doing so got a tremendous view of the green and blue waters of the Indus river way below us flowing very fast indeed. At that point the north bound train that we had stopped for came puffing under the fort on the far side, what a tremendous sight that was as it made it's way across, whistling as it did so, crammed full to the gunwales with people. The train eventually passing through our fortress, it's smoke blasting furiously up from beneath engulfing us all for a few moments as it continued it's journey northward to Peshawar. While the station master continued to explain to both of us about the fortress, we looked out from it's tower back at the Attock Kurd station, the passenger train that was following us had now pulled in

Anni, me, Nanni & Alexander, January 11th 1972
(picture taken by our driver)

behind our train still full to the brim with people. Alexander and I were wondering about getting back to our train, so this train could move on but the station master was having none of this, saying they can wait until we had finished our tour, however long that may be.

Continuing, the station master showed us where the soldiers lived in these huge towers that straddled each side of this important strategic location, eventually finishing some thirty minutes later back on the platform. The two police guards standing at the far end of our train, *lathi* in hand, so not to let any of the people who had ventured off the second train to encroach towards us or our train, thus leaving the platform totally empty at this end for the three of us while we had a nice cold drink, sitting on a bench in the sun.

After saying our goodbyes to this extraordinary man with what can only be described as a wondrous moustache we stepped back into our carriage to be greeted by the traditional cup of *chai*, served in a china cup and saucer, along with an array of sweet cakes and pastries one even had a lit candle in it for my birthday, (Oh, how the other half live!).

The train blew its whistle and moved very slowly under the fortress and out onto the bridge, the sheer drop looking out below was quite frightening, but if you looked straight out at eye level you would think you were floating in mid-air on some type of magic carpet.

The second fortress came far too quickly, then Attock Bridge was just one fantastic memory, as the train again reached top speed, heading towards Rawalpindi entering a couple of very dark smoke-filled tunnels on the way while Alexander and I consumed as many cakes as we could.

It was early afternoon as we approached the city of Rawalpindi, and after having to be shunted around its sidings for about an hour, we finally came to a halt in a secure area away from the main station.

We were then greeted by Annie and Nanni, our cousins, Dads' brothers' children from Islamabad and their driver. They took us to see the sights and sounds of this city, visiting a large dam on the outskirts of the city which supplied the majority of water for that area, but these sights did not come anywhere near the sight of Attock Bridge we witnessed earlier that day, in fact the best part was returning to the train, where all four of us sat down to yet another meal prepared for us by the cook, a type of tandoori chicken, with fresh salad — delicious.

After playing a few card games our cousins went back to Islamabad, less than an hour's drive away, while Alexander and I had hot chocolate before eventually retiring to bed, the police armed guards still on duty for our protection as we did so.

What a birthday for a child, my own train for the day with all the trimmings, how wonderful! But as I lay there in bed before I eventually dropped off to sleep to the constant humming of the night life of Rawalpindi I thought to myself, 'a birthday to remember!', unfortunately though without the company of my parents. I would have swapped it all for a simple visit to the park and a go on the swings, before heading back home for tea and cake that would have undoubtedly been just as good, if not better, as long as both of them could have been there to have shared it with me.

Awoken early by our private alarm, not a clock with a bell on the top, but the sudden clanking of our carriage being buffeted by its engine, as it hooked up to us and started to pull us out of the siding, that had become our resting place for the night. The sun not anywhere to be seen as our train gathered speed, Alexander and I staying in our beds as the train clicked and rocked its way along the tracks heading south, eventually both of us rising with the sun that started to beam through the small windows at the side of the beds. Again sitting for breakfast at the dining table with fresh fruit in abundance followed by chapatti with scrambled eggs mixed with rice and currants, sounds odd but very nice indeed.

As we gazed from the window the landscape was now becoming green and flat, the smoke from our engine going at full tilt, drifting by every so often, slightly masking our view as it did so. It was now around nine o'clock as our train pulled into Wazirabad Junction, an area which had loads of tracks side by side with disused and abandoned carriages on them that looked as if they had been there for years just decaying in the heat of the day. The train waited here for over an hour before moving off steadily, the sun moving round in the bright blue sky as we now began to head eastwards to what was now to be our final destination and the town of Sialkot, on this quite unbelievable but true chance of a lifetime train ride for two very lucky young boys, one now ten years old.

War Zone

Sialkot was a small town on the eastern side of Pakistan, about ten miles from the border with India. It had now been less than four weeks since the war had ceased between these two countries. As Alexander and I stepped down from the train saying goodbye to the cook and guards that had looked after us so well, it was very noticeable that many armed soldiers stood on the platform of Sialkot Junction, the station itself having sandbags at its windows and more soldiers packed around the many machine gun posts dotted along its platform.

You could feel the tense atmosphere, a definite sense of worry in case the violent hostilities were to suddenly return to this potential war zone.

'Tell me please, why we are getting off here?' In fact, it had been arranged by our father who was to meet us here the very next day, with Uncle Hashim and Uncle Hyat after driving down from Peshawar in our Triumph Vitesse, a very easy trip for a car of that stature. The three of them, after a night's stay here in Sialkot, taking the train that we had just arrived on to the city of Lahore to meet some old friends, leaving Alexander and I to stay with Dad's sister and family for a week or so here in Sialkot.

As Alexander and I stood on the platform with our two police guards the soldiers instantly stood to attention as this grand figure, Uncle Abid, in full military uniform, the general and the husband of Dad's sister strolled majestically down to meet us. Military formalities totally disregarded as he held us both in a warm and long embrace, his profound Qizilbash moustache tickling my face as he did so. Dad's sister's husband Uncle Abid was the general in charge of the whole of the Sialkot region which included a large military base and it was fully operational for the defence of Pakistan against an invasion by India, a place my brother and I would come to know very well over the next couple of weeks.

Alexander and I with Uncle Arbid

We then made our way out of the station and into a fully armed escort of several vehicles for the hasty journey to our uncle's residence. During the journey Alexander and I told him of all the wonderful things that had happened on my birthday and today on Uncle Hyat's train. He then replied by saying that he would have to keep up the high standards Uncle Hyat had set and the expectancy that we both are now used to and would be thinking very hard how to achieve this.

Arriving at the house, a very large white bungalow set within a white high walled garden we were greeted by the rest of the family; Dad's sister and their children who we had met before in Peshawar, Raza aged twenty-two, Shakeela aged twenty, Saira aged seventeen, Hashim aged thirteen and Qasim the youngest. It was felt that time spent with children of our own age would be good for Alexander and myself and might ease some of the pain we both had had to suffer over the last few weeks or so. It was Friday afternoon, so the schools finished early before afternoon prayer. All of the children were escorted by armed military personnel from their different schools or in Raza's case the international university in Lahore, back to Sialkot to meet us once again, all of us mixing together happily and very much at ease with each other, as though we were all brothers and sisters.

Having woken gently on Saturday morning, and not to the clunking of our bedroom being hit with a steam engine before the sun would rise, we took breakfast.

After breakfast all of us played cricket in the large walled garden while waiting for Dad to arrive, Alexander managing to strike the ball over the high wall, and Shakeela sending two of the servants to eventually find it while we all sat waiting in the shade drinking lemonade, the ball finally retrieved, so we could continue our game, only to be hit straight back over again. Back home in England we would have had to fetch our own ball and you wouldn't get that back if it went in Mrs Beryl's garden that's for sure.

Two days of real fun and laughter was had, with Dad arriving on the Saturday night, joining in on all the different types of games we played on Sunday, along with his sister and all three of my uncles, many of the servants taking part to make the numbers up for some of these games.

Dad left us on Sunday night for Lahore, after a large buffet meal enough for all of us twice over, happily knowing we would be in good hands here with his sister.

After another good night's sleep having been worn out from the weekend's activities, my cousins would return to their schools, leaving Alexander and I with Dads' sister for the first day. She taught us, along with their cook, how to make nan bread and chapattis in a traditional very hot tandoori oven, then making samosas and pakora from flour and ghee, very messy, but well worth the effort.

The Brigadier

Uncle Abid took Alexander and me to his headquarters inside the military base here in Sialkot in a very shiny staff car with a flag adorning its front. It was flanked by armed Jeeps, full of soldiers, a very nice target for the Indian Air force if they wish to re-start the war, hopefully for my brother and I, not today. Once on the military base we watched the soldiers train in hand combat and fire their rifles on the target range. Alexander then being allowed to fire a pistol, not too certain if he hit anything or not, but knowing him like I do, I'm sure he would say he did.

We then had our lunch with all the soldiers in the mess, before heading out to the parade ground to watch the Drill Sergeant put some unfortunate new recruits through their paces, our uncle joining us to inspect these men by walking up and down each line allowing us to follow, stopping momentarily before moving on once more.

Late afternoon while having a nice glass of *chai* with our uncle in his office and talking about the day's events, a Brigadier on the base was summoned by him, and because he was well educated and could speak the Queen's English to a very high standard was told — no, ordered by our Uncle Abid to keep us occupied and look after us over the next two days, while he dealt with more important matters. Basically this Brigadier, who probably had just fought in the war, was down on baby-sitting duties, not that he had any choice, so it was arranged that he would come to the house and pick us up around ten the very next day.

After returning to the house again in the staff car, yet another opportunity missed by the Indian Air Force, we told our auntie and cousins about the day we had just had and that we were looking forward to what tomorrow will bring.

The next day, as agreed, the Brigadier turned up at the house with two army Jeeps and a Toyota pick-up truck. The first Jeep had an open back and had two soldiers in the front and four soldiers in the back all armed. The Toyota truck had two soldiers in the front and one standing on the back in charge of a very large machine gun fixed to the truck on a pivoting mount, the third Jeep was driven by the Brigadier, open sides and canvas roof and one armed guard. The Brigadier also brought along another man, not armed, but in uniform and while Alexander went out to admire the vehicles that had just entered the compound, my auntie, the Brigadier and this man along with myself went back into the house.

Now Uncle Abid had arranged a late present for my birthday and in doing so trying to top Uncle Hyat`s birthday present of a train for two days, (uncles — they are a breed of their own and I had many of them here in Pakistan, who was I to complain if they all wanted to treat me?). The man the Brigadier had with him was an army tailor and he was here to measure me for a Pakistani Army uniform, to be made as quickly as possible so Uncle Abid could then see me wear it before we returned to Peshawar.

Tape measure ready, arms out, waist circled, inside legs done and auntie having a joke with the Brigadier about which side I dress, at that age I would say straight down the middle, wouldn't you? All done in a quick and methodical way, just what you would expect from the armed forces. The Brigadier said after ordering the tailor to make his own way back to the base. We were now to head out to inspect a dam on the Chenab River about an hour's drive away, a type of dam built only a couple of years earlier to control the flood waters.

Jumping in the back of the Jeep, the armed guard sitting to my right, Alexander in front of me sitting next to the Brigadier who was driving, we exited the house compound at great speed, the Jeep in front with the armed guards continually sounding its horn as we travelled through the streets of Sialkot and out into the countryside. Alexander and I enjoying every minute of this speeding convoy as it left a trail of dust in its wake. After passing a few small farms along very bumpy dirt tracks we finally reached the Chenab River and the new dam, which is known as the Marala Barrage Dam, which consisted of many large iron sluice gates set on concrete structures to form a type of bridge across this vast expanse of water.

This area was highlighted as a strategic point in the eventuality of an armed invasion from India, and for that reason it was heavily guarded with large gun emplacements set along it's length, to repel either air strikes or attacks from gun boats coming up the river. The Barrage had a road running its full length so remaining in the Jeep we went all the way to the far end to inspect the gun emplacement there. The Brigadier making the soldiers open their gun barrel so he could look inside to see if it was clean, then checking the live shells that stood ready in a box at the side, standing back and ordering them to go through the procedure of battle stations and then loading the gun ready for firing. Once satisfied we proceeded back along the Barrage stopping at the next gun emplacement, the Brigadier going through the same routine as the first one before moving on once more, Alexander and I watching intensely every time. We had now reached the middle of this structure and the third gun emplacement, a smaller type of gun sat here out of the five that were on the

Barrage. The Brigadier giving the order to load the gun as on the previous two occasions only this time the order was to fire. Well, what a noise! A very loud pumping sound that caused the wildlife to scatter in every direction, the used shell cases spilling out hot onto the ground from this double barrelled machine gun, all very frightening at first, but also very exciting for two young boys. Then the Brigadier offered Alexander the opportunity to fire this gun, but first putting on some ear defenders before climbing up behind the gun and grasping the two handles, then being shown how to fire by the gunner soldier in charge.

All of a sudden letting it rip, the bullets pounding the calm waters of the Chenab River intensely about a hundred meters away, Alexander having a second go after gaining his confidence the noise seemingly less noticeable to him, when concentrating on the firing of the gun. It was then suggested to me that I should have a go, Alexander really prompting me, as at first I was reluctant but I was made to feel at ease by the Brigadier explaining it would be fine and to take this once in a life time opportunity to do what most boys my age would only dream of.

I was then lifted up onto the gun platform, ear defenders in place and because of my height, or the lack of it one might say, the gun which I now held by the trigger handles was pointing skywards, rather than out across the river, being told when I'm ready to start firing. Well forget the noise, as I pulled the trigger the intense shaking of this gun went right through me and the force that this thing had was mind blowing. It appeared for what seemed like ages but perhaps only about fifteen seconds, that I was somehow frozen to the handles. The thought of letting go did not appear in my train of thought, because as I held onto this beast it lifted me up off the ground, the two barrels eventually pointing straight down into the water as the bullets continually disappeared into the river directly below, my feet now dangling somewhere off the ground. I was then eventually lifted off by one of the soldiers, the noise of the gun ceasing, but being replaced by the shear laughter and enjoyment of everybody around me including my brother at what they had just witnessed.

Back in the Jeep and still feeling the shaking motion in my body, we continued with the Brigadier to inspect the last two gun emplacements, one of them firing a large shell to show us how it worked, the whole gun jumping backward from the force it had produced, a loud bang echoing backup the river as the shell hit the water way off in the distance. The Brigadier said we would be going up country next after lunch to see an army outpost very close to the border with India.

We then all sat by the river eating nan bread and a type of dal out of a billycan supplied by the army around an open fire. Fully satisfied by the food provided, although rather spicier than I had been used to, we headed out in our little convoy going at a great rate of knots where we could, slowing right down where the road turned into large dried mud ruts, the Jeeps rocking back and forth, Alexander and I hanging on tightly as they managed to overcome these obstacles.

Eventually after nearly an hour of driving we parked the Jeeps and walked quietly along the river bank, the large clumps of bulrushes keeping us from seeing the edge of the water but also concealing us from view as we reached this remote outpost hidden deep up-river, just like a den we would build in the hedgerows near our village in the summer holidays. Set here amongst the reed beds was another gun emplacement, four soldiers always occupied this position, the Brigadier then fully inspecting this remote gun position, after surprising the four occupants with our arrival.

Then Alexander and I were ushered forward on our stomachs to a hide right on the water's edge, where through a pair of binoculars and a small fixed telescope we were able to see across the river a fully operational Indian machine gun post, the turban headdress of some of the soldiers clearly visible, as we watched on in silence.

Returning to the Jeeps mid-afternoon we headed again at great speed back to the safety of the base in Sialkot, eventually meeting up with Uncle Abid in his office. With faces beaming with delight, telling him of the great day we have just had with our guide the Brigadier, Uncle Abid constantly raising his bushy eye brows across the room at the Brigadier when we mentioned anything controversial, which Alexander and I were not supposed to do.

Rows of Heads

Day two of the Brigadier's babysitting duties and from the speed of the Jeeps when leaving the compound and the serious look on his face, told us that Uncle Abid must have had a word or two in his ear, after yesterday's events.

He first took us to the railway station to inspect the gun posts that we had seen on our arrival here in Sialkot, a few days previously. We then headed the short distance to Sialkot Fort in the centre of the town, mainly a large hill with lots of steps. The army had a lookout post at the top, not much in the way of a fort-like structure, as I have known and seen recently. From there we visited the clock tower on Iqbal Square, several guards on a machine gun post standing behind sandbags, watching the long day go by, our convoy returning to the base in an orderly fashion for lunch thereafter.

Just as we were finishing our food the Brigadier asked us if we would like to go to the cinema to watch a film, it was a new war film called *The Battle of the Bulge* and had just arrived at Sialkot picture house. It would be shown in English but with Urdu subtitles, I think the Brigadier was more interested in the film than we were, as it was a war film. Alexander agreed to this and asked the Brigadier on which day would he like us to go, the reply coming back that now would be a good time. Back in the Jeeps our convoy returned to the centre of Sialkot after winding our way through the chaos of the bazaars, eventually pulling up in line outside the local picture house (cinema). The people in the street gathering round in high numbers to see why three heavily armed army vehicles had arrived at this location. Climbing out of the Jeep, the men who were in the pickup truck with the large gun attached to its rear, remained in the street on surveillance, while the rest of the soldiers stepped inside this old building that had seen far better days, behind the Brigadier, Alexander and I. We entered through the double doors and approached the tiny kiosk at the front, a man behind its glass had a look of total bewilderment on his face, as he tried to comprehend why and what had just entered his building. The Brigadier barking orders at him the closer we got, while at the same time our ears could hear the loud soundtrack from the movie that was being shown inside, cascading out into this small foyer. As good as dragging this poor man from his kiosk, we then proceeded to enter the screening area of this picture house, myself glancing up at the screen to see a picture of a tank firing its gun, the noise of the film so much louder now as the light from the screen shone down to guide our way forward. Then suddenly, the screen went blank and the sound stopped, a moment of darkness prevailed before the house lights went on.

Looking up from the front of this cinema, the screen directly behind us, the many seats climbed quite steeply, rows of heads with faces that showed all kinds of expressions, from stunned surprise to alarm and fear as they all looked on. The first five rows of seats were ordered by the soldiers, who were still armed, to vacate their seats, making all these people either leave or find another seat further back, some of them having to sit on the stairs, it started to appear to me how the train must have been like when all the people started to climb inside back in Peshawar station, very crammed indeed.

Without saying a word Alexander and I looked at each other with a look that said, we can't believe what we were seeing but once everybody was sort of settled, if you could call it that, the Brigadier then told us to sit in the third row right in the middle. He then positioned four of the guards on the end seats of rows one and five and another two guards on the door, so nobody could come in and the poor people behind us were not allowed out. The Brigadier then came and sat next to me, the man from the kiosk sat to the left of the Brigadier on the end of our row. The Brigadier then shouted out in Urdu, which I could easily translate to lights out and start the film, 'how?', you may ask — because that is exactly what happened next.

After about five or ten minutes into the film I began to realise that all the people behind us had actually seen this part before, as they were already watching the film when we all rudely barged in and turned it off. I then started to look for the place in the film when I saw the tank firing on the screen when we first entered. Well it was nowhere soon because after about an hour, the Brigadier had told the man on his left to stop the film and go and get us some cold drinks and with that the house lights came on again. I looked round to see all the people still with the look of amazement on their faces, I suppose it's something to tell their grandchildren the day the army came to the cinema with two young boys, just as I am telling my future generations in this book.

Drinks in hand and the film started again and I eventually saw the tank firing scene I had been looking for, and not too long after that the film ended.

All the people behind us still had to wait while we left the picture house in no particular hurry at all, into the bright sunlight of the afternoon, the Brigadier not stopping for one moment to wax lyrical about the film he had just seen as we climbed aboard our Jeep. On our return to the house and compound our little saffron yellow Triumph Vitesse was being cleaned by two servants. Auntie coming out to greet us to tell us the news that Dad would be arriving from Lahore tomorrow by train. Alexander and I very happy indeed and couldn't wait to tell him about our last two days running around with the babysitter, I mean the Brigadier in an army Jeep convoy.

Dad's arrival prompted another week's stay in Sialkot, so he could spend some quality time with his sister, making up time for the years they had both lost from not being together. This also gave Dad some very important light relief and comfort, to the rigors that he must have gone through over the past six weeks or more, caring for our mother, only to see the love of his life eventually slip away, knowing nothing he or anybody else could have done to change the plight of the situation that had acted itself out in a bedroom back at Agha Manzil in Peshawar.

The day before we had to leave, Dad, his sister, Alexander and I went off to the army base in another armed escort, where we were met by the Brigadier who introduced himself to Dad, he then began to give him a tour of the base with Alexander.

My auntie and I going off to the office of Uncle Abid for what I now know was the fitting of my uniform, made to measure and finished some days earlier. A little bit itchy at first but fitted perfectly, and a small beret to top it off, you might say. Uncle Abid was to inspect some of the soldiers out on the parade ground shortly, and I was to go with them as if I was a part of the regiment. Dad and Alexander were to be taken there by the Brigadier, but unaware of the small spectacle that was to be performed shortly. Well I marched on to the parade ground the best I could not having a dress rehearsal you understand, more of a hop and a skip as my stride was nowhere near those of the regular soldiers. I could see Alexander and my auntie giggling profoundly at the sight before them as we came to a

Enjoying the plains of Pakistan near Islamabad, today totally consumed by buildings

halt, myself standing in the middle of the first row of about three or four. Uncle Abid began to inspect the ranks of soldiers somewhere behind me, eventually reaching me, then looking me up and down with great interest, dusting my shoulders as he did so, finally returning to the front. I was then ordered to step forward. The Brigadier was holding a tray, too high for me to see what was on it as then Uncle Abid reached over and pinned a row of medals on my chest, citing they were for not letting go of a machine gun when in full firing mode while protecting the Marala Barrage. ('Very good', I thought, as everyone burst into fits of laughter).

Leaving Sialkot behind for the last time we headed for Islamabad and the house of Dad's brother the judge. We stayed there for four or five days exploring this new city before eventually driving back to Peshawar and Agha Manzil. The return journey taking us across the Attock Bridge once more but this time going in the opposite direction and on the lower road deck, telling Dad again about our marvellous train journey and our crossing on the tracks above.

Aladdin's Cave

Whilst staying in Agha Manzil, Dad's elder brother Mohammad Khan suggested we should take a trip out to the Tribal Lands area south west of Peshawar and the small village of Dara Adamkhel. This was an unruly place, not governed by the police or army, our family having no influence whatsoever in

A trip to Aladdin's Cave

this region, an area mostly left to its own devices hence the words 'tribal lands', a place that you could get killed for no reason at all and nobody would do anything about it. They would say it would actually be your own fault for going there.

So was this another one of our uncles trying to spoil us? It seemed a funny way of doing it, in fact I can tell you my brother and I were definitely not laughing at the thought of this day out.

We all travelled in a small local minibus taking about an hour to our destination, Alexander and I along with Dad, his brother and his two sons Zia and Zaka. Taking our car would have drawn too much attention to ourselves and a likely target, to whoever wanted to be known as the person that attacked the little saffron yellow Triumph Vitesse and it's occupants just because they could, or even the possibility of being kidnapped and held to ransom, hoping the family could eventually get us all released — or not. Again, what a great day out, just one you must add to your bucket list if you get the chance, but you might want to put it last on the list in case it actually was the last one!

Reaching the small village of Dara Adamkhel, in the tribal area, we headed out along a dirt road, the minibus felt like it was about to fall to bits, as the driver failed to slow down for any of the ruts that had formed along its path. Then up ahead there was this large mud wall which blended nicely into the desert background, the only give away that it was not a mirage in the heat of the day was the very large wooden gates that drew you in to wonder what lay beyond. As we approached the gates heavily armed men with machine guns and rifles in hand spilled out from behind a smaller wall, like Smarties from a tube, their bullet belts in full view to give a more intimidating look, two of them coming over to our vehicle with one of them sliding the side door open to have a closer look at all of us in the back. Zia sitting closest to the door explained the purpose of our visit, the well bearded man giving no reply as he slammed the door shut so hard, it made me jump out of my skin, if I wasn't already scared, that just topped it for me.

The gates then started to open, me straining to look over the top of my uncle's head through the dusty windscreen to see what lay beyond, all was finally divulged to me as our minibus moved forward, the gates being quickly closed behind us. Well it was as if we had stepped through into a western type country, and definitely not what you would think was behind this very bland but high wall, yes there were men with guns, but once inside not in any threatening way.

I suppose they were there to keep the authorities at bay and quite understandable for their line of thought must have been, 'what we have, we hold'.

We were not the only visitors there, as our minibus parked in the centre of this very large compound next to all sorts of different vehicles, their occupants also deciding to take a day out in the middle of nowhere on the offchance of getting shot.

The area of this place was at least the size of the recreation ground back in Wootton, maybe five or six football pitches in

Zaka with one of the sellers of a rifle

total, with what appeared to be large garage type buildings all the way round the outside, there must have been twenty-five of them on each side. As we started to walk in front of these garages in a clockwise direction peering in as we did so they began to reveal their contents, nearly every one of them had something different inside to offer, their owners trying to entice us in to look.

What I can hear you ask would be inside, the answer to that question was literally everything you could possibly buy or want to buy; from a simple Mars Bar to a rocket launcher. This was their idea of a retail park out of the city and towns in the middle of nowhere, a place where you can come and buy anything on the black market, at a price of course, it was a good thirty years ahead of England at the time with an out of town retail park and people say this is a third world country. I was told by Dad that most of the goods had come by road, from Iran mostly, western goods and some of the items were probably in the trucks we had passed in Afghanistan on our journey; most of them likely paying the border guards a fee to let them go through uninterrupted. Dad had told his brother that he wanted to buy Agha Manzil a new washing machine and my uncle agreed telling him that this was the place to buy it, hence the day out, allbeit a nervy one.

I know they sold Mars Bars because my brother and I were bought one by our cousin Zaka, not sure how long it had been here as the chocolate had started to turn white, but it still tasted just how I remembered as well as the saying: *A Mars a day helps you work, rest, and well, stay alive today.*

As we walked past these garages packed with all sorts of different household goods, every so often you would hear the sound of gunfire, which made me still very uneasy and unsure, until we had reached one of the corners, where a small entrance led you out of this strange world, to what only can be described as a firing range.

Not at all like the army firing range at Simpson Barracks in our village, enclosed for safety and with red flags on show to say that firing was in progress, this was just an open piece of land behind the compound, with a few old oil drums scattered around on it. We all stood and watched a potential buyer of a Russian machine gun riddle a drum with holes while two other men fired a handgun and a rifle. Then my cousin Zaka tried a rifle, hitting a barrel about twenty feet or so away, as though he had done this many times before, I thought, 'that's quite handy to know, I will be sticking close to him in the near future'.

Back into the compound we ventured into a garage that had all sorts of electrical goods, from stereos to TVs, and at last some new washing machines. My uncle bartered with a man over the price, after having taken advice from Dad which make to buy and eventually settling on a Hoovermatic Deluxe twin tub, apparently all the rage back in England. This was the latest version, one that probably hadn't even reached the Shires by then, but here it was, all brand new and ready to go, deal done and re-boxed, we watched it being loaded onto a small truck then heading out of the gates there and then to Peshawar, and Agha Manzil. Now that's what you call service, not sure there was any guarantee with it or the chance to call a Hoover repair man out if needed, but I would not be surprised in the least if you could not get the parts you may need somewhere in this Aladdin's Cave of a compound. Continuing to browse through the garages, what was noticeable was seeing how many people were in this one particular garage, and to see the large amount of whisky that you could buy in a supposedly Islamic country, with Johnnie Walker Red Label being bought by the box load at a considerable rate of knots. We then all went and relaxed sitting at a table and having a cup of sweet *chai* under a makeshift parasol, watching the daily bustle of this place as though we were in a western shopping centre on a Saturday afternoon, the Wimpy bar being substituted for a local kebab stall on wheels, realising the world may not be too different after all, maybe a little strange, but not different.

Once refreshed we returned to our transport for the hour-long journey back to Peshawar, quite a placid end to the day, the total opposite to the nervy beginning that I had earlier felt out here in the tribal lands. We eventually arrived back at Agha Manzil and found the washing machine only purchased a few hours ago was already installed up in the servants quarters on the roof and ready for action, Dad showing the housemaid how to use it, quite a task but he got there in the end.

CHAPTER 8

Time to Leave

OVER THE SIX months or so we were in Pakistan, there were many such adventures my brother and I took, such as spending several days with the uncle we first met on our arrival in this country at the border with Afghanistan. He was the officer in charge of the Khyber Rifles, a very privileged position to hold and one that was held in high regard by his peers in army circles. We stopped a few days in the Khyber Fort at Landi Kotal, sleeping in the officer's quarters and eating with the regiment of the Khyber Rifles. We went out on patrol checking the lorries at the border crossing, then going out on foot patrol for a whole day high up in the Khyber mountains. It was as if you were on top of the world seeing some wonderful views of the Hindu Kush and the Himalayan foothills rising up to their snow-capped peaks, off in the distance the peak of K2, the second highest mountain in the world.

It would get quite cold at times from the swirling wind while following the border with Afghanistan, stopping and sharing lunch with a goat herder. He then showing us a recent kill of one of his animals from the night before. Thought to be by a snow leopard, now nowhere to be seen as it blended back nicely into the landscape of these mountains.

Another episode, if you would like to call it that, happened when we went out for the evening with our Uncle Sajard. He was head of narcotics for the whole of the northern part of Pakistan, other than the tribal lands, and again a very influential man, so much so that any sort of drug movement, of which I can tell you there are a lot in that part of the world,

Entrance to the Khyber Pass

The Khyber Rifles Fort

had to be authorised by him whether it was legal or illegal, and you could guess the benefits of that job.

Dad, Alexander and I went out with his family to a show in Peshawar, held in a very large and long tent at least four times bigger than the tent the circus would bring to Northampton. I'm not quite sure what the event was for other, than it entailed lots of dancing and music, although that was not the thing that stuck in my mind, but what followed did. There were about ten of us in total arriving in three cars surrounded by a lot of security just as the show was about to start, the doorways and surrounding areas to the event were crammed with people who could not get in, or even afford to get in. A path was cleared for our passage — something similar to the parting of the Red Sea that our rector told us about back at my school on a Friday morning, (See, I did take some of it in!) but still hard to believe.

As we eventually entered this place it was crammed full with people, most standing to try and get the best vantage point they could, we on the other hand were shown straight to the front of this large mass of people by the organisers of this event. The police moving ten well dressed and prominent people from their seats right in the middle of the front row, so to accommodate our entourage. The look on their faces, not entirely impressed, as we now moved onto their nicely warmed seats, a tray of drinks along with snacks immediately brought forward for our comfort and, as one would say, 'let the show begin'.

Alexander and I, as mentioned before, often went out with Zia and Zaka on the back of their scooters which was fun and exhilarating, but Pakistan was in a bit of turmoil at this particular time. On a couple of occasions, we headed out to very large political rallies. I am not sure of the exact month when these trips occurred it could have been either in 1971 or 1972, but these rallies were on behalf of the Pakistan People's Party, known as the P.P.P. One was in Peshawar near to the university, which I then thought at the time, was a very

Bhutto rally in Peshawar 1971/1972

*My Uncle the president Yahya Khan, with Khanan Khan,
Dad's eldest brother in Agha Manzil*

large crowd much larger than the football match that I had watched, the one George Best took part in, at Northampton.

Following that we went to another rally in a park in Rawalpindi where the leader of this party Zulfikar Ali Bhutto was due to speak, well we left in the morning and didn't return back until late at night, myself totally exhausted from the day's events. After having been carried aloft by Zia for what seemed like ages, as we made our way along with what was reported as nearly a million people from all walks of life who tried to attend that day, and with what I could see from my elevated position, I couldn't really argue with that.

We got into the park and from my vantage point on Zia's shoulders I could clearly see, and at the time, a direct opponent to my uncle the man all these people had come far and wide to see. Not knowing or understanding a single word he was uttering, but like any good politician the way he whipped up that crowd he must have been saying all the right things they wanted to hear. I had never, before or since, seen so many people in one place for one cause.

Now, due to losing the war with India, our uncle President Yahya Khan was placed under house arrest whilst being investigated, and the man I had seen in that park in Rawalpindi and in Peshawar had now become the new president.

Pakistan started a transition from one of military rule to one run by the Pakistani Peoples party and this made our Dad conclude that now was the time to leave.

Torn

I know for a fact because she told me, that sometime after our mother had passed away Dad had phoned Grandma Blaney and promised her, 'I'm bringing the boys home'. He wanted Alexander and I to be brought up and schooled in the western world away from all the poverty and corruption that surrounded us here. What I cannot say is true, but I have had many a thought on the issue and still do as I write this, is the fact that Mum and Dad loved each other intensely, so much so that they were willing to follow each other across the world. It takes a special relationship to do that, and so the day my brother and I sat below that window telling our mother the story about the tank factory so she could hear our voices once more, I believe that Mum knew then she would not pull through her illness, making our father promise to take the boys home back to England.

A lot had happened to our little family from number 18, Springfield, Wootton in the last six months or so, some good things, some things you would never think would happen in your lifetime or anybody else's for that matter, and obviously some sad things, but I would say that's what life is all about — nobody said it would be easy. So considering the tragic event that unfortunately befell us while we were away, and the fact that our family was one of the most influential families in the Punjab at that time, you would imagine that when it was decided it was time to leave we would just go to the nearest International airport and board a plane for a flight to London (Well you know what's coming next!).

Not this family and not my Dad, and don't forget the little saffron yellow Triumph Vitesse in all of this! Yes, you guessed it, bringing the boys home in Dad's eyes meant we were to drive all the way back to England. Why I hear you cry, 'that makes no sense', 'because he could', he would reply, and that's the man he was, and I would say he would do it every time given the choice, knowing now what I know about my Dad — and you will think the same as you read on.

It must have been hard for my father, torn between the promise he made to Gran and more than likely our mother, and the thought of leaving his family here in his homeland for the second time in his life not knowing when he would see them again, if at all. Although he did not have his parents around, you could tell that the lost years mainly due to religion from his brothers and sister must have been a big draw to him, but delaying the process of leaving would have made the task a lot harder, and a promise is a promise.

Losing a Family

It was now late March, time for us to pop back out of this extraordinary bubble we had decided to enter approximately six months previously, and now that spring was upon us, the winter snows that would have fallen on our route back to England would have receded well enough to give us a clear run on our journey home.

Car all packed along with a few extra goodies, mostly food given to me by the cook, Dad wanted to slip away quietly, which was quite understandable, but we had no chance of that given how close the family were and how they all had taken us in without any concerns whatsoever during our time out here. So, as usual a large, and what can only be described as an elaborate banquet, was laid on in the courtyard of Agha Manzil, my father's childhood home, the one he was brought up in then left for England as a young man, only to return many years later with his wife and children with great expectations, only to see her pass away in front of his eyes in a bedroom only feet from where we are now standing. What must his memories have been of his old family house, which memories would he want to remember, if any — you really couldn't say or begin to wonder, could you?

Our family and friends came from everywhere to say their goodbyes arriving at different times throughout the morning and beyond. I was kissed and cuddled to the point of exhaustion from all the aunties, uncles and cousins that preyed upon me that day, but at the same time felt very sad

Agha Manzil, our leaving banquet

in leaving them all behind, especially the ones that in my eyes I had a unique bond with and had showed me plenty of kindness and affection over the time I had spent with them, not knowing if I would ever see them again in my lifetime.

My Dad's brother's children; Rukhsana, Irfana, and Imrana from Agha Manzil, along with Zia, Zaka, and Sabath, Annie and Nanni from Islamabad and Dad's sister's children the girls Raza, Shakeela, and Saira and the two boys Hashim and Qasim, all had a special place in my heart in that period.

To me it seemed as if I was losing a family as well, because at that age they had been a real influence on me. This day, which was our day of leaving, just kept gathering pace well into the afternoon as more people came to say farewell, Dad's school friends, local shopkeepers, everyone you could think of who we had been in contact with in one way or another. Unfortunately not my uncle Agha Muhammad Yahya Khan who had really instigated this epic episode of ours two years ago in London, but now he was no longer the president of the country and was under house arrest in Rawalpindi, put there by his friend the new president of Pakistan Zulfikar Ali Bhutto. So due to reasons beyond our control he could not attend this momentous day for the Agha family.

It takes around four and a half hours to our first stop, Kabul in Afghanistan after we have crossed the border and two hours to the border from Peshawar with a good wind, so I think Dad agreed sometime in the early afternoon that he would postpone our eventual departure until the next morning.

That changed this banquet into an all-day feast of eating, drinking and dancing which lasted well into the night and just added to the enjoyment for everybody, and the most important ingredients of all — laughter, instead of the sad and teary occasion it might well have turned out to be.

Recollecting

Alexander and I were up early the next day along with Dad, Agha Manzil was still recovering from the events of yesterday and last night with a lot of family members staying over in one of the many rooms. We on the other hand had a very important place to go, not the journey home as you may be thinking, although that would definitely happen today, but to a place we all visit when we are in the city of Peshawar, a place not to be forgotten, a place for reflection and contemplation. A place I wish I could visit while I write these words. That place of course was my mother's grave.

As the sun began to climb into the morning sky over the shadowy buildings of the city, it also had just started to shed its light upon the white marble of her grave where she lay. I myself was perched carefully beside her on the raised smooth coping stone, still cold to the touch from the night's air, while waiting for the sun to shed its warmth on the smooth marble plinth, as it rapped itself round her grave like a walled city to keep her safe. Soon we would not be here to look after her and for me not even since, being able to sit beside her once more, they say once lost is lost forever but I do hope not, as time starts to take effect. Trying to recollect the laughter and joy she brought to my life with her presence which begins to fade over the many years that have past, perhaps a visit in the future may reignite them for me. Eventually and most reluctantly, Dad told us to say our last goodbyes, and to this day I cannot remember what I said in those last moments, one can only wonder.

I only have the picture of her grave etched in my mind as I looked back before disappearing through the arched gate of this place, a gate I wished I had never ever seen, a gate which leads either to a place of sorrow or leads you away from the ones you have loved.

Mum and Dad 1971

Alexander Agha 1971

Jason Agha 1971

My father`s side of the family

My grandfather, Dad's father

My grandmother, Dad's mother

My great grandfather

My great great grandfather

My great grandfather with his four sons,
my grandfather second from the left

My great great great great
grandfather with his son

Dad with his sister 1947

Dads sister

*Uncle Arbid, Dad's
sister's husband*

*Uncle Hyat, otherwise known as Yul Brunner.
He gave me a train for my birthday*

Uncle Sajard, the head of narcotics with girls of the family in Agha Manzil 1972 the day before we left

Uncle Agha Mohammed Yaya Khan, who made this epic trip possible, shown here with Richard Nixon, the President of the United States of America, 1971

JASON AGHA

Peshawar City 1971/1972

Train leaving Peshawar

CHAPTER 9

Homeward-Bound

OUR SECOND ATTEMPT at leaving and this time we were more successful, Dad finally saying goodbye to his sister, both with tears in their eyes. The women of the family gathering outside on the steps in front of that old wooden door of Agha Manzil that we first saw six months previously, each vying for a better position, the cook pushing more food parcels into my hand as I climbed into the back of the car.

I was now to sit alone, Alexander had moved to the front of the car to sit alongside Dad, then as we pulled away I looked back through the rear window to see an array of the most wonderful people you could have wished to meet disappear from my view giving themselves up to the chaotic streets of what was Peshawar.

We were not alone by any means as we finally left Peshawar, only the women of the family were left back in the city, no doubt upset about us leaving, but leaving we were — in quite some style I can tell you. An armed convoy by the Khyber Rifles now led the procession of family vehicles all the way out of the city heading for the Khyber Pass. There must have been at least twenty of us going at full tilt; lights on, horns sounding, it was like the Munchkins following Dorothy to the end of Munchkinland and waving her goodbye, although at the end of this procession, which took over two hours was the Afghan border, not in any way the land of Oz!

We said our goodbyes to all the men of the family, who had ventured out to see us off from Peshawar, Dad saying his final farewells to his brothers, again with a heavy heart, then as if on cue the border barrier lifted and our little saffron yellow Triumph Vitesse headed off out of this strange world for me and my brother, not on some fancy yellow brick road but just a dusty windswept one heading for the city of Kabul.

Kabul reached in less than four hours, as Dad used most of the power from the two litre engine that was packed under the bonnet of our Triumph to propel us forward, leaving most of the local transport flailing in a cloud of dust as we zipped on past. Dad eventually finding us the same hotel that we had stayed in on the outward journey in this sprawling mass that was Kabul. It was now about five o'clock and after having something to eat close to the hotel, Dad said we should all go to bed and get some sleep, so that we could get an early start in the morning. I think this was more for Dad's benefit, not only having a difficult day leaving his family behind but then having the evening without adult company and knowing he would have a full day driving in front of him tomorrow, a theme that would repeat itself until our final destination was achieved. Awoken by Dad, who had left Alexander and me to sleep for as long as we could, he had packed the roof rack of the car on his own, so we were soon heading out of Kabul on the Kandahar road.

The morning light just starting to appear as we cleared the city boundary, me falling asleep once more as the endless sight of the sandy wilderness rolled past the window, only to be awoken by the usual fee-paying checkpoint stopping the car's motion along with it's constant humming, that had aided my relaxed state.

The journey back appeared to be less exciting although just as dangerous, maybe the atmosphere in the car was different now, the reason could have been that I was sitting alone in the back of the car, or the fact that we had been here and done that. It may be that I had just grown up and realised you take what life throws at you, and it had thrown a lot at me in the past few months. So just make the most of it and deal with whatever happens when it happens, that is one lesson I still carry with me today.

Travelling in the opposite direction has its advantages, with the sun rising behind us in the morning, allowing Dad to increase the car's speed at every opportunity as his view was not impeded by the sun's glare through a murky windscreen. With familiar sites beginning to appear on the horizon, like the strange eight-sided towers near Ghanzi, progress became swift.

Lunch was taken while we travelled, tucking into an array of goodies that the cook had managed to smuggle on board, not only through me, but we all laughed when we found out she had done the same trick to Dad and Alexander. Naan bread stuffed with mince and homemade pakora washed down with bottles of water were consumed between more paying checkpoints.

Kandahar loomed into view at the end of a hot and dusty afternoon, our little Triumph doing wonderfully in those conditions and was ready for a night's rest, along with it's occupants. Kandahar had not changed one bit, still a vibrant market town going about its daily business oblivious to our arrival. Again re-visiting the same hotel for the night, not that you had endless choices of four-star accommodation here in Kandahar, they may have had the sand but the sea was, well, not within any kind of walking distance I can tell you. As you can imagine the hotel didn't supply any evening entertainment unless you wanted to look at the scabby dog as it stretched itself across the entrance, not a pretty sight as it displayed its undercarriage to all and sundry, not surprisingly spicy lamb meat balls were declined for dinner as grilled chicken suggested a better option.

After dinner the usual sight of foreign hippies lounging around the hotel, the smoke and smell of hashish clinging to you like only it can from their constant use of it. Straight to our rooms for a hot welcoming shower, to clean away that

The hippies in our hotel, Kandahar

disinctive smell and the dusty grime from every crevice, before putting our heads down on a pillow for a good night's sleep.

Up early once more before the sun rose, this time for the nine hours plus drive to Herat in the west of Afghanistan, Dad managing to get some fried eggs and bread along with fresh milk to eat before leaving. Diana Ross and The Supremes making their presence heard as we trundled along the streets towards the Herat road. After about two hours we reached our first checkpoint since leaving Kandahar province and entering the province of Helmand. Alexander studying the maps our mother had used months earlier, pointing out where she had marked the checkpoints on the map along with the desert of death that we would be crossing within the next two hours, 'hopefully it won't be so hot this time', I thought — as you guessed I thought wrong.

Reaching Gereshk Dad decided to top up the car with petrol knowing what lay ahead, stopping at a roadside stall on the main street and purchasing several bottles of petrol from a young local Afghan entrepreneur. Dad emptied the bottles into the car eventually returning all the bottles to the young man, I don't think Dad got a penny for the returns like we did in our village every fortnight from the Corona man. (Ahh Cherryade and the guarantee of a red tongue). As we headed out of Gereshk on the two hour journey across the desert of death to Delaram, the sun was getting higher and higher in the hazy blue sky, while the wind whipped up small dust clouds at a moment's notice like small tornadoes, only to disappear just as quickly. The inside of the car was now getting hotter and hotter and beginning to feel like cook's bread oven back in Peshawar, Diana Ross struggling along with The Supremes to make any sense of *Stop in the Name of Love*, until they did stop, as the cassette player in the dashboard started to push the thin brown tape from its tiny mouth, sending it cascading towards the floor. Alexander just about managed to eject it before it destroyed itself, which as far as I was concerned wouldn't have been a bad thing! They had decided to split up last year anyway, and for the next thirty minutes Alexander got them back together again, it gave him something to do rather than look out of the window at completely nothing as we crossed this barren land. He had eventually managed to untangle the tape then wind it back up by putting a pen through the middle of the cassette — oh lucky us! On reaching the checkpoint of Delaram we had successfully negotiated the desert of death for the second time, Dad deciding to celebrate this achievement by buying us all a Coke in the town of Delaram while we tucked into the last of the food that cook had smuggled onboard. Fully nourished we started the last part of the journey to Herat paying another fee soon after we left the town and now that Diana Ross was taking a break from the heat, lucky her! We amused ourselves by pointing out old rundown mud buildings along the way, and suggesting that they were the Afghan embassy, the winner

The city of Herat

of this game spotting the best rundown place before Herat. I cannot remember the outcome but it passed the endless hours before we reached our destination, no built-in DVD system in the headrests back in those days, you just had to make your own entertainment the best you could.

Herat came into view, its mud citadel sitting proudly above the town as the last rays of the days sun shone across its worn-out walls all of us declaring it as an Afghan embassy in our little game. Dad filled the car up again with petrol on the edge of this oasis in this hot and dusty land, and then bought some cooked chicken and fresh bread along with several bottles of water.

We again headed for the hotel we used the last time we were here, Dad remembering there was no food available, hence the supplies so we could eat in our room before settling down for another early night. Dad must have been quite exhausted by now although he did not show it, that was a hard and tedious nine-and-a-half-hour drive for him in our little car with no air conditioning. It was now the morning after the third night stopping in Afghanistan and hopefully by the end of this day we would be firmly in Iran.

Dad had his sights set on the city of Mashhad to stop for the night, a place we visited on the way but not rested at, this was because according to Mum's notes on the map, past that point there were not many towns or even hotels that we could stop at for the distance we wanted to cover in a day. Also, not knowing how long it would take to clear the border between the two countries of Afghanistan and Iran, going on the previous events that had occurred at this crossing last time. After leaving Herat the old minarets that we saw on our outward trip came into view, standing very proud and clear as the morning sun shone upon them, one of the five still leaning far too much for my liking as we passed beneath it, probably today there are now only four standing, going on what I had seen all those years ago. As we approached the border around eleven o'clock there were many trucks parked at the side of the road, their drivers checking their loads ready for the crossing.

Then suddenly, the traffic which was travelling in our direction came to a halt, this must have been more than two miles from the actual border and the queue was moving very slowly. The traffic coming in the opposite direction was very sporadic, lorries with goods bound for Kabul and beyond most likely for the black market, mixed in with the usual hippy van that had successfully negotiated the Afghan customs. We sat for over two hours Dad getting a well-earned forty winks between Alexander telling him to move forward when needed, myself just huddled down in the back taking a sip of water every so often as time stood still. Dad being fully awake now got very frustrated at the length of time it was taking to reach the crossing. It was then he decided to break ranks and drive our little saffron yellow Triumph Vitesse down the middle of the road, not so camouflaged now I thought, Alexander pleading constantly with Dad not to do so knowing what lay ahead at the border. As we passed by the line of static vehicles a few European travellers in the queue giving us some strange looks as we sped on by, some of the lorries sounded their horns in anger, Dad was more concerned that he missed the traffic that was coming the other way, I found it quite exciting given that I had been sitting in the back of the car for the last two hours twiddling my thumbs in silence. We made our final approach to the border, Afghan guards with guns on all sides of us as the car rolled steadily forward after Dad had slipped it into neutral, time seemingly going into that slow motion mode again as I peered at these armed men through the dusty windows, the looks on their faces was one of utter bewilderment. Finally, a guard stepped out in front of us and with hand gestures told us to stop and go back, Alexander still insisting to Dad to turn round as plan 'A' had just failed. Enter plan 'B', handbrake on, engine off, Dad got out of the car and walked forward towards the guard, he in turn immediately raising his gun at Dad, finger on the trigger while people in the queue looked on. Not at all sure what Dad was saying but as he walked, he was continuously talking to the guard, Alexander and I wondering if we were to lose our second parent to another tragedy, in a matter of months.

Dad having reached the guard in the middle of the road, myself now perched between the two front seats and along with Alexander looked intensely out through the dirty windscreen, only to see this guard shake Dad's hand and beckon him to fetch the car forward.

On Dad's return to the car Alexander bombarded him with an array of questions which Dad said he would explain later, as he proceeded to start the car and we moved forward under the first barrier only to be stopped in what was a very recognisable place. This place was where I had stood with my mother clutching her hand as she shook with fear some six months previously, and as I stepped out from the back of the car a very familiar and noticeable face came into view. It was Amir the same man in charge, his very distinguished and memorable moustache even more prominent now than I had remembered. Alexander and I said, 'hello' before shaking his hand then promptly got back into the car, Dad having a few words with Amir before returning to the car. All barriers lifted as we headed onward without further ado towards the Iranian customs, a check of our passports was all that was needed, and we were released as quickly as we had arrived.

Once clear and on a good road, well any road is good compared to Afghanistan's roads, Alexander quizzed Dad about what he did back at the border and told him he could have got himself shot, then where would that leave us. Dad explained he was never in any trouble he just wanted to get some extra sleep in the queue before travelling to meet Amir at the border crossing. This was something that he had arranged and paid extra to Amir on our outward journey, he just didn't think to tell us, which would have been a good idea wouldn't you think. What if Amir did not work there any more what then?

Mashhad reached after about another three hours of travelling, having stopped in one of the small towns for some petrol and some welcome food and drink. We found a hotel not too far into this city, other European travellers appear to be stopping here as well, the gold dome and towers of the famous holy shrine we had visited previously was the view from our first floor window, in fact I think you would see this epic site from almost any window in this city. We ventured out not to far from the hotel for some food, this place although a Muslim country had a completely different feel to the towns and cities we had left behind in Afghanistan and Pakistan, so westernised and upbeat, lots of people dressed in jeans and t-shirts, almost gone was the traditional Muslim attire.

Chicken kebabs, nan bread and Coke eaten while watching the world go by then heading back for a good night's sleep.

Another early start, Dad wanting to cover as much distance as possible, as we headed westward and home.

Now, Dad's idea of an early start was usually just as the sun popped its head above the eastern horizon, but this morning it felt like I hadn't even gone to bed. No sooner had I fallen asleep I was being shaken by Dad to get up and get dressed, my eyes still being pulled together by the sleepy dust attached to each of them, myself finding it hard to resist the inevitable as my body just wanted to go back to sleep. Very dark outside, the small bedroom lamp on the table gave very little assistance to the task in hand but somehow I managed to get dressed and find the comfort of the back seat of the car, my head resting on my all too familiar pillow, as I drifted back off to sleep once more.

I don't know how long I was asleep, the smooth tarmac roads of Iran allowing me more time than usual to rest and eventually waking to the rumble of my stomach as it shouts for it's breakfast. A short drive further on Dad stopped the car in a small village, all of us got out to stretch our legs with the intention of having a bite to eat at the only type of restaurant visible. After three glasses of *chai* were ordered, Dad was trying to get some eggs and nan for us, but no matter what language he tried it just wasn't getting through to the owner of this place. This then prompted Dad to go into the kitchen to see if he could find anything that resembled what he was trying to describe, having no luck and now attracting a small audience he spotted some ducks across the road and in his best but unsuccessful sign language, like some strange game of charades, again tried to explain what we wanted, the owner of this place just pointing to his watch with a look of total bewilderment on his face. I swear you could make some sort of TV show out of what started to be quite funny, although my tummy didn't think so, from the noise it was now making.

With the conversation now in deadlock, Dad made the decision to move on, we were just about to get back into the car, when a young boy with tray in hand produced three glasses of *chai*. Dad said, 'no *chai*' and proceeded to get into the car, Alexander waiting for me with the front seat up, so I could clamber into the back, but as I passed this boy with the tray held aloft a round about my head height, I reached out and grabbed the sugar lumps that were conveniently on offer and immediately popped them into my mouth for a source of sustenance, well that's what I tell myself today! But the look on most of the people there, including the boy, was the look of that cheeky little rascal or words to that effect, words that I would not have possibly known at that age.

Back on the road and with The Seekers playing their repertoire from the now rested tape deck, more ground was covered at an even greater speed. Reaching the town of Shahroud for a mid-morning brunch of lamb, eggs and bread with *chai*, my stomach treating it as more of a banquet considering it had to wait so long, but well full by the time we had left.

Dad decided to change route at Damghan to miss the capital city Tehran, and all the hustle and bustle that it brings with it. This confirmed to Alexander and I that flying back home was never an option, as Tehran and its modern international airport would have been the ideal place to fly to London and home.

So instead we headed north into uncharted territory and away from Mum's original notes that she had made on the map, up into the lush green mountains the road being just as good quality, not slowing our progress at all, apart from the odd strain of a few steep inclines that were forced upon our over-laden Triumph Vitesse. The views looking out over the Caspian Sea from upon high were breath-taking to say

The shores of the Caspian Sea, Dad and me relaxing

the least and will stick long and hard in one's memory, Dad eventually stopping in the small town of Chalus, for the night and a well-deserved rest after being cooped up in our little car for well over twelve hours. Before finding the only hotel in the town we stopped off along the shore of the Caspian Sea, so we all could take a dip in the cool water in the late afternoon sun, Alexander and myself stripping down to our underpants so we could have a good swim. Now who could have predicted that the detour in Iran that Dad decided to take back in 1972, would lead us to an overnight stop in this small town of Chalus on the shores of the Caspian Sea?

And what are the odds that forty-six years later, I would decide to write this book telling our family's story from a desk just outside the town of Chalus in France, where's a bookie when you need one? Life can be strange as well as cruel, so just make the best of it — I know I do. The hotel wasn't too bad although we all had to sleep in the same room. Food was about the usual, chicken kebabs and more nan bread but it was good enough. Dad explained we needed again to have an early night ahead of another twelve hour trip if we were to reach our next target city of Trabriz, not that I needed much encouragement. After a swim and a meal I was out for the count anyway.

Up early as you might have guessed, all of us helping to load the car again before the sun rose, then heading inland away from the Caspian Sea, a detour which I think did us all good, like a mini break you might say, but given the choice I think I would have preferred to be in Great Yarmouth with the whole family. It was about four hours into our journey when Alexander announced that when we reach the town of Karaj we would be back on the original road set out on Mum's map.

With the roads being as good as any in Europe, apart from the autobahns in Germany, the twelve hours plus trip to Tabriz didn't appear to take as long as the same length of journey a few days previously. Just a doddle really with nothing much happening, then you wouldn't expect it in this much westernised and more civilised society, food stop in the middle of the day and Tabriz coming into sight early evening with the sun going down. Dad booked us into the same hotel in this small town but unlike last time where two rooms were required, only one large room with three beds was needed. Although spring was here and summer just around the corner there was a good chill to the air as we stepped out into the well-lit streets for something to eat. That something was grilled lamb with rice and peas and a nice change from chicken and nan bread. As the night got colder and remembering the air conditioning in the hotel that could heat a room as well as cool one, it was very welcoming as I snuggled down in bed before the lights went out.

Up after the sun had risen, which was a nice relief after the early mornings and long drives that we all had endured for the last couple of days.

Breakfast was a cold meat sandwich and a glass of milk, eaten in the street as we packed the roof of the car prior to leaving, heading out of Tabriz for the Turkish border, then on from there to Erzurum for our next overnight stop.

Reaching the border and clearing customs on both sides after about four hours of our journey, you may remember that this part of our trip was day eleven on the outward trek, very grey skies, snow falling at will and very misty. Well today was as far away from that bleak day as you could get, and the atmosphere in the car was poles away from what it was then. Very blue and clear skies as we headed for Agri, the beautiful site of which you could not fail to notice in any direction for literally miles and miles, was that of Mount Ararat, very sacred but very humbling as it soared skywards from the plateau which it sat on.

A smaller but just as significant peak trying to follow in it's footsteps to it's left, both covered with snow left as a winter's gift in the heat of a spring day. I say sacred for this is where Noah and his ark came to rest after the floods, so the story of

Mount Ararat, can you see Noah? I didn`t think so!

the Bible tells us. To me a little far-fetched, as the height of what I am now gazing at through the car window as we drive nearby, is so high (16,854ft or 5,137m) that if he did come to rest there at that height, how did the animals breathe in such thin air let alone where did all that water go? This actually substantiates what I was explaining at the beginning of this book, that the Bible was a book of narratives and stories, I think this world would have been a better place without religion, but that's just my opinion, but the facts do speak for themselves — wouldn't you say?

Eventually pulling into Agri, the small town where the good hearted Iranian lorry driver and us had parted company, I wish I knew his name, if only for the reason to write it in this book, but I hope that the world gave him all he had wished for. Filling up with fuel for the car, along with fuel for us in the form of chicken kebabs we headed out of Agri, no slush or snow, no grinding of snow chains or windscreen wipers today.

This day seemed so benign as we climbed past the location of our ordeal a few months earlier, all of us pondering quietly

Gravel road and a drop to who knows where?

to ourselves what might have been, stopping to take a picture of where our car perched itself over the precipice, as some sort of memento, I just glad we could although one of us was lost.

We continued our journey home, Erzurum reached as the cool air of the evening started to replace the heat from that afternoon, Dad finding the same hotel we had used previously, all of us going through the usual routine of offloading the roof rack as though it was some military excise, each man doing his job, or in my case, trying to carry the smallest things I could! Hey, they do say every little helps!

Evening meal was the usual choice of chicken, chicken or chicken taken in a small restaurant near the hotel, Dad telling us that we will be heading for the Black Sea tomorrow, back on the same diversion that we took last time, not risking saving time via the direct route across the centre of Turkey, due to the ultimate dangers that it might pose. At which point I thought what a good choice, I did not want this to be my last supper, not chicken anyway as I recall the memory of those four poor Germans in my head.

Up before the sun fully raised itself above the Kose mountain range (that's one place you don't want to be hanging around in — literally!), we packed the car before stopping at the same little restaurant for eggs, nan and *chai*, before setting off north for the Black Sea. As we travelled this section of the diversion Alexander was constantly looking at the map, then noticing an alternative way of getting to Ordu, our next predicted overnight stop on the Black sea. This would then cut out the city of Trabzon which our route took us through on our outward journey, this could gain us some vital hours, so we could progress further along the Black Sea coast. Dad double checked this time saving idea but was not sure of the condition of the road on that particular route, but felt it was worth a try, what else is there to do — we are driving anyway and it's not a race? Detour taken and although the road was narrower it was still tarmac, following a small river through high steeped sided gorges — quite a magnificent sight and very different from the plateau of central Turkey, in which Ezurum nestled, appropriately The Supremes now back together singing *River Deep Mountain High* as we progressed.

This time instead of climbing high into the Pontiac mountain range, it was as if we were driving straight through it, carving it open like a hot knife through butter. Mile after mile as the road snaked parallel to the fast-flowing river, both of us heading for the Black Sea, but both of us on a different journey's end.

There was very little traffic going in either direction, mainly small local vehicles and I would say in wintertime this road would be inpassable.

With the Black Sea in view we turned left, leaving the fast flowing river that had kept us company for the last two and a half hours to bundle itself into the mass of water in front of its path, Dad increasing the speed of the car on the wider coastal road leading to Ordu.

We refuelled the car at Ordu, Dad also getting us some crisps and biscuits along with bottles of water to keep us going, as he said we would not be stopping but heading straight to Samsun another three hours along the coast, which was very achievable before the night set in. A good road running flat along the shores of this vast land-locked sea, it's only exit being the straights of the Bosporus, which we would hope to see in another day's time. After two packets of crisps and half a packet of plain biscuits we reached Samsun as the blue waters of the Black Sea started to turn grey from the night sky that was now fast approaching.

This was not a place we had stopped at before, only passed through on the first day of our unexpected diversion, eventually finding a hotel as this fishing port slowly lights itself up against the dark background which now surrounded it. The hotel wasn't too bad, again one room with three beds with the bathroom at the end of the landing but no lock on the door, all having a shower with one of us standing outside on guard, while we took it in turn to clean ourselves. All refreshed we stepped outside, embracing the cool night air that swept off the sea with much delight after being cooped up in the car all day. It was the closest we had been to air conditioning since Tabriz in Iran, but we used it then to give us some welcoming heat from the chill of the night in our hotel room. We found a street seller not far from the hotel serving food, yes you guessed right! Chicken, nan and Coke which we took and sat on a sea wall in front of the hotel, staring into the black mass in front of us; the small light of what we presumed was a ship twinkling way out on the horizon like a star that had dropped to earth.

It was quite late for us, around ten o'clock when we all lay our heads on our pillows, Dad telling us that we needed to be up early so we could reach Istanbul and cross the Bosporus before nightfall, so back onto those twelve hour days tomorrow, what fun I thought as my eyes started to close.

Up before light, my body going through the motions as if on autopilot, my head not really awake at all, and as I rested it softly on the pillow in the back seat of the car, the rest of me gave into the inevitable as I drifted off to who knows where.

I awoke to the sound of Alexander calling my name as he prodded me profusely two hours later, the car now parked in the town of Mirzifon. Dad had left us in the car in search of finding us something to eat, when all of a sudden I was slightly startled by a young face pressed hard up against the window, eagerly trying to look inside as though it was a shop full of sweeties. This young but well-rounded face belonged to a small boy dressed in traditional clothes topped with a colourful round cap. I can assure him there were no sweeties in here, just the smell of days of sweat, as he was pulled away quite sharply by the hand of his mother, small bag on his back presumably on his way to school. As I watched them walk away happy in their own little world it reminded me of when Mum used to take me to school, then wondering who would take me now. As Alexander and I watched the world go by from our little capsule the door suddenly opened to the unique smell of fresh bread. Dad climbed aboard then handed out what was to be our breakfast of cold lamb but warm bread; this was devoured very rapidly by all.

Heading swiftly out of Mirzifon we were now travelling straight on to Istanbul, completely missing out Turkey's capital city Ankara, which we had passed through on our journey outward, we were now heading across the top of Turkey instead of the unpredictable middle of this country. Although this story is about my family and writing it down on paper for it not to be forgotten, one must not forget how well our mode of transport in all of this has done.

Little did the Triumph factory back in England know that when this car came off the production line it would travel half way across the world and back, its two-litre engine purring across Turkey now for the second time, never missing a beat at all, not one. It has had no faults, other than the washer bottle for the windscreen running out of water, and the cassette player, not quite good enough to shut Diana Ross and The Supremes up completely. Not a single puncture, it's been running on the same four tyres throughout it's adventure, coping with extreme weather conditions on different road surfaces, when you think about it — what a car! I think it would have won the Monte Carlo Rally if it had been entered, Dad driving of course, Mum navigating (but not the usual navigator's jargon of, 'Forty, left five minus over crest opens over 40, tightens, right over big jump') no, more like 200 miles to next town and will we reach it by nightfall. I'd say was just as exciting, wouldn't you?

After several hours of what you would call easy driving considering the above paragraph and what this car has had to endure, with Diana Ross now exchanging places with The Seekers again, we were edging closer to the city of Istanbul. The roads improving even more, the volume of traffic increasing as the Sea of Marmara flanked our left side glistening in the sun as though it was a sheet of glass.

For no apparent reason that we could see, the traffic came to a sudden halt, Alexander then realising that there wasn't any traffic coming in the opposite direction, as a large black plume of smoke appeared from beyond the next rise, I myself commenting out loud, I hope this is not another war! (been there, done that). It was late afternoon as we sat motionless in the queue of traffic, Dad constantly looking at his watch, pointing out that we would not be able to cross the Bosporus by tonight if we are delayed any longer, thus making it more difficult to find a hotel. The plume of smoke had long disappeared when what seemed like *déjà vu* to us, our little Triumph Vitesse stepped out of line once more as Dad did his same old trick and headed down the wrong side of the road, not too fast as people from the other vehicles were scattered randomly along this route, each one giving us some extraordinary looks as we passed. Reaching the brow of the hill we now could see what had been causing our delay, two or maybe three large vehicles smouldering away in the evening light, Dad still continuing to project us forward to what appeared to be the front of this queue, a melée of people now blocking our progress as Dad sounded his horn to the surprise of the onlookers. This action somehow managed to part the crowd that stood in our way, each individual turning and stepping back as if this little saffron yellow Triumph Vitesse was a part of International Rescue from the well-known television series *Thunderbirds*, an important vehicle sent to deal with the situation that lay only a few yards beyond this human wall, which closed rapidly behind us as we progressed through it.

We were no such thing, which became very clear to the policeman that stood beyond this wall of people and stopped us in our tracks without delay.

So here we were stuck in no-man's land as you might say, unable to go back, completely on the wrong side of the road, and with this heap of smouldering metal blocking our path. It was now more than likely that we would not even reach Istanbul, let alone cross the Bosporus by nightfall.

Well, just like I had seen back in the film studio in London, it was like someone had been waiting for us to appear before shouting 'Action' as a large bulldozer that was hooked up to the first vehicle, which we could make out to be a petrol tanker of some kind, started to drag it to one side revealing the second vehicle beyond. The air was full of a smell the likes of which I had never smelt before, and would never wish to smell again, very pungent very distinctive, very unusual shall we say. The second vehicle that had now been revealed and was clearly the shell of a bus, just as black and charred as the petrol tanker, making you wonder who, if anyone, was in it. Because the road was quite narrow at this point, which may have been a factor in this terrible accident, our manoeuvre earlier had placed us in the position that if any traffic was to come from the opposite direction it could not go any further as the road was now blocked by us. This was realised by the police, therefore they motioned us to go through immediately after a route was cleared, result I thought — plan 'A' worked, as Dad moved the car slowly under the policeman's instructions.

As we passed the bus the heat from its side panels could be felt through the glass of the car's windows, which were shut due to the smell that continuously lingered in the air. As we passed the end of the bus and only a few feet away was a sight that the smell then gave away its origin, a sight I can still see today. Twenty, maybe more, bodies lined the side of the road, not distinguishable, be it man, woman or child, just completely blackened, white clumps of fat still bubbling away on each one, as though they were pieces of meat strung out on a late afternoon barbecue, you tried not to look but the smell drew you to stare in disbelief. Dad tried to accelerate as quickly as he could but the circumstances would not allow the car to move beyond a slow crawl, due to the fact that another crowd had gathered on this side of the accident watching every move as it unfolded. While the police moved the crowd back to aid our progress the car literally halted alongside the last few bodies, giving me an even clearer view of this tragedy, while the heat and the smell was one thing to take in, the image of the last bodies so fused together, you would have had great difficulty to clarify what they actually were, this sight is etched in the back of my mind even today.

The car moved forward through the crowd, again immediately closing behind us as before, thus shutting out the horrible sight that had projected itself into our eyes and minds forever. As soon he could, Dad picked up speed as we passed the queue of traffic that had been halted on this side of the accident and with windows down and the fan blower on full tilt, we tried to clear the very distinguishable smell from the car. It took our sensitive noses much longer to clear, in fact all the way to Istanbul, and the warmth of the hotel shower, before it had totally disappeared; although as I said, the memory still lives on today.

The hotel Dad found in this vast metropolis was more of an upmarket establishment for holiday makers of all nationalities, not the usual places we had been used to, not in the slightest.

It was around seven o'clock when we decided to leave and go for something to eat, from what we regarded as our plush rooms, it had a telephone by the bed — would you believe?

The hotel restaurant was closed, and Dad did not want to venture out into the back streets of such a large city, so approached the front desk for advice. He returned with three pieces of paper, thus booking us on a trip with a meal, to view Istanbul's delights. I think he just wanted to erase the sights and sounds of the afternoon from our heads the best he could, I just thought, 'I have just sat in the back of the car for the last twelve hours, do I really want to be sitting in a vehicle for several more? Just give me the posh hotel with a bed'.

Waiting in the lobby for our transport to arrive, more and more people of different nationalities had gathered along with our guide for the night, who then called out the surnames of those going on this trip. Well the uproar when the other parties realised that there were two children on the trip, had the guide really flustered, and his attempts to ease the situation then resulted in him asking Dad if he would leave us at the hotel, while Dad went on his own. Dad said, 'my boys go where I go, and I will not leave them behind, not ever', he also stressed that he has paid good money for this, probably more than the other guests. Having won the argument much to the disgust of many of the others, we went outside to get on our transport, well Dad's idea of erasing this afternoon events went straight out of the window as we queued to get on a bus, really!

Istanbul was buzzing, to say the least, we headed down towards the Bosporus, street sellers of all kinds stood out in the brightly lit streets, side roads closed to traffic as pop-up restaurants with hordes of people sitting down at make shift tables blocked the way. Reaching the Bosporus, we all stepped off the bus much to my relief, the other passengers totally unaware of the thoughts going through my head as we travelled that relatively short distance. The guide then ushered us quickly on to a boat and without delay it started to move away from the shore.

As our craft reached about the middle of the Bosporus it slowed down then began to slowly rotate giving us all a fantastic view of this city by night, all the bright lights shining as one, illuminating Istanbul on both sides of this water divide, the Blue Mosque standing out so prominently as if to stress the importance of this Asian metropolis, again a marvellous sight to behold at such a young age. Heading along the shorefront, the noises that you could hear from the city blended as one, creating its own type of music out on the water, this place was so alive, it's a pity our small Kodak Instamatic could not take a picture because it would have been such a sight to keep, one of the better ones taken on the twenty-four exposure Kodak film. What seemed like ages bobbing about in the dark on the Bosporus along with many other craft, I was feeling quite cold as the boat headed towards the northern shore to dock.

Also by this time, I was getting quite hungry as we again boarded a bus still a little apprehensive, well could you blame me? As it headed off through the streets of Istanbul. We finally came to stop in a side street and looking out of the window expecting to see some sort of nice restaurant that my stomach was now craving, saw only a large wooden door much like the door that adorned Agha Manzil back in Peshawar. As we departed the bus, I could see the first passengers stepping through this now open entrance and disappearing inside. When we reached the door, Dad was stopped and there was some sort of confusion, until our guide sorted it out by passing what I only could presume was money, to two large men smartly dressed in suits at the door. After entering we immediately headed down a large flight of steep stairs, the distinguishable sound of Turkish music rising from below, as we continued on down.

At the bottom it came apparent that we had entered a rather plush nightclub full of tables, a band was playing on a stage to our left as we were shown to a seating area. I now could understand why so many people had objected to us coming on this trip back at the hotel, as Alexander let alone little old me were way too young for this type of place — I wasn't old enough to go to the youth club back in Wootton, — let alone a nightclub in the heart of Istanbul!

Drinks ordered, Coke of course, as much as you liked along with an array of different types of Turkish foods, it just kept coming and I just kept eating.

Well it would have been rude not too, wouldn't it!

Now I did say that I suppose Dad thought it might be a good distraction from today's events to visit all Istanbul could offer, and apart from the slight misjudgement of the bus for transport I would say distraction was a very good description, as throughout this banquet of food and drink, came what was to be the entertainment.

Well imagine two boys one aged fourteen the other ten, deep down in an Istanbul night club in 1972 (The *Kervansaray* night club to be precise). Drink flowing, not alcohol for us mind you, and then we would get these young women, several of them at the last count, traditional Turkish belly dancers literally thrusting themselves right before our very eyes, I am all for tradition if this is it! Alexander's eyes were literally popping out of his glasses, talk about being distracted, the more the girls came our way the more the club appeared to erupt, as though we were part of the entertainment.

I said at the beginning of this journey it was time to grow up, well if this is growing up, in Oliver's words, 'can I have some more please?'

I also mentioned that our Kodak Instamatic was not the best and I don't think in the dark depths of this nightclub that would have changed, but I must say I would have used a whole film of twenty-four to expose some of tonight's sights, being exposed to me, they say what goes on in Istanbul stays in Istanbul.

It was just as well we were on the European side of the Bosporus; I am most certainly sure we would have been stoned to death or at least put in prison if this was on the Asian side. It might be hard to understand two different cultures in the same city but that stretch of water is such a dividing line in so many ways. Although our camera was not up to the job unbeknown to me when we left the club that night to head back to our hotel, Dad was given a photograph by one of the managers saying it was one of the best nights they had in there for a long time, and I wouldn't argue with that one. Dad showed the two of us a photo when we were back at the hotel many hours later, that photograph is still available for viewing to this day and shows the three of us along with one of the many traditional girls enjoying ourselves!

Woken the next day by Dad, around nine, late for us although we had one of those late nights, the car already packed to go, straight after we had grabbed something to eat from the buffet breakfast supplied by this hotel. I wasn't very hungry after gorging myself between private dances of the adult kind, but still managing a drink and some toast, also smuggling out some fruit for the journey that day.

We headed for one of the many ferries that took you back across the Bosporus, a stretch of water I was becoming very accustomed to. The eastern sun now high in the sky searching out every nook and cranny in this vast city, although this metropolis didn't look quite the same by day as it did by night, and you could even say, some of the nooks and crannies that I saw last night never get a chance to see the sun! As we eventually cleared Istanbul and its Turkish delights, (full of eastern promise) my head rested on it's very familiar companion the pillow, and with that late night I soon drifted off to sleep to the hum of the car's engine. My dreams must have been good ones, and I can only guess what I was dreaming about, as I was still in a deep sleep as our little car crossed the border from Turkey to Bulgaria.

We were heading for the capital Sofia, around a four hour drive, our next stop for the night, a city we had not stopped at before, a communist city so don't expect the thrills of Istanbul. There was a petrol shortage on our way out, but things appeared to have gone back to normal, as we made our way from the border to the capital city. I was now awake as our little car hit one of the unavoidable pot holes that appeared on this route, when an almighty crack suddenly worked its way at lightning speed from the right hand side of the windscreen right across to almost the top left, as though it was splitting it in two, Dad stopped to assess the damage saying that a new windscreen was now required. Driving much slower so as not to cause any more damage to the screen or the possibility that it would cave in on Dad and Alexander, Sofia was reached as darkness fell. We found a hotel for the night, very much a downgrade from Istanbul to say the least, but then again, we had been spoilt.

Dad organised some soup and bread for supper, a far cry from that all you could eat banquet of the night before — they say good things don't last.

While Alexander and I got ourselves ready for bed Dad had gone to see if there was anywhere close by to get the windscreen fixed. Returning about an hour later he said that there was a garage at the end of the road that might be able to help in the morning.

Up early, tea and toast for breakfast. We headed out around eight o'clock to find the garage. Yes, it was a car garage but not one that could help our predicament, but Dad got some directions to a place that might be able to help us. Eventually finding this place over an hour later down some dingy back street well off the beaten track our little Triumph Vitesse was presented to two guys, well the look on their faces it was as if we had just landed in an unidentified space craft.

They could see the problem we had but I don't think Triumph sale staff had ever got near this communist country, so a spare windscreen was as rare as hen's teeth. These two guys measured the screen and kept yapping on to one another as though they were designing the car from scratch. They spoke to Dad and in some sort of communication with drawings and hand gestures came up with two solutions. Parked outside was what I know now as a Volkswagen type 3 and one option was to exchange the car taking this back to England, leaving our little saffron yellow Triumph Vitesse in the middle of communist Europe at the hands of two grumpy Bulgarians, after all it has been through, only to be let down by a piece of glass not even made at the Triumph factory. Option one as far as we were all concerned was not an option. This journey was made with a car and four people, we had already lost one of these to an unforeseen tragedy, we were not about to abandon another over the small issue of a windscreen, 'not on your nelly' as they say. This left option two and it was communicated that it could take up to four hours or more to achieve. This radical second option was to use the Volkswagen as a donor car, taking its good windscreen out and putting it into our Triumph, as though it was some type of body part. Old windscreen removed, Dad keeping the tax disc, we left our little car in the hands of these two Bulgarians to hopefully work some magic, while we looked for somewhere to get a drink. After going into a shop and buying some cans of pop we found a pocket park, giving some light relief in the middle of this grey concrete mass of a city, well the part we were looking at any way. I am sure there are some nice parts in this capital city, but for now this park will suffice. As we sat on a bench Dad getting some more shut eye as you might say, some local boys came to play football in the park, this place probably giving them some relief as well. It didn't take long before Alexander and I were kicking that ball alongside those boys, language not required for this universal sport, although they knew who Bobby Charlton was, shouting out his name when they wanted the ball passed to them from my brother or me.

Fame at last, as we spent ages burning off our energy before Dad said it was time to go, shaking hands while saying 'bye' to the boys, they most likely went back and told their parents they had played football with Bobby Charlton today.

Back to see those two grumpy Bulgarians and more importantly our little saffron yellow Triumph, they had indeed done their magic, in fact David Nixon would have been well impressed I can tell you. (A 1970s TV magician) They had somehow moulded the Volkswagen windscreen into the existing rubber seal of the Triumph by cutting the glass to somehow make it fit. The one difference being the new screen was more curved than the original so they had to alter the windscreen wipers, they now only covered part of the screen's area when turned on, not perfect but should be good enough to get us back to England.

Half a day lost although we had all the time in the world, and again it wasn't a race, it was just the journey back, it was Dad bringing his boys home after all, and home we were heading. Leaving Sofia and then hopefully within just over two hours, we would also be leaving Bulgaria and entering our second communist country, Yugoslavia. The border reached and apart from the usual queuing and heavily armed border guards, the crossing between these two countries was fairly easy for us, I don't think we posed a national threat to communism, not in the slightest, mind you we were in the new secret prototype Triumph/Volkswagen, this could have been valuable information, who knows.?

It was quite clear we were not going to reach the capital of Yugoslavia, Zagreb before nightfall, and as we didn't want to risk hitting any more of the large potholes which may cause our makeshift windscreen to pop out, Dad decided to get as far as we could in the remaining daylight, eventually stopping in a place called Slavonski Brod. A very peculiar name I know, just a small town on our route, Dad finding us another hotel, again very basic, but they served a nice lamb chop with potatoes and cabbage, no gravy though.

A good nights sleep had by all, Dad getting us up at around six, bread jam and milky tea for breakfast, then off towards Zagreb only two hours away before the morning light appeared. Not too much happened on this part of the journey not like many of our little escapades we had to endure on previous days, Yugoslavia very pretty in places but also very industrious in others, Zagreb and its surrounding area being one of these.

While The Seekers now blasted out *The Carnival is Over* and *We Shall Not be Moved*, all three of us singing along knowing the words off by heart, well you would too, and all the other songs in their repertoire, along with Miss Ross and those silly Supremes if that's all you had to listen to halfway across the world and back. The border between Yugoslavia and Austria reached by late morning and the queue for non-communist registered vehicles was us and one camper van with German plates; we cleared it within twenty minutes or less, accelerating into the fresh clean air that was Austria.

My favourite looking country I had seen on this trip, snow-capped mountains changing to green slopes, valleys carved out by streams that turn to large rivers, all this along with picturebook houses dotted between quaint villages, very scenic indeed. Although the roads were very winding in places, we still made good progress as the traffic was very light, stopping for a bite to eat before heading towards Salzburg. Not quite reaching the city of Salzburg but gaining more progress by its more up-to-date road system we turned to reach the German border by early evening. The border, although heavily policed, was just a case of slowing down to show our passports through the window and then waved straight on as though we were some sort of VIPs.

So once through the border, Dad pulled in to the first rest area on the main road, a restaurant with a small motel attached to it, this was to be our stop for the night. Car parked and unloaded outside our room we headed for the restaurant. Having spent most of the last eight months in a Muslim based world the pork schnitzel was the thing for me along with chips and a Coke, very nice indeed. While eating our food Dad said we were going to try and reach Ostend in Belgium by tomorrow night then catch the ferry across the channel and home.

This may have seemed quite a trek, but knowing what the roads were like in Germany made it very possible, if we only took small comfort breaks on the way. Food eaten, then while Alexander and I got ready for bed, Dad just nipped to the garage at the front of the motel to fill the car with petrol ready for an early start. Awoken while it was still dark, hands and faced washed, teeth cleaned, clothes on and car re-loaded, off we went onto these very impressive German Autobahns.

Well under two hours later we were going around the outskirts of Munich, the Olympic Stadium standing proud as the morning light started to show it in its full glory reflecting off its magnificent glass roof, many of the cranes that had dominated the skyline only a few months earlier were now reduced to just one as the start date for the 1972 Olympic Games was now only weeks away. After stopping at a service area to collect some sandwiches we continued to head north and reached the outskirts of Nuremberg by late morning. Petrol stop and comfort break after clearing Nuremberg our little saffron yellow Triumph was making great strides across Germany, passing Wurzburg where we stopped the night on the way out and on to Frankfurt another two hours further on. The great thing about how they built these autobahns was they took the route around all the large cities, giving those who wish to a continuous journey, still today they haven't built ring roads around many of the towns back in England.

Another stop for food, petrol and the toilet just after Frankfurt then back on the road for Cologne, myself falling asleep at this stage having eaten and with the constant views of trees out of the window on each side made my eyes eventually shut. Awake now due to the car not moving as the traffic had come to a stop just outside Cologne, the Autobahn appeared to be shut as the traffic was being diverted off.

This had obviously slowed our great progress across this country as we made our way on this diversion route at a slower rate due to the amount of traffic doing the same thing. We came to a type of underpass where the road opened into two lanes, but the traffic slowed even more, and no one was entering this second lane. Dad did his usual for the third time on this trip back home and took our little saffron yellow Triumph Vitesse out of line and down this extra lane, all of us not quite understanding why no one else had done the same. As we began to pass the other vehicles, not at a great pace but still faster than this queue to our right, we could see at the end of this stretch of road a bend and as we continued to pass these cars they started to beep their horns and some of the drivers were waving furiously at us. Dad took this as a form of complaint because we were progressing better than they were, but as we went round the bend, we could all see their reason for trying to stop us from doing what we did.

As the bend started to straighten, tucked out of sight was the German Police or Polizei as it was written across the side of a very nice Porsche 911, perks of the job I guess.

Well they immediately pulled us to one side, the queue now going faster than us, Dad winding down his window as this German policeman in a green uniform approached.

Then Dad tried to explain to him that he does not speak any German, only English, this policeman didn't speak any English, but that did not bother him as he produced a card from his pocket in English and passed it to Dad, we said later perhaps he had one for every country in the world or just those who beat them in the war. For this traffic offence which we had just committed but did not understand why, was to produce our passports and accept a one hundred German Marks fine, Dad doing exactly what it said on the card as the traffic kept moving past us everyone looking in our direction as to say, 'told you so'.

The policemen seemingly enjoyed holding us there to prove a point that queue jumping was going to be a lot slower than actual queuing, either that or he didn't like the English, which you could understand a little, as Cologne was badly bombed in the war with over twenty-thousand civilian casualties.

Eventually letting us back into the traffic after about half an hour, we travelled through the outskirts of this city rejoining the autobahn system some two hours after leaving it and one hundred Marks lighter, heading now to the German border with Holland only an hour away.

It was now about five o'clock in the afternoon as we crossed the border into Holland, eleven hours after leaving this morning by the Austrian border, just showing how fast even back then in a little Triumph Vitesse, how quick you can cross Germany. Stopping for a short break it took us less than one hour to cross this part of Holland into Belgium, the borders open freely to traffic. All you had to do was slow down when passing the control booths, guards watching for anything suspicious, like a little yellow Triumph packed to the gunwales, which had crossed two continents. The last leg now of our journey across Europe as we headed for Brussels then on to Ostend the channel port where we would catch a ferry to England.

Easy driving, not that I was doing any, trouble free should be the description as we reached the port of Ostend by ten o'clock that night, the darkness of the channel appearing beyond the bright lights of the port. There was a ferry due to depart at two in the morning catching the high tide that was available at that time, Dad booking us on the ferry before finding a small café to get some food and drink. Loaded onto the ferry along with all the other vehicles, we headed for the lounges that were provided upstairs for the passengers, taking my pillow and blanket with me so I could rest. We all fell asleep on the seats in the passenger lounge, to the continuous hum of the ferry's engines, Dad earning his more than anyone having driven hard for the last twenty hours.

It was five o'clock in the morning when the ferry docked at Dover, the white cliffs that we saw when leaving and wondered to ourselves when we would see them again, were too close to view, as our car drove down the metal ramp and touched the *terra firma* that was England.

Clearing customs, one small man in a peaked cap reading a newspaper as we went past, not even lifting his head to see this amazing saffron yellow Triumph Vitesse along with its Volkswagen windscreen fitted by the Bulgarian pit crew, arriving back on British soil after its epic journey, covering more miles than the famous Mexico Rally of 1970 (Another good PR opportunity missed there by Triumph — wouldn't you say?).

It really was quite uneventful considering what we had achieved and endured. We headed out of Dover along the A2 dual carriageway and we had not travelled far when the flashing of a blue light appeared through the back window of the car, Dad pulling over to see what on earth the problem was. A police car then pulling up in front of us lights still flashing, Dad winding down his window for the second time in twenty-four hours for another policeman. Dressed in a black trench coat and supporting a very prominent police helmet with a large shinny badge attached to the front you could not help but notice, the policeman leant forward towards Dad's window and began to speak in a very softly but precise tone, 'Excuse me sir I know you have just got off the early ferry but in this country we drive on the right-hand side of the road'. Dad apologised immediately, he had just driven completely up the wrong side of a dual carriageway totally unaware, lucky for us it was so early in the morning there was no oncoming traffic, imagine driving across two continents from Peshawar, a total of thirteen days, about 312 hours, then bumping straight into something as we arrived back here in England and all because you were on the wrong side of a dual carriageway. After correcting our mistake and now driving up the right side of this road with a police escort in front of us, we literally all just burst into laughter with relief, not just relief of that particular incident which could have resulted in an accident but a greater relief all round that we had made it back to England.

A relief that you could sense among the three of us within that tiny space of our little car, a laughter that almost turned you to tears, and when the laughter eventually subsided the silence then made you ponder in earnest, what will be in store for the three of us in the future?

There is one thing for sure, we will never forget what actually has happened over the past thirteen days on this journey back across the world, and the unexplained whirlwind that had set upon us in the previous six months for the rest of our lives, and you know that we definitely will never, ever forget our mothers love which she gave to Alexander and me, and a much loving wife to our Dad, Sardar Hassan Agha.

As the morning light rose behind us we approached the outskirts of London, eventually climbing the crest of Blackheath Hill, a place I remembered we stopped at on the way out, a place where Mum broke out the thermos so we could all have a hot drink, whilst looking at the lights of the city disappear.

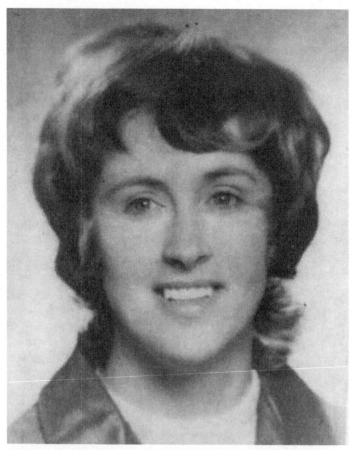

Eileen Brigid Agha, *June 7th 1938 — December 16th 1971*

It's those little things that Mums do that you don't really notice at the time, but now thinking about it, I will remember them a lot more, but knowing eventually they will fade in time as I automatically just do them myself.

London was in full flow as we tried to work our way across this vast concrete jungle, no ring roads around this city, in fact the complete opposite to Germany, the M25 motorway had not even started construction until 1975 some three years away, and was completed eleven years later in 1986.

Two and a half hours it took us to go from the top of Blackheath Hill in the south of London to Scratchwood Services in the north at the start of the M1, Dad pulling in so we could get a hearty breakfast, which turned out to be a good old English fry up with all the trimmings. We must have sat for well over an hour, while watching the traffic go past the window on the motorway, Dad ordering another mug of tea, the third so far. It appeared that time was not an urgent thing as it had a been over the past few days while travelling across Europe, it's not even that Dad was trying to get forty winks to catch up on his sleep. It just seemed so strange, as the fourth mug of hot tea was delivered to the table along with two Bar Sixes for Alexander and me.

So, sitting there at the time I never gave it much thought about why we sat for so long, well you wouldn't when you are getting chocolate, would you?

The conversation didn't appear to be anything significant as time just slipped by that morning at Scratchwood services. Although today as I write this and look back at that moment, we were about one hour away from home, one hour away from Grandma and Grandad Blaney. Only one hour away to have that great feeling to be held in the arms of your family and to have that reassurance once more. As my Dad sat there, mug of tea in hand starring out of that window, give a thought to what he might have been thinking. Yes he was only one hour away and yes he had brought the boys home as promised, but he was also one hour away from trying to explain why he had not brought their daughter home, one hour away from the actual unknown.

How on earth would he, could he, explain the circumstances to our mother's parents, her sister and her brother, where does one start? What reaction was there to be when first meeting them after all this time and three months after Mum passed away, those things must have been rolling around in his head non-stop? Eventually climbing back into the car for one last time, the engine starting again without fault we headed north for Northamptonshire.

I remember very clearly to this day the sign for junction 15, our car exiting the motorway up the slip road until it came to a halt at the top, Dad then turning left instead of right for Northampton and our village of Wootton just a mile from here. What I cannot remember is Grandma and Grandad moving to a new house, from Northampton to Blisworth, a small village about five miles south of the town. I am not sure if they moved before we left or they moved while we were away, and that Mum's death was the trigger for them to move, knowing a lot of memories were to be left in their old terrace house back in Jimmy's End, where they lived. Anyway, the village of Blisworth was our destination and it didn't take too long to reach, pulling up beside a row of six houses just outside of this village known locally as Pine Ridge Cottages.

Now, as seeing it through the eyes of a ten-year-old the initial reunion appeared fine and there was no underlying current that I could tell or feel.

I suppose what really mattered at that time was Alexander and me, although the inner grief of my grandparents must have been tremendous, now being able to give us a welcoming cuddle after so many months of uncertainty.

Our grandparents were not ones for giving cuddles lightly, in fact I cannot really remember any at all, maybe when we used to leave them on a Sunday after getting one of the many toys, but it came more from us boys than from them, it was just the way things were. There may be an easy explanation as both grandparents came from well hardened Irish Catholic families with little emotion shown, but cuddles we got that day, most likely to comfort them than us. Both Alexander and I had now in a kind of way had time to come to terms with the current situation, as grief for us lay some months back in the city of Peshawar. I am not quite sure how long we visited my grandparents that first time back, but I do remember returning to the village of Wootton, and the little street of Springfield while it was still light, our saffron yellow Triumph Vitesse once more gracing its familiar territory by rumbling over the concrete road as we headed for number 18, at the end of this small cul-de-sac. At the top we turned right, and the car rose up and over the tarmac ramp then glided down the incline of the drive passing that now familiar sign that sits on two continents, Manzil. After slowly coming to a halt, and with the reliable engine that we all had come to take for granted switched off, a real eerie silence immediately descended inside the car, broken only after what seemed like ages, but must have been seconds, of the driver's side door cranking loud on its hinges as Dad opened it.

CHAPTER 10

Home

AFTER DAD UNLOCKED the front door, I took my things from the back seat of the car into this cold uninviting place we called home, not really recognising it as the happy fun loving place we had left some months earlier. I am not sure what I had expected returning back to 18 Springfield Wootton, certainly not balloons flags and a brass band, but certainly not this as I slipped back into realisation, throwing my good companion of a pillow onto the top bunk in our bedroom. I said that when I left this house on our incredible journey that it was time to grow up and as I surveyed the reality of this cold place, I think this is when I knew I had to grow up. That child who had lived in this bedroom aged nine was gone, the new guy aged ten had to knuckle down and get on with it, no matter what life was going to throw at him, nothing could be worse than losing your mother's love aged nine — nothing.

They say time is a great healer with these sorts of matters, then on the other hand they say you should never forget, well let me tell you there is no written book on events like these, none at all, whatever they say would not be right because everyone is different, you really have to deal with the matter yourself, find your own strengths and build from there, accept and go on in your life knowing you have done all this from within yourself each and every day. Once you can do this you then go out and enjoy life which has been offered to you, for there are many people who do not get to enjoy a full life because of various circumstances. There are lives that had much more to offer this world, but sadly couldn't, I had known one of these people for nine years, and I think most of you would also know some who could have offered a lot more. So now it was three men and a bungalow, and as long as we have each other I was sure we would be alright, but over time how wrong I was about that, how wrong indeed!

Dad contacted our schools to get us both back as soon as it was possible, trying to return some sort of routine into our lives. Alexander went back first but had to drop back a year to catch up on his secondary education, thus making him the oldest in that year. Dad took me back to primary with just four weeks left of the school year before breaking for the summer, holding my hand as we entered the school gates just as Mum had done on many occasions previously, the headmaster greeting us before telling me I would be going back into the same year so to keep as much familiarity as possible at this unfortunate time. Well those first few days back seemed quite strange, yes, I still had the friends that I had left some six months or so earlier, but it was like starting school all over again. At playtime children from the other classes looked at you as if you had two heads or something, they came in packs maybe for some kind of security gained in numbers, they came to look at the child with no mother, as if I was some kind of act left behind by the circus, when it had left town. It wasn't name calling, it wasn't bullying it was just what I would call child curiosity and it was something I had to deal with, just another part of growing up, I guess.

I settled in quite well after the first week, Dad taking me every day while he organised himself with all things to do with the house and sorting the paperwork out, getting us a new colour television from Granada rentals, and applying for a new job. The one time I really realised at school that Mum was not around was in the last week and the annual sports day had arrived, it seemed that all the other children's Mums were attending the afternoon's events, myself just trying to stay out of the way as they appeared to somehow want to reciprocate what their children had done previously, and stare at the boy with no mother. The answer I had for all of them and the only one that afternoon offered to me, were the three races that I was entered into for my year, two sprint races over different distances and the obligatory obstacle race. I won all three races receiving three red ribbons from the headmaster, neatly attached across the front of my shirt. I then proudly walked round for all to see, maybe just making those mothers think twice why they had been staring at me in the first place.

It also made me think anything is possible, then wondering in the back of my mind if any of them would now protest that I had triumphed in adversity just because my mother was not there to witness my achievements.

Clear of the gates once school had finished and with tears cascading down my face from not being able to share that moment with my mother, but then realising that it was the first time I had cried over my mother's passing, the grief exploding all of a sudden without any control, but also without anyone else to share it with. Pulling myself together as quick as that moment had installed itself on me, I began to run, as fast as I possibly could, not breaking stride once until I had reached the top of our drive.

The adrenaline that I was feeling made me realise that nothing could hold me back, it just made me more resilient, a trait I still hold today and a trait my mother would be proud of, but of course it is thanks to her unfortunate passing that I have been able to absorb that trait. I know my mother gave me the strength and start in life that all mothers hope to give their children, it's whether you choose to embrace it, that's what matters, and I did, 'thanks Mum'.

Summer came and with our new colour TV we watched the events of the 1972 Olympic Games in Munich unfold from our front room, having passed this wonderful stadium only months earlier.

We watched how Mark Spits won seven golds in the swimming, giving Alexander the inspiration to swim for his school and then for the county in the butterfly event, I on the other hand watched Valeriy Borzov win the one hundred and two hundred metres, he most likely getting his inspiration from my sports day achievement a few weeks previously. Although all the sports were very good and inspirational this thing called religion reared its ugly head again, as terrorists attacked the games killing eleven Israeli athletes, just because of what they believed in.

Every summer Simpson Barracks, the local Army camp held an open day, where most of the people from the villages around the area came to have an afternoon out and look round, viewing several stalls and to see what the army could offer them. They came in their hundreds to watch the soldiers parade and stage a mock battle, my favourite part was the traditional piano smashing contest between the local men and the army cadets, very entertaining. That year I wore the army uniform Uncle Arbid had made for me along with my medals brought back on our long journey, and subsequently was introduced to the visiting Colonel of the Pioneer Corps, who said I had seen more action than most of the soldiers attending that day. I was given a VIP seat alongside him for the annual tug of war competition and started the proceedings by waving a flag then handing out the winning team their medals, like some sort of royalty.

As the autumn of 1972 merged into the spring of 1973 our lives, if at all possible, returned to some sort of normality, school was school as I can remember, no real drama occurred since sports day, and if there was anything it sure wasn't going to be a problem to me, just deal with it and move on, 'life's too short' as they say, whoever keeps saying these things, they should think about writing a book.

Dad started his new job working for the Co-op bakery in Northampton, this allowed him to go to work at around four-thirty in the morning leaving us boys in bed until our alarm went off at around seven-fifteen, Alexander making sure we had breakfast before leaving for school. Mrs Hammond from across the road was on watch duty from behind her net curtains for Dad, making sure Alexander and I left for school on time, nipping across to check all was okay when we were running late, which was at least three mornings a week guaranteed. Alexander would walk me down to the school gates in the morning before catching his bus to the secondary school, I would then have my lunch at school leaving at three forty-five and walk home to Springfield with the other school children who lived in our street. This routine went on for the rest of my primary school and my secondary school education. It was the type of routine that concentrated the mind with a little responsibility, but not taking anything away from those important childhood days that we all needed to proceed in life. Dad took this job deliberately so that on most days it would give him the opportunity to be back home by two-thirty, allowing him to prepare a meal and be there for when I returned home, Alexander following shortly after.

Fridays were sometimes different, when Dad would be waiting outside the primary school gates in his old Commer bread van. This was a large blue van with two front seats split by the longest gear lever you ever did see, that crunched away happily every time the van was on the move. There was a central walkway right through the van from front to back, shelving floor to ceiling on each side where the bread and most importantly the cakes were kept slightly at a tilt for easy access. At the back of the van was a small dropdown counter before two steps allowed you to dismount the van through a two-glass paned sliding door. On most of the days when Dad picked me up, all the children from the top end of the village would clamber on board filling the central isle of the van. Sometimes there would be over ten of us in there, doors wide open as we sped up the village, Dad taking the corners a bit quicker around the village green making us all scream out loud as though we were on a funfair ride, hanging on to the bread shelves for dear life and the fear of being thrown out of those double doors.

Where was health and safety back then? Nowhere to be seen, but overall it didn't do any harm and gave all of us some great childhood memories, along with some of the fresh cream cakes that were left over from the round that day, cream horn, apple turnover, and the odd éclair just to name a few. Dad would park his van outside our house, then do his paperwork while waiting for Alexander, he would then come in with a tray of goodies for tea. Crumpets followed by as many custard tarts as it was possible to eat and a fresh cream cake if there were any left after passing them round to all our friends earlier. These leftover items were from Dad's bakery round which he didn't sell that day resulted in us having a rather different Friday night dinner, but if there weren't any cakes left Dad would make his *piece de resistance* bread and butter pudding from a full pre-cut loaf, with lashings of milk and a large bag of raisins and sultanas, extravagance beyond belief — well it was the 1970s after all.

Dad had a few friends that rallied round him in this time of need giving him the adult friendship he undoubtedly needed, there was Diane and Lazlo who he knew from college, Lazlo being from Hungary so was away from his family just like my Dad so a common bond grew between them. Bob Brewer and his wife Dorothy kept in touch going out for meals, Dad working with Bob as a Hoover salesman in the mid-sixties. Dad would venture out into Northampton with Brian, a work colleague from the Co-op bakery.

Dad's best friends were Ted and Enid, a friendship that started on the off-chance and lasted for well over forty-five years, a friendship that some people could only wish for.

Ted was a local policeman in the village of Roade, and

at that time Enid was so fed up because they had very little money and times were extremely hard for them, she said the next person to knock on our door she would invite for dinner even though it would only be baked beans on toast. My Dad was that person who knocked on their door and accepted their invitation, supplying the bread for the toast and other goodies to keep their family going on many occasions, taking a current out of a fruit loaf and claiming it was a fly so the goods could not be sold to the general public — and asking Enid if she would like these 'contaminated' items. So from a meal of beans on toast a friendship grew Ted and Enid having three children of their own Katherine, Caroline and Peter, a friendship between two families from very different beginnings that saw Ted, Enid and my Dad go on holidays regular together, even touring the USA for a month.

The summer of 1973 has stuck hard in my memory, the second of July to be precise, the first week of the school holidays. Alexander had an old record player and had been playing David Bowie's *Space Oddity* album for the past nine months or so, I would also play it when he was out of the house as younger brothers were often told 'don't touch or else'. Knowing I was safe from a good whack I would sit comfortably on my top bunk, singing the words to every song printed on the inner sleeve repeatedly as it played. With the large poster of Bowie which came with the record, stuck neatly with Sellotape to the free standing G Plan wardrobe door on the opposite side of the room, eventually engraining itself as a photograph on the back of my mind, and as this picture stared out across the bedroom I became encapsulated into the world of David Bowie.

A few weeks before school broke for the summer of '73, Alexander purchased *Life on Mars*, David Bowie's latest single from Boots record department with his paper round money, again I played it at every chance I got, memorising every word then doing the same with the B-side, *The Man who Sold the World*.

Alexander came in one evening from school and said a girl in his year who lived in our village had two tickets to see David Bowie and wanted Alex to go with her but he didn't really fancy it, so in stepped little brother and after some real knee bending to my Dad, he said if the girl came to our house and explain to him the actual itinerary then he may consider it. Well the next day I told Alexander to make sure he let her know, and instead of going home after school I waited for the buses that brought the school children from the secondary school, the first bus had the boys onboard the second the girls, making sure Alexander pointed this girl out to me, as she got of her bus.

Claire Ruskin was her name, a school prefect and I followed her like a puppy dog all the way to her front door at the other end of our village, pleading with her every step of the way that I would have the ticket and go with her, if she would just come and explain everything to my father. Well typical girl keeping you hanging on until the end, turning round as she stepped through her front door, tell Alex I will be up at seven o'clock, and tell your Dad I will explain all about the day to him.

Well I don't even remember running all the way home, just piling through the front door and shouting she will be here tonight, Alexander saying he knew, and so did Dad. Alexander had already spoken to her at school and she already had agreed to come over that evening. Girls, who needs them anyway? I did, or I wouldn't be going to see David Bowie.

Monday the second of July 1973, jean jacket on, flared school trousers cascading over my one and only pair of platform shoes, we boarded the two o'clock train for London Euston, then catching a tube train to Hammersmith, following this Clair Ruskin again like a puppy dog (well I had been

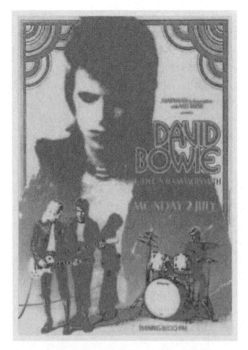

Poster on the Odeon wall, 1973

practicing), the difference this time was she was not in her school uniform, and had really gone to town with colourful makeup, easy to spot I thought, that was until we stepped outside Hammersmith tube station. Well it was like nothing I had ever seen before, totally captivating the number of people with their faces painted and their hair dyed all heading in the same direction to the Hammersmith Odeon where Bowie was performing that night.

I remember queuing along the street under a motorway flyover at least four deep around about five o'clock, some two hours before doors opened, the crowd singing his songs at the top of their voices, the noise echoing under this flyover making it even louder and more in tune. The actual performance was quite something else, very extravagant as Bowie changed his clothes several times throughout in what seemed like some theatrical show, rather than a concert. The music turned up so loud trying, but failing, to drown out the screaming of the many girls in the audience, myself trying to listen the best I could whilst being jostled from side to side singing along to many of the songs I had learnt back home on the top bunk in my bedroom.

All in all an experience not to be missed and over far too soon as Dad picked us up from Northampton train station around half-past one in the morning, my ears still ringing as my body started to tire from the day's events, an experience I would repeat twelve more times over the next forty years.

September 1973 would see me start secondary school, the same routine getting up as before, but Alexander and I would now be catching the bus together. Dad bought me a school uniform from Northampton, blazer sleeves far too long but the thought process would be that I would grow into it, yes most likely by the time I would leave school going on the size of this thing, it was more like a two man tent. The night before school started, I put on my uniform so Dad could see me in it as he would not get the chance due to his early starts for work. Dad had been teaching me how to tie my tie for the last few weeks, but I was still struggling, so I had to rely on Alexander to help me most mornings, until the penny dropped. As I stood in the middle of our front room in Springfield the new uniform overwhelming the small body that lay inside, Dad said to me, 'your Mother would be proud of you and you should be proud of yourself' more words that just somehow you knew would stick with you for the rest of your life.

Secondary school was a good learning process and I made good friends; the studying was okay. Alexander left school a year later leaving me to take up the flak from the kids he used to regularly pick on, 'thanks Alex', but at least I could keep up

Dad, me and Alexander 1976

my running on a regular basis if nothing else.

Home life changed as three men and a bungalow became only two as Alexander decided to join the Royal Navy, signing on for nine years after eighteen months training leaving me a bedroom to myself and of course that all important record player.

1975 and 1976 saw Dad and I take many a trip to London, meeting several uncles who had flown in from Pakistan, sometimes picking them up from Heathrow Airport or meeting them in an apartment in Neasden, a suburb of the capital city. Dad would have many conversations about home life back in Pakistan, mainly over a large bottle of Johnnie Walker Black Label, these meetings lasted hours but then they would always end with the so-called uncle producing several large tins of Imperial Leather talcum powder, which was very strange at first, but became very much the norm.

These would be placed on a large piece of newspaper on a coffee table, then the top section of the tin would be split from the bottom section, revealing plastic bags full of money in the bottom half, but still talc in the top half. Sometimes there would be at least twelve bags strewn across the table — I did not know how much money, but I knew it was a lot, and it all came home with us. It wasn't long after one of these trips that I came home from school to see a brand-new java green Triumph Spitfire parked down our drive, the usual site of our trusted saffron yellow Triumph Vitesse no longer to be seen.

Dad had traded it in for this two seater sports car but I still much preferred our old car, the one that had travelled halfway across the world and back with very little trouble, apart from borrowing a windscreen from a German surrogate. I suppose for sentimental reasons if truth were told but life moves on, and as Elton John would sing, goodbye yellow Vitesse.

On many a Saturday night, Dad and I would take trips to Ceaser's Palace in Luton, a night club where you would sit down to a meal and would watch a variety show with all the latest talent, not the sort of talent that an Istanbul nightclub can offer, more's the pity. I saw Bruce Forsyth, Bob Monkhouse and Dave Allen along with Shirley Bassey, Tom Jones, the comedy was good, well the bits I understood anyway, the music well you guessed right, it wasn't Bowie — not by a long shot, although the food was good and plenty of it, so there was the compromise. I had the same every time we went, prawn cocktail, steak and chips, followed by black forest gateau, very up to date I can tell you, although the menu offered very little else apart from chicken or scampi, again with chips.

Dad took my best friend from school, Stuart Mann, and me, to watch England versus Northern Ireland in the home Internationals conveniently calling in at Neasden again, to meet allegedly another uncle, before going on to Wembley in the next borough. England won four-nil but not the result

I wanted, as I was cheering for George Best and wearing a Northern Ireland rosette that had been given to me by Grandad Blaney, he told me to back the Irish side of the family and I did, we all enjoyed ourselves that evening, the only problem was the transport.

Dad picked Stuart and me up from the middle of the village of Roade, thinking we were clever after slipping out of school before lunchtime without telling anyone, although we got detention the next day, 'not that bright', we were told by the school, even though they were the ones teaching us! Work that one out, I say. This Triumph Spitfire with its two seats worked well for Dad and I but put another body in the equation and that's where the practicalities end, as I had to scrunch down and lie behind the seats all the way to London and back, was it worth it? Well any time off school has to be a bonus, but don't tell your children that. Two weeks later another car appeared on the drive, a brand-new Renault 17 TS a very unusual car, it was a cross between a sports car and a saloon, not the best but at least it had four seats.

Alexander would come home the odd time on leave, but you could tell he was like a fish out of water, not exactly fitting in, just killing time before he would head back to his ship, before setting off around the world to try and kill someone else, well that's what they sign up for, that's what the job entails, right?

On many a weekend in the summers, to give Dad a break as much as anything else, Grandad Blaney would invite me over to their house at Blisworth. So on a Friday afternoon I would cycle the seven miles across three villages, my cow horn handle bars stretching out proudly from the hand painted silver frame rat bike that I had built myself, eating up the tarmac footways and roads to reach their cottage, in great anticipation of the dinner awaiting my arrival.

Grandad and Grandma would usually have fish on a Friday, regular as clockwork. I am sure it was a Catholic thing, but

JASON AGHA

when she knew I was coming over Gran would still have her fish but make Grandad and I a bacon and onion clanger. For the food connoisseurs among you, this is bacon and onion roll made from suet pastry twisted in the middle so the other end has jam inside, all cooked at the same time in the oven, one complete meal makes total sense to me — and they say the Irish are not quite all there!

I am now quite sure Grandad liked inviting me over just for that reason alone, but I am also sure he would tell you in his distinguished voice, it was because he liked seeing his grandson, whatever the reason they were good grandparents to me. Stopping the night I would then go with Grandad to his works on Saturday morning in St James Mill road Northampton, Gran supplying blackcurrant jam squashed between two large cut pieces of bread and butter all wrapped in greaseproof paper for our morning break.

Home for lunch, usually Gran's famous fruit cake with a mug of tea, then we would walk the garden and the back field, before returning to the warmth of the house, so Gran with a bottle of Mackeson Stout in hand after opening it with her teeth would you believe, would watch the wrestling on *World of Sport* shouting profusely at the television in the corner of the room. Once Gran had stretched her vocal chords to the astonishment of Grandad and I, she would disappear into the kitchen to dish us a full-blown fry up, as soon as Grandad had finished checking his pools coupon in complete silence, the total opposite to what had occurred twenty minutes earlier. The following morning, I would spend with my grandparents before heading home on my bike but not before devouring one of Gran's Sunday roasts.

One weekend a year, in the summer, the British Grand Prix for motor bikes came to Silverstone, a village only a few miles further on from Gran's.

I would stop three nights sitting outside the front of their house on the footway, a chair and a small table provided from Grandad's garage, front row VIP seating for the whole of Saturday and Sunday. Not daring to moving an inch, in case I missed something, Gran would bring me my lunch and tea on both days, my eyes and ears totally fixed on the A43 that ran right past the ends of my toes, as these two wheeled monsters would roar up the hill from the village below, sometimes three abreast racing each other before disappearing out of sight as fast as they had arrived heading for the race track then back again at night. What wonderful times at Gran's.

The 1976 school year passed without too much going on, I got ribbed at school as Manchester United lost the FA Cup Final in May to Southampton, then breaking up at the end of the school year for what was to be one of the hottest summers on record. Spending most of my time either at Castle Ashby lakes or the open-air swimming pool down on Midsummer Meadow in Northampton great times had by all.

The first of September saw another new car, a Toyota Corolla with the new registration year — oh did I tell you? This was after several more trips to Neasden in London, but at least one of these trips became fruitful for me.

While waiting for Dad to conclude his usual business, I was captivated by the large Waltham stereo that completely covered the length of the sideboard that this monster of technology was on. A large record deck with two built-in cassette players, all protected under a smoked glass top, there were buttons to alter the music you listened to that I never knew existed, if that was not enough it had a built-in radio, and the whole system was topped off by two large speakers that stood proudly on each side.

Well the question was asked to me by one of these so-called uncles and before it had finished the answer was yes, although the three week wait was totally unbearable until our next visit, the sight of this new Waltham stereo still in its box, was something you could only dream of as a fourteen year old boy, but Bowie never sounded so good especially when Dad was out and I cranked up the volume to its max.

Sometimes after visiting Neasden instead of heading back to Northampton, Dad and I would head off to the Odeon cinema by Marble Arch which had the biggest screen in Great Britain, when you were sitting down it felt like it nearly wrapped itself right around you. They would screen classic films specially adapted to fit this extra-large screen. I remember watching the film *Once Upon a Time in the West,* a favorite of mine still today, and the epic *Ben Hur,* the chariot race that was in the film was something to behold, it was so real it almost made you duck under your seat, as the clatter of horses hooves echoed around us with such volume, you wondered if the rest of London could also hear them.

In May of 1977 I got the chance to get my own back at all the kids that ribbed me at school the year before, as

Silver Jubilee celebrations, me far right
on the wall of Manzil, 18 Springfield. June 7th 1977

Manchester United won the cup-final, beating Liverpool two-one, the front room of our bungalow was packed with a few friends of mine, but mostly with many of the Dad's from our street, there to watch it on our latest colour TV, courtesy of Granada Rentals via our sponsor, the tins of Imperial Leather talcum powder from London.

June of 1977 was the Silver Jubilee year and Springfield decided to hold a street party, all the tables and chairs were set up outside our house at the end of the cul-de-sac, Dad supplying all the bread and cakes for the day as the street celebrated the Queen's Silver Jubilee.

It was also that year I decided to get a paper round in the village like my brother, so I could buy more records to keep the Waltham stereo as happy as I could.

Mark Page, our next door neighbour, was a year older than me and together we use to catch the 301 United Counties bus into Northampton on a Saturday morning, then off to Boots at the top of Gold Street to disappear downstairs to their record department, where his older sister Geraldine worked.

The store had six record booths where you would pick a record and she then put the record on a turntable behind the counter, telling you which sound proof booth you could go in and listen to it, it was mainly for customers so they could listen before buying, but most of the time we hogged a booth for hours listening to records chosen by each of us alternately, it made the department look busy while satisfying our appetite for the latest music. I bought David Bowie's new album *Heroes* with the money I had earnt from my paper round, after listening to it several times over in one of these booths.

Things were good at home, Dad and I would venture out together, Bletchley Leisure Centre to go swimming, the new shopping centre in Milton Keynes and a few football matches at Coventry, Leicester and Northampton on a Saturday afternoon. Dad liked his cricket, so most of the summer holidays I was left to my own devices, lying in bed knowing the mafia from across the road would not be poking her nose in, then going out the rest of the day with my friends, mostly trying the patience of many of the villagers, generally getting up to no good, before heading off home to find Dad asleep in the front room, while allegedly watching the Test Match on the television. I would get myself something to eat before heading back out to meet up with my friends again, to play some sort of sport at the recreation ground, finally leaving for home before it got too dark, around nine o'clock.

1977 and 1978 brought me back to the world of Manchester United after having seen George Best and then win the Cup Final in May that year, my friend Stuart Mann and I decided to go to all their games the following season, in fact we went for the next four years home and away. The stories we could tell about our days out following United, would most likely fill another book, and maybe one day they will.

1978 saw me leave school, not with the greatest of qualifications, four CSEs to be precise, but with more common sense than was necessary and plenty of life experiences to say the least. Now sixteen and let loose on this world I got my first job at Cosworth Engineering in Northampton as an apprentice. The money was very good as it was known to be one of the best firms to work for in Northampton, allowing me to pursue my three favourite things; David Bowie, Manchester United and motor bikes, oh yes, didn't I tell you? I bought my first motor bike that year, a silver Yamaha RD 200, well it was a natural progression after watching all those bikes outside my grandparents house for over three years running.

I passed my bike test in 1979/1981, followed by an emerald green oriental dragon otherwise known as my Kawasaki Z650, winter saw a Suzuki 250Ts alongside it and just for fun a BSA Bantam 175.

These years were good years, late teens, working and enjoying what life had to offer me on my own and with my

Dad, but every year remembering the sixteenth of December with private reflection.

In 1982 I took my car test and passed, as riding a bike through the winters was becoming a very wearing task, then the following year was to be my twenty-first birthday. Although I had bikes Dad didn't like the fact, and I have thought for many a year that he conspired with my grandad to get me off those motor bikes. The thought was if Dad had mentioned it, I would resist as a son, but if Grandad could reach out to me then it might be possible, well the latter prevailed. My grandad said he would buy me a car that was only a few years old, but the choice was mine, on the condition that once I had the car, I would sell my bikes. Well my friends had Ford Capris, Cortinas or Escorts but my eyes were totally fixed on what was known as the Japanese E-Type, a Datsun 260Z, and that's exactly what I got.

Shiny blue paintwork with very little mileage on the clock, bought from a doctor, myself and my grandparents having a day out to Cambridgeshire to collect it, Grandad paying in

Me and my Datsun 260Z 2+2, 1983

hard cash, which by now you probably have worked out came via Dad and the famous talcum powder tins.

Driving it back home over fifty miles with my grandparents following was a moment I never have forgotten, my face stuck permanently on smile mode, as the constant purring of the straight six-cylinder engine pulled me effortlessly along the road. 'Could life get any better for a young man?', you might ask, although I would swap it in an instant to see the smile on my mother's face once again.

The eighties were good for me and Dad up to a point; he would now collect me from Northampton station every Saturday night around eight-fifteen after I had caught the train back from the football, picking up our usual Chinese takeaway on the way home, then consuming it while sitting in front of the television watching *Dallas*, followed by *Match of the Day*. My brother, now out of the Royal Navy was married, he and his wife Anne lived in the new city of Milton Keynes. Alexander not being able to hold down a job on a regular basis, he eventually ended up at Her Majesty's pleasure for over a year for some criminal act. When Alexander eventually surfaced and after taking in a considerable amount of alcohol, most likely for courage, he and Anne went to visit Dad. I believe to this day that Anne had no prior knowledge of what was about to happen, and at first I think it was just to ask Dad for money to help them out, but as one thing led to another, things got really ugly.

I had no idea how long my brother had been at the house, but in the time he was there, Alexander had blatantly accused our father of killing our mother back in Pakistan for his own benefit, and that he could have saved her if he had tried. I had just returned home and caught the end of this conflict, as Dad grappled with Alexander in the hallway telling him to get out of the house, this was not at all what I thought would be greeting me at that time, it came as a complete shock and still is to this very day. Dad continued to shout at Alexander and then proceeded to tell me what he had just accused him of after all these years, with that I pulled Alexander out of the house backwards by his collar, both of us fighting fist to fist on the driveway, me telling him in no uncertain terms how cruel he was. Although older, the fact that he had consumed so much alcohol gave me the advantage, after what seemed like ages and a few nasty cuts and bruises on each side, Alexander walked off down the road, still claiming at the top of his voice what he believed Dad had done to our mother, Anne driving their car after him as he disappeared round the corner and out of sight.

My father, after marrying our mother became a 'black sheep' of his family — cast out for going against his family's wishes; after this, Alexander became another, if not the new 'black sheep' of the family, Dad had totally disowned him as a son and with his words and actions that day, I lost a brother.

As I said the eighties were good times, if you had the right attitude you could work and prosper, apart from the odd domestic hiccup that came along, but I guess that was the same for most families throughout history.

I met my beautiful wife to be, Julie at my twenty-first birthday party, ensuring she liked David Bowie, fast cars and Man United before finally getting married in 1987, moving into our first house the same year, (well it's better if you are both singing from the same hymn sheet as they say, well Bowie's songs in our case). We have two wonderful children, Rachael Eileen born September 1989, then Richard Jason born 1991 in the month of June, my Dad delighted and thrilled at having grandchildren spoiling them both with his love every chance he got.

I lost my grandad in October of 1991; we were very close, still giving me his worldly advice right up to the end. He called me up on Saturday morning making sure I would bring

Grandad & Grandma Blaney with myself

the children round to see him that day, just as we had done every Saturday at around one o'clock.

He sat in his armchair in the front room playing with Rachael and Richard making them giggle with laughter at every opportunity, we stopped for well over two hours while eating Gran's freshly made fruitcake, but as we left he put his hand on my shoulder and told me to look after the children, they are the most import thing in life, your children, and with that we said our goodbyes. That very afternoon just after five, Grandad had a heart attack and never recovered, it was like he knew what was going to happen, he somehow sensed it. Well Grandad, you now can go and look after your own child, my mother Eileen.

My own family life grew but we would always include my Dad where we could, Christmas, New Year and family days out, just as he had done all those years previously.

Hashim Khan, Dad's best friend visited every few years and on one such occasion brought with him another old school chum, Humayum Khan, then the High Commissioner for Pakistan in India. Both were keen golfers and although my Dad did not play, my wife Julie's father was a member of a local club in Northampton, so a game was arranged. The whole course was shut down while they played as the Embassy car stood in the club carpark, flag proudly sitting on the front bonnet waiting for their return.

The year 2000 crept up so quick, as we all saw in the New Millennium, we had a party for all of Julie's family and of course Dad at our house. The evening going out with a bang — literally, Julie's brother Nigel, setting the garden shed alight with all the fireworks inside, a good way of introducing in the new century, wouldn't you say?

Grandma passed away in the June of 2007 at the ripe old age of ninety-three, she had had a hard life but hopefully a rewarding one, she was also a very hard woman, not shedding a tear for my grandad at his passing, in fact the opposite literally saying 'good riddance', to our astonishment!

Although Dad and I always thought of Mum on the anniversary of her death, the only picture or recollection I had of my mother's resting place was the one that was ingrained in my mind when I was nine years old. Although Alexander soon after coming out of the Navy in the 1980s had a trip back to Pakistan, not telling Dad or myself that he was going. He took some pictures of Mum's grave before returning home, although mentioning his trip and the photos he would never show them to me, even though I asked repeatedly. This, over the years played on my mind, and having lost all contact with my brother due to his unforgiveable and treacherous thoughts amongst other things, made me privately look to see if I could locate my mother's grave, not telling Dad in case it would upset him enormously.

So around 2008 I contacted several authorities in the Peshawar region, as well as speaking to the British Embassy of Pakistan, who suggested to me to contact the Foreign Nationals Graves Society for that area. The overwhelming consensus from those who I spoke with was that my mother's grave was now not traceable and more than likely destroyed when all the refugees fled Afghanistan in 1979, after the Russians invaded.

They headed to Pakistan in their many thousands, where the only places to stay were the graveyards of Peshawar, so these areas became their permanent encampments for several years. It was just as well I did not tell my father of my continuing search for Mum's resting place, for the results I found were disappointing for me, and would surely have been devastating for him.

Dad lived alone but remained very active in his day to day life, but he also liked his peace and quiet, especially when the cricket or tennis was on the television, just so he could relax and close his eyes, he deserved it.

I would call in most days on the way home from work to check he was OK, we would exchange stories of the day with each other, before he would insist that I should go home as in his words he would say to me, 'you go, you have a family to look after, I'm fine'. It's now that you wish you had stopped for much longer as it's now you realise how precious time is, so if you get the chance to stop that extra moment with a loved one, stop. They mean well in what they are telling you, but the meaning of staying will resonate with you more in the years to come.

On the sixteenth of November 2010 Dad passed away, he had been feeling unwell for about three weeks, I found him in excruciating pain when dropping in one afternoon, taking him immediately to hospital but unfortunately, he never returned. I would sit for hours daily in hospital telling him the date and what had been going on in the world waiting for him to tell me to go home but he never did.

He slowly came to the point that I think he thought it was time to go, the last few days he would be just lying there as though asleep as I would find him in his armchair on many occasions supposedly watching the cricket.

I think, no, I know, he could still hear me, as I held his

hand saying 'Dad it's the fifteenth today, and tomorrow is the sixteenth'.

That may have just been his last thought, 'it's the sixteenth tomorrow', as I got a call from the hospital at two in the morninig to say Dad had slipped away, and you may ask yourself, 'what is significant about that'? Well I did not tell Dad the month, not once, I just told him the days in numbers, then finally telling him it was the sixteenth tomorrow, Mum died on the sixteenth and the time difference between the two countries put their deaths exactly in the same hour although thirty-eight years apart.

You may think this would be the end of this true and extraordinary family story, but as I mentioned at the beginning of this saga, it would have to start in the middle, where I started, and although it might have been the end of Sardar Hassan Agha's life, his story will now continue as you read on. Life is strange, but death can be strange as well.

The events that follow were either told to me by my father or his family and friends, from family documents or research by myself, to find this extraordinary saga of the man known as Agha Sardar Hassan Zahid.

After a couple of days coming to terms with what had happened, I decided to contact Hashim Khan, Dad's old school friend who we met in Pakistan and who had also visited us here in England over the years on many occasions, Dad always claiming he was a prince from a well-known family. Well he was, and after I told him the news, he said he would contact all the relevant people to give them the sad news of my father's passing. The following week I received a call from Dad's School, the Bishop Cotton School in Shimla, India, telling me what a great man my father was and that they were sad to hear of his passing. I thought nothing of the call, only a gesture of goodwill on behalf of the school, but then came more.

All week, I received calls from Hong Kong, South Africa,

USA, India, Pakistan, Singapore, Dubai, Kuwait, and here in England. 'Who were these people calling me from across the world', was the question I kept asking myself, but in the fullness of time I would find out exactly who they were.

The calls all said the same thing, how great my father was and that they wouldn't be where they are today if it wasn't for him. On a Saturday morning we received another call, this time asking to speak with a Mr Jason Agha. My son Richard answered the call, and then proceeded to search me out so I could speak with this caller. A voice at the other end asked if I was Jason Agha, son of Agha Sardar Hassan Zahid, before telling me to hold the line. After a short interlude another man's voice came on the phone, this well-spoken individual again telling me that my father was a great and honourable man and his thoughts, as well as his nations were now thinking of my father.

The man to my astonishment at the other end of this phone call on a dreary English Saturday morning was none other than Mr Asif Ali Zardari, the serving President of Pakistan.

Well to say I, along with my family were totally bemused was a real understatement, with all these calls coming in from all four corners of the world, topped off with the one from the President was just so overwhelming, he was just Dad to me and my wife Julie and Grandad to Richard and Rachael.

Dad's old school in Shimla got back in touch to ask when his funeral was taking place, then telling us that they would open their chapel and hold a service with the whole school in attendance, this then would coincide at the same time my father was to be laid to rest here in England. They also would hold prayers everyday up until the funeral, also sending flowers along with a bottle of single malt whisky with the Bishop Cotton School badge as its label. I had a phone call from a man who was in Riyadh, the capital city of Saudi Arabia, telling me that he would walk from Riyadh to Mecca some 900km (600 miles) to be there at the exact time that

Dad would be laid to rest, so he could then pray for him at the *Kaaba*, the holiest shrine in the Muslim world. He said he would do this pilgrimage because he believed this would be his way of honouring my father, that was some task indeed.

I then had a call from my cousin Zia, the son of my father's brother, who I remembered fondly from our times back in Peshawar. We had a good talk, remembering my father who now was the last child of my grandparents to pass away. I asked Zia if he would know where my mother might have been buried in Peshawar all those years ago. His answer was the response I had waited to hear for many years, the one that lifted my heart at the very same time that it was supposed to be sad. He proceeded to tell me that my mother was buried in the family graveyard, along with all my other relatives, great grandparents, grandparents, uncles and aunties, from generations back.

The same graveyard where I once sat, back in 1971, on that white marble plinth, to say my last goodbyes to Mum, that same one that is behind that plain but unforgettable arched gateway.

IN MEMORY OF
SARDAR HASSAN AGHA
1927 – 2010
LOVED BY ALL HIS FAMILY
DEPARTED THIS LIFE TO BE RE – UNITED
WITH EILEEN ONCE MORE

Cheers Hassan, one of life's unsung heroes

All those years searching then not realising that our family, because they were so prominent in that region of the world, owned their own piece of the world in which to lay their loved ones to rest. Not destroyed as everyone I spoke to concluded, but there, just there in a corner of Peshawar as it always has been and still is today. I now concluded that if I had asked Dad where Mum was laid to rest, he probably could have told me straight away, preventing all those years of not knowing. I asked Zia if it would be possible for him to send me a picture of my Mum's grave, and then within the hour, lots of pictures came over the internet of all the graves of my ancestors, and there alongside them lay my Mum's grave, just as I had remembered as if it was yesterday, a simple white topped marble grave but with all the meaning in the world to me.

After my father had been happily laid to rest facing Mecca in a green burial ground in England, his best friend Ted saying a few poignant words at his graveside, Enid his wife distraught with grief by his side along with the rest of us at the loss of someone so humble but so precious.

I then had the task of sorting out all his personal items, it is now you find out the person who you thought they were was also somebody that you never knew they were, but to me he was just my Dad.

While sorting out the family affairs, Dad's bank contacted me and told me of a safe deposit box that was in his name. I then visited the bank to view the inside of the box which consisted of lots of paperwork, but unfortunately no Imperial Leather talcum powder tins. The family plot thickened when reviewing the birth certificates of Alexander and myself.

My certificate reads as follows:
Jason Agha   11/01/1962
Mother   Eileen Brigid Agha
Father   Hassan Sardar Agha

My brother's certificate reads:
Alexander Blaney   12/03/1957
Mother   Eileen Brigid Blaney
Father   Unknown

As I trolled through the paperwork further, all would be revealed in the fullness of time why the above certificates read as they did.

CHAPTER 11

Agha Sardar Hassan Zahid

BORN ON THE twenty-ninth of August 1929 in Peshawar, the youngest son of Agha Sardar Ghulam Hussain Zahid and Amna Begum Zahid, also having one sister and three other brothers. Hassan's father worked as a judge on behalf of British India, as did his father and my great grandfather before him.

The family name Agha stands out in a long line of prominent figures throughout history, and originated from the dynasty of the Turcoman Qizilbash, a militant Shia group and a part of the Ottoman Empire from the 15th century which reached out across Persia. The meaning of Agha is that of great lord, chief, or nobleman and was given to only a few, but very prominent dignitaries.

The privileges acquired, not only made our family well respected in the area from Kabul to Peshawar in the eighteenth, nineteenth and twentieth centuries, an area better known as the North West Frontier, but also gave my father the chance to go to the top English school in the heart of British India. Each dignitary was allowed to send one son from their family to the school, and from the four boys in our family at that time my grandfather, for reasons known to him, had chosen the youngest of the four; my father, a privilege and honour he grasped with both hands, even though he was so young.

So in the spring of 1938, aged eight, my father headed for the foothills of the Himalayas and the well-recognised English Bishop Cotton School for boys, one of the oldest schools of it's type in Asia, run by the British authorities at their summer capital and hill top retreat of Shimla or Simla, as it was first known since 1864. This retreat was so typically English, more of a very large village than a small town sprawling out horizontally as well as vertical, whilst clinging precariously to the side of the lower hills of this well known mountain range.

Typical Victorian architecture of tea rooms and shops line up along the Mall and the Ridge, where the English paraded daily in their fine clothing supported by fancy parasols to hide their white complexions from the sun, all this capped off by a traditional English stone church.

Just outside Shimla in its very well-manicured grounds stood the Grand Lodge, it was very regal indeed and the residence of the Viceroy of India, you would hardly think that you were in the middle of Asia, more likely to be in one of the many shires' back in England. Shimla was a well-established town when my father's eyes glimpsed it for the first time through the murky window of the narrow gauge train, that had taken him from Kalka station, where his father had said good bye, before putting him on the train for the seven hour mountainous journey to Shimla at the other end of the line.

This was quite a task for an eight year old boy on his own, probably for the very first time, but I suppose that was just the first in a long line of journeys that he would eventually take, journeys that would model his life in so many ways.

My father boarded at the school for most of the ten years of his education there, one of the reasons being the winters can be long and hard, let alone the trip all the way back to Peshawar, which could take over two days by train if you were lucky. But he did tell me, the times he did return as a boy growing in years, were times he spent joyously with his mother and especially his sister. They would spend their days endlessly laughing and talking about life in general before he would head back again on the long journey to those foothills of the Himalayas.

In 1945 my father, along with his school chums of all nationalities, gathered at the side of the road to the Viceroy's Lodge along with hundreds of others, to watch as the leaders of the then national parties, including Mahatma Ghandi, Muhammad Ali Jinnah, and the then Viceroy of India, Lord Wavell passed by.

They were being pulled through the streets on individual rickshaws, each by two men in full uniform from Shimla Station to the Grand Lodge, for the important meeting known as the Shimla/Simla conference, which was convened to decide the future of India in a constructive and peaceful manner. With my father's hopes in their hands, little did he know that this gathering and momentous occasion taking place less than a mile from his school, would shatter the hopes of that young boy, and thousands more like him within two years.

Academically I think he did well, this type of school would not suffer failure, but the path Dad's life took didn't need top qualifications, just honesty and integrity mixed in with lots of love, affection and common sense, qualities the school most likely taught him but would never give out in diplomas and certainly not to a boy of ethnic minority, not in those days that's for sure. My father did well at sports, hockey, cricket and boxing, becoming school champion for his weight. I used to pull his leg later in life, that he only became champion at his boxing weight because he was so fat and overweight, myself just managing to stay out of reach of his right hand in case of a good clip to the head.

Something must have stood out for the school in the ten years or more my father was there, because in 1946 he became School Captain, a great honour and privilege for a sixteen year old boy from the far outreaches of the North West Frontier of British India.

This then also must have given great pride to his father

Bishop Cotton School, Shimla

The first Indian boys permitted to join the school were Suren Tagore in 1881 and Vishnu Singh in 1883. The first four Indian School Captains were RJ Gandhi in 1928, Harry Chukerbuti in 1936, Jahengzeb Khan in 1941 and Hasan Agha in 1946-47. These four boys were prominent examples of the predominance of a student body that was being groomed for leadership of Indian affairs, which training was proof of the far-sightedness of the Founder and successive Headmasters.

Dad second from the left, front row as school captain

Dad second from the right, top row, hockey team

Dad far right top, cricket team, 1945

and mother along with the rest of the family, who with a heavy heart sent this young boy aged 8 away to hopefully achieve a good education, the results then bringing him great things in his life. Continuing to be School Captain in 1947 and only the fourth Indian boy to achieve this throughout the school's history up to that date, my father must have had a year full of mixed emotions.

In early August of that year the then Viceroy of India, Lord Mountbatten, came to the school to give a reassuring speech, as the rumours of ethnic killings reverberated from all four corners of this vast country, because of the British deciding to vacate India as they knew it, in the middle of August that year.

My father sat alongside him at the top table as school captain. Mountbatten spoke about the momentous events happening around the world now the war was over, a world living in peace and harmony with India being an equal partner with Britain, it would then become one of the great nations of this world. Great words for young boys believing and applauding the Viceroy as he spoke loud and clear, and why shouldn't they have? They had believed the British for the last hundred years, and all that they brought with them.

Unfortunately this thing called religion reared its ugly head once more in history, as the brutalisation of both Hindus, Sikhs and Muslims went on totally out of control across this vast nation, the worst area affected being that of the Punjab with some people calling it retributive genocide, as between two hundred thousand and two million people lost their lives and their homes in an ethnic cleansing process that was only matched by the Nazis a few years earlier. As the tide turned and the British started to lose control of this spiralling situation in late September of that year, Lord Mountbatten, along with the schools hierarchy wanted the Muslim boys of the school to stay boarding, believing this would be their

*My Father on the right in his best suit ready to
meet Lord Mountbatten at The Grand Lodge, Shimla 1947*

safest option. The families of those boys feared the worst and wanted them home as reports suggested and history confirmed, no Muslims managed to survive in the area known as East Punjab, and Shimla with all its regal buildings, was to become it's capital. So, it was decided by those in authority only a few weeks later, that the wishes of the Muslim boy's families would come first.

In 1947 there were some forty-two Muslim boys left attending the Bishop Cotton School at the time, My father being one of them. Some of the younger boys had been collected in person by their families before partition was completed on the fifteenth of August.

As the genocide continued to ravage out of control in what once was a glorious and somewhat peaceful and tranquil nation full of colour and gaiety, it fractured overnight into unrecognisable chaos. Caused by the British dividing the country into three without any real thought to the consequences it would bring to bear on normal family life of the population at the time.

On the twenty-second of October 1947, in the presence of the whole school and its staff, the Headmaster addressed those forty-two Muslim boys in the Irwin Hall, then immediately after my father as School Captain stood and gave this short speech, which he hoped would be ingrained into those boys as one of their last thoughts at the school:

Remembrance is the presence in the absence,
It is spoken in silence,
It is the past few memorise,
In which the heart gives immortality
                                    SARDAR HASSAN AGHA

Let love be without dissimulation,
Abhor that which is evil;
Cleave to that which is good
                                    SARDAR HASSAN AGHA

Irwin hall, Bishop Cotton School, Simla/Shimla

Bishop Cotton School motto

*And so, from those who have gone before, to those who are yet
to come, we pass our motto loud and clear, all evil overcome.*

*As true as is a brother's love, as close as ivy grows, we'll stand
four square throughout our lives to every wind that blows.*

Irwin Hall, according to old tradition, out of the three doors
which gave access to the hall, the middle door is only opened
for Presidents and Viceroys to enter, and School Captains
to leave at the end of their year, to tumultuous cheers from
their school colleagues. On this occasion after my father's
words had finished reverberating round this iconic hall, the

middle doors were then opened by two prefects, and in utter sorrowful silence my father led those forty-one boys slowly out in single file, it's as if those doors themselves knew something was awry, closing gingerly and quietly in unison behind the last boy, as he began his decent of the curved stone steps outside leading down to the courtyard.

This day, the twenty-second of October 1947 has been classed as the saddest day in the entire school's history, and those doors were never opened again until 2009 as a part of a reunion for those Muslim boys that left that day, but unfortunately although invited, my father could not attend.

As school captain and now the figurehead of this unusual but precious platoon, my father gathered those forty-one boys aged between eight and seventeen years into pairs, before leaving the school grounds, then marching proudly through the streets of Shimla in their school uniform. Their destination in Shimla was the railway station, the very station that gave hope to every one of those boys as they disembarked for a life in Shimla and the Bishop Cotton School, but now gave great fear as they all headed from the saftey of Shimla back out into the unknown.

As they strolled on to the platform, one of the small gauge engines, smoke bellowing from its funnel and steam coming from it's under belly was ready and waiting to take them on the agonising seven hour plus trip down this ever winding track to the town of Kalka. It was from there that they were to head to Lahore in East Punjab and the new country of Pakistan, one can only imagine the trepidation of those boys considering their age. The older boys including my father were probably as scared as the next boy, although not allowing it to show as they sought to comfort and offer encouragement to the younger ones on this trip that no one wanted to take, through what was to be known as the mouth of hell.

It was given that name as the genocide continued. No Muslim was safe in East Punjab and no Sikh in West Punjab, what sights must have been exposed to those young eyes, that more than likely etched themselves in their minds for the rest of their lives, as they headed westward for the new border line, and then the safety of their families in Lahore, atrocities beyond belief, which you can read in most history books today.

Lahore was reached and my fathers' objective achieved, he had brought those boys home, without losing anyone, something he would repeat twenty-four years later with his own boys, as he promised Grandma and our mother, 'I'm bringing the boys home'.

Maybe his thoughts were, 'if I can lead forty-one boys to saftey and return them to their homes — I can sure take my own boys back to theirs'.

How long it took those forty-two boys to make that perilous journey of around 350 kilometres (218 miles) and which route they took, I am not sure, but make it they did.

But it was from Lahore that the forty-two disbursed to their homes, scattered right across this infant nation.

You may have already figured it out, that when my father passed away, those phone calls I received in the following weeks from every corner of the globe, who describe him as a good and great man, were some of those boys he led out of those doors of Irwin Hall in late October 1947. Passing through the mouth of hell to the city of Lahore, thanking me profusely knowing they would not be where they were in the world today with their own families, without my father's courage and guidance. My father never once mentioned to me that he guided those young boys home or what his eyes must have seen, although it must have been a gruelling memory to carry all his adult life.

I only found out once these boys, now men, started to contact me after his passing, delving into the history of the school, piecing it together bit by bit the more I looked the more this untold story of a private, strong-willed young man aged just seventeen came to light, that man, 'My Dad'. Perhaps what he saw was best left back on the road he travelled, and the only answer to what he saw was religion, turning on itself, as it had done for many centuries, religion is mostly the root of all evil, and the reason he and my mother would not take Alexander and I in that direction whatsoever.

My father headed for Peshawar and to the bosom of his own family, where he did not have long to enjoy the comforts of home before his father pulled a few strings with the British as they continued their final efforts of leaving and in quite a hurry, what was formally known as British India.

His efforts got my father along with three other boys of around the same age from the school, one being Hashim Khan, his best friend, on a British plane out of Lahore to RAF Northolt Aerodrome on the outskirts of London.

From the aerodrome these boys were transported by road to the city of spires, otherwise known as Oxford, where they continued the last two years of their education at one of the many collages that this city was renowned for, thus keeping him away from all the delights, but also the turmoil a new country can bring to a young man. On completing his education my Dad then contacted Agha Manzil for instructions on how to return home, but the answer was not the one he expected. The returning telegram from his father had different instructions, one that had not even crossed his mind, but must have been conceived and agreed by the family back in Peshawar. The instruction was not to return at the present moment but to make his way to Silverstone in Northamptonshire, today a Formula 1 racing track and headquarters of British motor sport, but back then in 1949 it was an RAF station that had been used during the war for heavy bombers. This then became a small facility for the British Commonwealth countries, to get some of their elite pupils trained in the art of flying combat aircraft. Now that

Training days, my father on the left, Hashim Khan far right

Pakistan was a new country it was felt that if my father learnt how to fly these aircraft, he could then return home and teach these skills and techniques to his fellow citizens to improve the country's new air force, thus giving him a prominent position within the government for decades to come. On this course run by the RAF along with the other boys from Pakistan, there were also boys from India, as well as other commonwealth countries. Dad explained to me how at first, he trained in an old Tiger Moth, a two-seat, two-winged biplane as well as plenty of class studies, then learning all about the Hurricane fighter before flying in a special two-seat version adapted for training. It wasn't long after Dad had just started this part of the course that the British Government stopped all training with immediate effect.

Dad explained that out of the blue the base was visited by an important person from Whitehall in London, and all training was stopped for the Indian and Pakistani boys, this was because the British government could not be seen helping one country or the other, or to show favouritism before the up and coming Declaration of London was to be agreed between the hierarchy of the Commonwealth countries later that year. It wasn't long before my father received another telegram from his father, telling him that he had now been enrolled in the Northampton College of Technology, which was only a short distance from Silverstone where he was training.

Northampton was known for its work in leather and in particular the boot and shoe industry, and the thought process from Pakistan was if Dad could study this subject and all that this entailed, he could return fully qualified and run the textile department for the Pakistani government.

My father stopped in a bedsit in the town along with Hashim Kahan whilst attending the college, and as well as his studies he kept up some of his sports from school, playing cricket on the racecourse for the college, and hockey for the county of Northampton. My father acquired the nickname Red due to the beard he was now sporting having a red tinge to it, and if you trace Dad's family history back to the Ottoman Dynasty *Qizilbash* translates to red-headed, which our family are well-known for.

My father was due to return to Pakistan and Peshawar when his education had been completed, but one might surmise that the relaxed nature of the western world and a

BISHOP COTTON SCHOOL
SIMLA

26th March 1948

To whom it may concern

I have known Hassan Agha for over seven years and I have
seen him grow up in our midst into a fine strapping young man.
In the class-room he took pains with his work and was always
willing to learn. He appeared for the Cambridge School Certificate Examination last year and but for the unsettled
conditions which he experienced towards the end of the year
I am sure he would have given a better account of himself.

He excelled on the playing field and won his School
colours at Hockey, Cricket, Boxing and Football. He possessed
more than ordinary talent in Hockey and Cricket and Captained
the School First XI, with good results. He was also an
outstanding boxer, possessing great courage and skill and had
the reputation of not having lost a single fight whilst at
School. He was the Captain of the School Boxing team and
was for some time jointly responsible for the training of his
team. He showed promise of developing into a fine athlete and
with proper training he should do well. A firm believer in
keeping fit, he took great interest in physical training and
very often was called upon to take sole charge of a P.T. squad.
For his outstanding sportsmanship he was elected a member
of the School Spartan Club-a much coveted honour.

He was a School Prefect, House Captain and held the
enviable post of School Captain for nearly two years with
distinction. He was a born leader and commanded the respect
of his colleagues and mentors alike. He was an excellent
disciplinarian without being harsh and never indulged in
partiality. He had nearly two hundred boys under his charge
and to a boy they honoured and respected him. His reliability
was generally acknowledged and frequently important duties
were entrusted to him which he executed thoroughly and with
great conscientiousness.

His conduct and character were exemplary and it can be
said of him that he truly carried away the stamp of
Bishop Cotton School.

I wish him every success in the future.

Ibbetson House Master

*This letter dated 1948 shows my father's strong character,
why he did what he did throughout his life, making him the
man I came to admire and be one of life's unsung heroes*

college campus got the better of him, or maybe he was not ready for that arranged marriage that lay in store for him on his expected return home. Whatever the reason that was rolling around my Dad's head at the time had a profound effect on his decision, it must have been so overwhelming that it led him to defy the person that gave him this opportunity in the very first instance, his own father. The reverberation this sent around the family was so heartfelt to the point that the family who held him in such high esteem, anticipating his joyous return back into their fold, turned almost immediately as one to cast him out from the family, thus becoming that black sheep.

CHAPTER 12

Eileen Bridgid Agha, née Blaney

EILEEN WAS BORN in Dundalk in 1938, in the county of Louth, Ireland, the eldest child and daughter of Ambrose Blaney and Mabel Alice Blaney, they had two other children Seamus and Deirdre. Eileen only an infant still cradled in her mother's arms, the Blaneys headed for England, and the town of Northampton, where her father had been promised work as a mechanic in a garage. Eileen, born into a very strict Catholic family attended the all girls Catholic school of Notre Dame in the centre of Northampton from an early age.

It was from here with her excellent exam results she was given a placement at the Northampton College of Technology on St George's Avenue and enrolled at the age of seventeen in 1955.

Next to the college was the Masonic Hall where they held dances most Saturday nights, and it was at one of these dances Hassan and Eileen met. Love blossomed between an Irish Catholic girl and a Pakistani Muslim boy, a problem in the middle of the 1950s in England. A problem at that time in society was not that of religion — who knows what religion someone is at first glance? But the fact a young ethnic man was stepping out with a young white girl, this was very much frowned upon. Put into context that she should be going out with her own kind, a strange thought today, but one that was not uncommon not so long ago.

As our family albums show, my father was a keen photographer taking pictures of Eileen at every opportunity, she returning the favour having been taught by Hassan. The pictures of Hassan show a very young-looking man, much

Eileen aged seventeen

younger than his actual age, which put him in 1955 at twenty-six; Eileen at that time was just seventeen. Either Hassan told Eileen his real age, or a very common thing to do like a lot of foreign young men travelling from east to west for work; reduce their age so they could work longer, that's just the way they thought. As their two religious cultures were so very far apart they had to be careful where they would meet and enjoy each other's company, Dad often borrowing friend's cars so he could venture away from Northampton and those prying eyes that would spread gossip like wild fire.

Whether they met in 1955 or 1956 is up for debate, but we definitely know Alexander was born on the twelfth of March 1957, a child conceived out of wedlock but also conceived from love. My grandad was furious with Eileen to say the least, that she could ruin her future prospects and bring shame to his door. So much so that it became a rift between my grandad and grandma, a religious rift between what was right and what was wrong, a child to be born out of a woman's sin, that had brought itself crashing into the middle of their tranquil life in the heart of Northampton. Eileen being Catholic, could in God's eyes only have one option, and that was to have the child, but grandad did not want the scandal that would come with it through the Catholic community and beyond here in Northampton.

After speaking with the Bishop at the Catholic Cathedral in Northampton, Eileen who now in my grandfather's eyes was the black sheep of his family, had arranged for her to be sent away to Leicester, and before she started to show signs that she was with child. Excuses were given to the college and the word among the Catholic community was she had returned to Ireland to help Grandad's ageing sister. Hassan in all of this was at the time banished from seeing Eileen, and in the words of Grandad, 'Haven't you done enough damage lad?' My father's love must have been one of utter devotion,

Hassan, 1949

Eileen, 1955

*Dad with a friend's
borrowed car*

Eileen aged 18

as he persisted to find out where the church had sent Eileen. Looking at some of the pictures just tell you that.

Leicester was his answer, after badgering grandma for weeks, telling her he would do the honourable thing and stand by Eileen if she wanted him, just one of those traits I was telling you about that the Bishop Cotton School in Shimla must have taught him back in India.

Grandma gave Hassan the address where Eileen was staying in Leicester, and he caught the next available bus to be at her side. As I mentioned early in this family saga, we used to visit an aunt Gladys on our Sunday trips back in the 1960s, well this aunt Gladys was the place where my Mum (Eileen) stayed when Alexander was born, my Dad visiting every chance he could.

Eileen was banished by her father for three years to Leicester, and so this black sheep not being allowed to return to Northampton, or even letting Gran go and see the new-born child. I think this grated with my grandma until the day she died and could have been one of the reasons she did not mourn my grandad's passing as you would have expected. The more you investigate what can only be described as one hell of a family puzzle, the more the different pieces start to fall into place.

As I keep saying, although my parents never introduced my brother and me to religion it has got so much to answer for throughout our lives. So, as we try and piece this puzzle together in that period of the 1940s and 1950s, religion be in no doubt, was the underlying factor that caused our family's turmoil.

My mother and father must have wished or even hoped for family backing with all that life had thrown upon them at that time, but none was forthcoming. With religion, came the scandal, and with scandal came the denial, families would try to deflect the truth the best they could instead of facing reality. Hassan and Eileen were both cast out from their

families in Pakistan and England due to religion, and both were very much classed as black sheep. My father at that time was totally disowned and banished from his family for not heeding Muslim traditions, my mother scorned just for having a child out of wedlock and sent away by the Catholic Church, when in fact they should have been supporting her as she tried to deal with all the turmoil that was put on her at such a young age.

With Alexander born in 1957, his birth certificate said father unknown, but my grandma told the Northampton Chronicle and Echo when interviewed in the 1970s, Eileen and Hassan had been married fifteen years, which then would have placed them getting married in 1956, thus making Alexander's birth a year later and quite legitimate. So why then send her away?

Grandma also said Eileen was thirty-three years old, which is correct, but Hassan was thirty-five, that then would mean Dad was born in 1936, this would mean Dad left school aged eleven, although history and facts tells us this can't be true, all this just to deny the truth and to save the family name, when the real truth was, they just loved each other intensely.

Alexander was baptised in July of 1957, in Leicester at the Catholic Church of St Edwards Aylestone, as Alexander Hassan Blaney, with just two local unknown witnesses on the paperwork along with my mother, no family or even my father present. Did he even know his son was being baptised? And even if he did, he could do nothing about it. Then again, the Catholic Church would not even care one way or the other as it turned a blind eye once again, as it has done throughout history, in the name of religion.

Grandad and I had a real understanding as I had mentioned earlier, it was a very good relationship when I was growing up and I was oblivious at the time to this scar that was etched so deep in our family's past. But was there guilt inside him? Or was he just trying to gloss over what had gone before, by putting his efforts to the one child of Eileen, in his eyes who was not born out of sin but born to his beliefs. You would think you know your family — but do you really? Hassan and Eileen did marry on the twenty-fifth of March 1960 at Northampton Registry office in the town hall, again with no family members attending. They had most likely decided between themselves it was best to tell no one, and who could blame them? Considering the size of the eruption it would have caused based on their previous history.

My aunt Dee and mum's sister explained to me a few years ago that she never met my brother until he was three. Eileen waltzing into her parents' house with Alexander, put him on my aunt Dee's knee and said, 'this is your new nephew', to her utter astonishment, 'oh and by the way, I am now married to Hassan'.

Auntie Dee with Alexander, 1960

18 Springfield Wootton, (Manzil), 1960

Whilst Eileen was in Leicester, Hassan gave up his education and left college to take up work as a salesman, this was so he could provide for Eileen and Alexander. He eventually saved enough money to put a deposit down on a small two-bedroom bungalow in the village of Wootton, just South of Northampton. 18 Springfield was the street address, and Manzil was it's name.

This is where they started to build their own lives, trying to ignore their turbulent past, this was their time and they were definitely not going to let anyone or anything distract them from their path, an attitude born out of their love for one another and rightly so, but an attitude that was ultimately forced upon them by religion.

What appears out of this, is one answer, love definitely conquered religion but it was hard fought.

Nineteen sixty-two

On the eleventh of January 1962, in a small two-bedroom bungalow in the county of Northamptonshire I was brought into this world by a man, who over time I would admire and deem in my view to be one of life's unsung heroes.

I can say that literally due to the heavy snow that lay outside in our little cul-de-sac in the middle of England, with my mother, Eileen, well into the final stages of labour, the midwife who was called over an hour earlier was nowhere to be seen.

The event about to happen in the front bedroom of this bungalow was totally in the hands of a thirty-three year old man, who years earlier had travelled halfway across the world to deliver me safely on this cold and bleak winter's day.

This man firmly instructed my elder brother, by five years, to remain in the front room of the house until otherwise told as he helped my mother to deliver me safely.

As the snow continued to fall outside, I was now being held securely but tenderly in the arms of this man and at that precise moment that I entered into our world this man became my father Sardar, Hassan, Agha.

We have now returned to the end of this family saga that unfolded before your eyes, a family saga that threw up so many questions, and I hope has given many of the answers. My brother who has taken a prominent part in this story still remains a black sheep of the family. My father excluding him from the family will, not forgiving him for the words he spoke all those years ago, my Dad unfortunately taking those words with him as he passed away. Alexander and Anne had a son, Sean now aged thirty-two, my nephew, who I still have contact with today, but I have not spoken to Alexander for well over twenty-five years. I believe he now lives somewhere in Chile.

But if you're still not sure what this family story's conclusion is, then let me just leave you with the following.

The Aghas, Manzil, 18 Springfield, Wootton, 1962

Sardar Hassan Agha travelled halfway across the world following the turmoil that the British had inflicted on his education. A journey that eventually found him love in a strange but modern world. Eileen Brigid Blaney was that love and after setting down their own roots and values together they decided to journey halfway back across the world with their new family, only for tragedy to strike at the very heart of this family, just as all their problems appeared to be behind them, as Eileen passed away.

Hassan then travelled back across the world once more with his boys, a task in itself, but one he was sure he could achieve knowing what he had done before as a young adult, but not knowing how this new chapter in his life would pan out, his own private thoughts and memories concealed within him, until he passed away.

Eileen Brigid Agha raised as a Catholic now resting in peace in the Muslim world — the very place that Sardar Hassan Agha grew up in as a child.

Sardar Hassan Agha raised as a Muslim now resting peacefully in a mainly Christian world — the very place Eileen had grown up in as a child.

So, was this book just a true love story or just another family saga, maybe it was more than that? Or in the end did it just boil down to being *Three Black Sheep and Me?*

ACKNOWLEDGEMENTS

THANK YOU to everyone who encouraged me to put pen to paper for the first time so that this fascinating true story could be shared to a wider audience. It took me a while but I hope it did not disappoint.

A special thank you to:

Kelly Walsh and Hilary Sadler of Gorila Grafica, for the professional design of the book cover and internal layout which this story deserved.

I also must thank Steph Fell for his valuable advice and input.

To my wife Julie, for her continuous encouragement throughout the process of writing this book.

And finally to my parents:

Firstly for the family photographs many of them over fifty to sixty years old, but once put to print, although not the best quality and taken mostly with a Kodak Instamatic, they definitely bring this story to life.

Then most importantly for their indestructible love for each other that no religion could ever conquer, only tragedy could split them apart and without having that great attribute this story would never have existed.